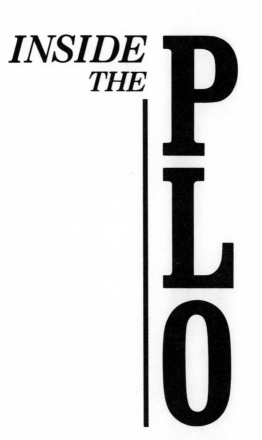

INSIDE THE

P
L
O

Neil C. Livingstone and David Halevy

in cooperation with
the Ethics and
Public Policy Center,
Washington, D.C.

WILLIAM MORROW
AND COMPANY, INC.
New York

INSIDE *THE*

Covert Units,

Secret Funds,

and the War

Against Israel

and the United

States

Recognizing the importance of preserving what has been written, it is the policy of William Morrow and Company, Inc., and its imprints and affiliates to have the books it publishes printed on acid-free paper, and we exert our best efforts to that end.

Library of Congress Cataloging-in-Publication Data

Livingstone, Neil C.
    Inside the PLO : covert units, secret funds, and the war against
Israel and the United States / Neil C. Livingstone and David Halevy
in cooperation with Ethics and Public Policy Center.
        p.   cm.
    Includes bibliographical references.
    ISBN 0-688-09335-3
    1. Munazzamat al-Taḥrīr al-Filasṭīnīyah.   2. Jewish-Arab
relations.   I. Halevy, David.   II. Ethics and Public Policy Center
(Washington, D.C.)   III. Title.
DS119.7.L58   1990
322.4'2'095694—dc20   89-38232
                                                                   CIP

Printed in the United States of America

First Edition

1 2 3 4 5 6 7 8 9 10

BOOK DESIGN BY LEVAVI & LEVAVI

Neil C. Livingstone dedicates
this book to his father, Neil.
David H. Halevy dedicates this
book to his parents, Emil and Marin.

Authors' Note

This book began with a grant from Ernest Lefever and the Ethics and Public Policy Center in Washington, D.C. Initially it was envisioned as a modest monograph or short work detailing the PLO's actions and operations against the United States. However, over time it took on a life of its own and gradually emerged as a far more comprehensive and ambitious project. This was chiefly due to the wealth of new material regarding the PLO and its constituent elements that was made available to the authors by various intelligence and law enforcement sources here and abroad.

The problem with writing a book about an organization like the PLO, which places a great emphasis on secrecy and regularly uses disinformation to cloak and shield its activities, is that much of the material appearing in open sources is outdated, inaccurate, and distorted by the passions evoked by the Middle East conflict. In addition, any serious investigator's task is complicated by the organizational chaos and lack of institutional record keeping that characterize the PLO.

In writing *Inside the PLO,* the authors have relied heavily on information developed in cooperation with six intelligence services: three in the West and three in the Middle East. In addition, numerous law enforcement officials, journalists, and scholars who regularly follow the PLO and events in the Middle East contributed their time and insights to the authors. As a rule, the material in the book has been authenticated by multiple sources, and the entire book has been reviewed for accuracy by several senior intelligence officials who closely watch the activities of the PLO and its various splinter groups. Whenever controversial material that could not be checked against other sources was included, the authors have noted its presence in the text.

The views expressed are those exclusively of the authors.

Contents

11

Glossary of Names

ABU ABBAS (MOHAMMED ZAIDAN ABBAS). Leader of a faction of the Palestine Liberation Front (PLF) and the mastermind of the *Achille Lauro* hijacking.

ABU A'ALA (MOHAMMED HASSAN MILHAM). Member of the PLO's Executive Committee and head of the Occupied Homeland Department.

ABU A'ALA* (AHMED QUARY). Chief executive officer (CEO) of Samed.

ABU AMAR (YASIR ARAFAT). Chairman of the PLO and commander in chief of its largest faction, Fatah.

ABU DAOUD (MOHAMMED DAOUD MACHMUD AUDA). A top Black September operator involved in the Munich Massacre, who was later captured and tortured by the Jordanians.

ABU GHASSAN (SALIM RIZAK). Operational leader of the PLO/Black September squad that seized the Saudi Embassy in Khartoum in 1973. The U.S. ambassador and two other diplomats were subsequently murdered by the terrorists.

ABU HASSAN (ALI HASSAN SALAMEH). Former operational chief of Black September and later head of Force 17.

ABU IBRAHIM (MOHAMMED AMRI). A Syrian of Palestinian descent and master bombmaker, who headed the May 15 group.

*It is not unusual for more than one individual to have the same nom de guerre.

15

ABU IYAD (SALAH KHALAF). Current number two man in the PLO. He is overall chief of the Intelligence and Security Apparatus and is responsible for the PLO's and Fatah's covert and clandestine units.

ABU JIHAD (KHALIL IBRAHIM MACHMUD AL-WAZIR). Former number two man in the PLO and overall military commander of the organization. He was killed by Israeli commandos on April 16, 1988.

ABU LUTF (FAROUK QADOUMI). Head of the PLO's Political Department and a member of Fatah's Central Committee.

ABU MARWAN (FAWAZ YASSIN ABDEL RAHMAN). PLO terrorist involved in the takeover of the Saudi Embassy in Khartoum, which resulted in the murder of three diplomats, two Americans and one Belgian.

ABU MUSA (COLONEL SA'ID MUSA MURAGHA). Leader of the Fatah Provisional Command a pro-Syrian organization that is not part of the PLO.

ABU NIDAL (SABRI KHALIL AL-BANNA). One of the most notorious terrorists in the world and leader of the Fatah Revolutionary Council (FRC).

ABU SHARAR (Bassam Majid Abu-Sharif). A PLO spokesman and confidant of Yasir Arafat. Abu Sharar formerly served as deputy to PFLP leader George Habash.

ABU TARIQ (ABDEL LATIF ABU HIJLAH). One of the PLO operatives who killed the U.S. ambassador and two other diplomats in Khartoum in 1973. Currently part of the PLO delegation involved in talks with the United States.

ABU TAYEB (COLONEL MOHAMMED NATOUR). Current commander of Force 17.

ABU TUFIQ (JAWEED YACCUB GHUSAIN). Chairman of the board of directors of the Palestinian National Fund (PNF) and a member of the PLO's Executive Committee.

ABU ZAIM (BRIGADIER ATALLAH ATALLAH). Former head of the Intelligence and Security Apparatus (ISA), who defected to Jordan in the mid-1980's.

ARAB BANK LTD. Known as the PLO bank, the Arab Bank Ltd. handles much of the PLO's money and oversees many of its financial transactions.

ARAB LIBERATION FRONT (ALF). A pro-Iraqi Palestinian faction that is part of the PLO.

ARAB ORGANIZATION OF 15 MAY (MAY 15). A terrorist group led by Abu Ibrahim that is not part of the PLO. It is believed that May 15 cooperates, on a covert basis, with Fatah's Special Operations Group.

ARAB REVOLUTIONARY BRIGADES (ARB). A covert unit of Fatah based in Beirut.

ATTAVARIOUS. Greek ship sunk by the Israelis on April 21, 1985, with several squads of Fatah terrorists on board, who were planning a clandestine landing on the beaches near Tel Aviv.

BEKAA VALLEY. Valley in eastern Lebanon controlled by the Syrians that serves as a base of operations for many Palestinian and other terrorist groups.

BLACK SEPTEMBER. Secret PLO-controlled terrorist organization that carried out the attack against Israeli athletes at the 1972 Munich Olympics and other outrages.

DEMOCRATIC FRONT FOR THE LIBERATION OF PALESTINE (DFLP). A pro-Soviet Palestinian splinter group with close ties to Syria. Headed by Naif Hawatmeh, it is part of the PLO.

FANON, FRANZ. Author of the famous revolutionary book *Wretched of the Earth,* which had a major impact on Arafat and other Palestinian leaders.

FATAH. Harkat al-Tachrir al-Watanni al-Falestinia, or Palestine Liberation Movement; in reverse order its acronym is FATAH, which, in Arabic, means "victory" or "conquest." Today Fatah is the largest constituent element of the PLO and is headed by Yasir Arafat.

FATAH PROVISIONAL COMMAND (FPC). A pro-Syrian Palestinian terrorist unit led by Abu Musa which is not part of the PLO.

FATAH REVOLUTIONARY COUNCIL (FRC). Also known as Black June, the FRC is a Palestinian terrorist group led by Abu Nidal.

FORCE 17. A semiautonomous Fatah unit that serves as Arafat's Praetorian Guard and also carries out covert operations.

GUPS (GENERAL UNION OF PALESTINIAN STUDENTS). Palestinian student organization once headed by Yasir Arafat and, later, by Abu Iyad.

HABASH, DR. GEORGE. Leader of the Popular Front for the Liberation of Palestine (PFLP).

HADDAD, WADIA. The late operational chief of the PFLP, who broke away in the mid-1970's to create the PFLP—Special Command.

HAMMAM EL-SHAT. Seaside village near Tunis that is the location of the PLO's headquarters.

HAMUDA, YECHYE. Second chairman of the PLO.

HAWARI, COLONEL (ABDULLAH ABED AL-HAMID LABIB). Head of Fatah's Special Operations Group (SOG).

HAWATMEH, NAIF. Leader of the Democratic Front for the Liberation of Palestine (DFLP), an independent Palestinian organization under the PLO umbrella.

HIZBALLAH (THE PARTY OF GOD). Lebanon-based Shiite terrorist organization controlled and directed by pro-Iranian nationals and often tasked from Teheran. It maintains secret ties to the PLO.

INTELLIGENCE AND SECURITY APPARATUS (ISA). Under the overall supervision of Abu Iyad, ISA is the primary intelligence and counterintelligence arm of Fatah and the PLO. Abu Houl is the operational chief of ISA.

INTIFADA. Uprising by Palestinians living in the West Bank and Gaza Strip that began in December 1987.

JIBRIL, AHMED. Leader of the Popular Front for the Liberation of Palestine—General Command (PFLP-GC).

JIHAZ EL-RAZD. The onetime chief intelligence section of the PLO, which was under the overall command of Abu Iyad.

MUGNIYEH, IMMAD. A Lebanese Shiite and leader of the Musawi clan, who serves as the chief operations officer and head of security of Hizballah.

NAHR AL-BARD (COLD RIVER). Palestinian refugee camp and terrorist training facility near Tripoli, Lebanon. "Nahr al-Bard" was also used as a code phrase to instruct the terrorists in Khartoum to kill the Western diplomats.

PALESTINE LIBERATION ARMY (PLA). With a total strength of between twelve and fourteen thousand men, the PLA serves as the PLO's military arm. Its name was officially changed to the National Palestinian Liberation Army in 1983.

PALESTINE LIBERATION FRONT (PLF)/ABBAS FACTION. A pro-Iraqi unit loyal to Arafat and the PLO, and headed by Abu Abbas.

PALESTINE LIBERATION FRONT/GHANEM FACTION. A pro-Syrian faction that is not part of the PLO.

PALESTINE LIBERATION FRONT/YAQUB FACTION. A pro-Iraqi unit that broke with Mohammed Abbas in 1983 but returned to the PLO fold in the mid-1980's.

PALESTINE LIBERATION ORGANIZATION (PLO). Umbrella organization dedicated to achieving an independent Palestinian state. Headed by Yasir Arafat.

PALESTINIAN NATIONAL FUND (PNF). Fund established to finance all PLO activities.

PALESTINE WELFARE ASSOCIATION (PWA). Formed by wealthy Palestinian businessmen, the PWA is a private organization based in Geneva that provides humanitarian assistance to needy Palestinians.

POPULAR ARAB LIBERATION MOVEMENT (PALM). A splinter group that broke away from Abu Nidal's FRC in 1979.

POPULAR FRONT FOR THE LIBERATION OF PALESTINE (PFLP). Headed by Dr. George Habash, the PFLP was formed in 1967 and is a part of the PLO.

POPULAR FRONT FOR THE LIBERATION OF PALESTINE— GENERAL COMMAND (PFLP-GC). Led by Ahmed Jibril, the PFLP-GC is a pro-Syrian terrorist group that broke away from the PLO in 1983.

POPULAR STRUGGLE FRONT (PSF). A pro-Syrian faction that is part of the PLO.

REVOLUTIONARY PALESTINIAN COMMUNIST PARTY (RPCP). A pro-Soviet Palestinian Communist organization financed by Moscow. The RPCP is a member of the PLO.

SABBAGH, HASIB. Reputedly the wealthiest Palestinian businessman in the world, Sabbagh was a founder of the PWA and has been known to engage in secret diplomacy on behalf of Arafat and the PLO. He is the chairman of the Consolidated Contractors Company (CCC).

SA'IQA. A Damascus-based Palestinian organization that is not part of the PLO.

SALAMEH, ALI HASSAN (ABU HASSAN). Known by the Israelis as the Red Prince, Salameh was the operational chief of Black September and later headed Force 17. He was killed by the Israelis in 1979.

SAMED. Set up as a pragmatic, nonsubsidized commercial and manufacturing entity that would serve as the economic arm of the PLO's fighting forces, today Samed is a global operation with revenues expected to reach seventy million dollars in 1989.

SHAATH, NABIL. Special emissary of Yasir Arafat and one of his closest advisers.

SHOMAN, ABDEL HAMID. Founder and longtime chairman of the Arab Bank Ltd.

SHOMAN, ABDEL MAJEED. First chairman of the PNF and current chairman of the Arab Bank Ltd.

SHUKEIRY, AHMED. First chairman of the PLO.

SPECIAL OPERATIONS GROUP (SOG). Also known as the Colonel Hawari Force, the Special Operations Group was established as part of Fatah to provide internal security within the PLO and to carry out covert international operations.

WESTERN SECTION. A covert unit of Fatah headed, until his death, by Abu Jihad.

Introduction

Hammam el-Shat is a pleasant, if shabby, seaside village, situated on the Gulf of Tunis some thirteen miles east of the Tunisian capital.[1] Long a favorite escape for government clerks and the petit bourgeois from Tunis, Hammam el-Shat's beaches are dirty but scenic. There are a few shops and cafés in the village and a number of changing houses near the shore, but none of the usual amenities associated with a beach community. The handful of villas perched along the coast are modest and surrounded by small gardens. Prior to 1982, Hammam el-Shat was the kind of town in which almost nothing ever happened.

To reach Hammam el-Shat from Tunis, one drives in an easterly direction to the village of Hammam el-Lif, where the road from Tunis intersects the coastal highway that leads north to Hammam el-Shat. In the winter and spring the landscape is green and pastoral, but in the summer the vegetation burns away, leaving only dry grasses and scraggly shrubs. Tamarisk trees, with their narrow leaves and fragile blossoms, line the road leading to Hammam el-Shat.

Since the end of 1982 Hammam el-Shat has been the political and military headquarters of the Palestine Liberation Organization (PLO), the seat of the PLO's "government-in-exile." When the PLO was forced to evacuate Beirut, Lebanon, in 1982 after being besieged by the Israeli Army, former Tunisian President Habib Bourguiba offered the battered revolutionary movement sanctuary, despite the legacy of death and destruction—first in Jordan and later in Lebanon—that seemed to accompany the PLO wherever it went. Bourguiba's longtime companion and mistress, Wassila, selected Hammam el-Shat as site of the PLO's new headquarters in large part because she didn't want to antagonize Tunisia's elite by choosing a more desirable location. In addition, it was deemed prudent to keep the PLO headquarters outside the capital and away from the population at large.

A large area in the center of the village was simply handed over to the PLO, which arbitrarily compensated former property owners for their homes and inconvenience. Most of the structures were small, few more than two stories in height, and were hardly adequate to accommodate the massive PLO bureaucracy and the thousands of militiamen and dependents who streamed into Tunisia. Thus, the PLO rapidly undertook an ambitious construction program and purchased additional buildings adjacent to the central compound.

Today a visitor to Hammam el-Shat must first stop at a guardhouse at the edge of the village and show his identity papers to Tunisian soldiers in gray uniforms who are armed with 7.62 mm Steyr submachine guns. After passing through the Tunisian checkpoint, the visitor is required to pause again a short distance away at a PLO checkpoint. The PLO men, all members of the elite internal security unit known as Force 17, wear civilian clothes and keep their arms out of sight. They are courteous and efficient and check with their operations center to verify that the visitor is expected. Once the visitor's identity has been confirmed, an escort officer accompanies the visitor everywhere he or she goes inside the compound.

As the visitor and escort officer proceed into the compound, they pass by the bombed-out ruins of buildings destroyed in the Israeli air raid on October 1, 1985, which left forty-seven dead and fifty-six wounded. One of the buildings leveled in the attack was the headquarters of Force 17, the shadowy covert unit that serves as PLO Chairman Yasir Arafat's Praetorian Guard and is used to carry out various deniable operations. The only thing left is the guardhouse that once stood in front of the building; the building itself was reduced to a pile of rubble. The Israeli planes narrowly missed killing Arafat, who had left the building only seven minutes before the attack.

A building that housed a group of former Sa'iqa commanders who remained loyal to the PLO after their organization broke ranks with Arafat in 1983 was another casualty of the Israeli attack. Nearby, however, stands the one-story building that serves as the PLO's communications center; its roof bristles with a forest of antennas. It was not damaged in the Israeli bombing raid, nor was Arafat's personal headquarters, a one-story structure that also stands in the midst of the ruins of other buildings. It is an unassuming structure in which Arafat maintains an office and a small apartment.

Today there are approximately fifteen to twenty small office structures, none higher than three or four stories, in the compound. Few of the PLO's top leaders live in the immediate area; most have moved to the more affluent suburbs of Tunis and commute to the compound each day to take care of administrative tasks.

The PLO compound was only lightly defended at the time of the Israeli air raid largely because it was thought that Tunis was too distant from Israel for the Israelis to consider seriously any kind of air attack against it. Tunisia, moreover, had never been a belligerent in any of the Arab-Israeli wars and had correct, but largely secret, relations with the Jewish state. Prior to the raid, neither the PLO nor the Tunisians had ever seriously considered the possibility of an Israeli air strike against Hammam el-Shat.

In the aftermath of the bombing, a joint committee composed of PLO representatives and Tunisian military officials was set up to review the security of the PLO compound. The Tunisians, however, refused to concede any independent authority to the PLO to provide for its own air defense, regarding this as an infringement of Tunisian sovereignty. They did finally agree to replace the old antiaircraft guns at Hammam el-Shat with four batteries of Chaparral short-range surface-to-air missiles, together with sophisticated target acquisition radars. (Ironically, the resulting situation witnessed U.S.-made missiles being used to protect the PLO from attack by a close American ally, Israel, armed with U.S.-manufactured warplanes and precision munitions.) Two of the missile batteries were placed between the compound and the shoreline, and the other two were located south of Hammam el-Shat near the coastal road, although they are camouflaged and not visible to travelers on the road. All four batteries were fully operational by late 1985. The Tunisian military, embarrassed by being caught unawares and unprepared in 1985, upgraded its own long-range radar capabilities with the acquisition of two new land-based systems from France and a new naval radar system.

After the PLO's number two man, Abu Jihad, was killed on April 16, 1988, by Israeli commandos who had infiltrated from the sea (see Chapter One), the Tunisian government came under heavy criticism, both in the parliament and in the local media, for having spent money on radars and weapons systems that apparently were incapable of offering any real protection to either Tunisia or the PLO. As a result, the defenses around Hammam el-Shat were shored up with the addition of several batteries of 20 mm M-163 Vulcan antiaircraft guns. Even with recent improvements, however, the current defenses around Hammam el-Shat are likely to prove inadequate since the Israelis have demonstrated more than once that they can shut down all of Tunisia's early-warning systems and reach the Tunisian coast without detection.

A GOVERNMENT-IN-EXILE?

If there is a certain ramshackle quality about the PLO "capital" at Hammam el-Shat, it is because most Palestinian leaders regard it only as a temporary way station on the road to realizing their dream of an independent Palestinian state. Why put money into something that is not permanent? they explain. Besides, everyone knows that the Israelis can strike Hammam el-Shat again, whenever they want, and the next bombing raid may not be so surgical.

Yet, when Arafat and the PLO arrived in Tunisia in 1982, they seemed defeated, their revolutionary goals more distant than ever. Most observers, including many within the PLO, conceded that Hammam el-Shat would be home to the PLO for the indefinite future, perhaps for a generation or more before the organization could recover the momentum and power it possessed before its expulsion from Lebanon. There was talk of Arafat's impending ouster as chairman and of unrest within the ranks that would lead, within months, to an open revolt against his leadership by some of the Palestinian units left behind in the Syrian-controlled Bekaa Valley of Lebanon.

But like the proverbial phoenix, the PLO has risen from the ashes of its defeat in Lebanon, as it did earlier after being driven from Jordan, and is closer than ever before to realizing its goal of an independent Palestinian state. As of this writing, there remain many hurdles for the Palestinians yet to overcome, not the least of which is Israel's adamant refusal to negotiate with the PLO or to entertain the idea of an independent Palestinian state composed of the West Bank and Gaza. Even if Israel were suddenly to reverse its present position, thorny problems like the future of Jerusalem and the seventy thousand Jewish settlers living in settlements on the West Bank could conceivably undermine any final agreement.

Nonetheless, the past twenty-four months have witnessed a series of dramatic events that have revitalized the PLO, solidified Arafat's leadership position, and brought the Palestinians into direct dialogue with the United States. Ironically, once again it was when things seemed darkest for Arafat and the PLO that opportunity was just around the corner.

The move to Hammam el-Shat forced the PLO to take the political road and largely to abandon, after some bloody outbursts, violence as the key to achieving its political goals and aspirations. The departure from Beirut, which the PLO had turned into the world's terrorist capital, marked the end of its ability to prosecute successfully an armed struggle against Israel and its allies. Hammam el-Shat, located sixteen hundred miles from from the land once known as Palestine, could not serve as a staging area for terrorist and military operations. By the mid-1980's it was clear to Arafat and most of the top leadership of the PLO that the freedom and sway they had enjoyed in Beirut were gone forever and that Lebanon could no longer serve as a model for their future strategy. They needed a new strategy appropriate to their present circumstances. Thus, Hammam el-Shat became the PLO's first "political," rather than military, capital.

The Israelis tried to destroy the PLO in Lebanon but failed. What they did, instead, was force the PLO to reconstitute itself into a much more politically oriented and effective organization. It was the same adversary; only it had a new conciliatory face. Its goals were the same, but it spoke the language of diplomacy rather than violence. The struggle for an independent Palestinian state had not been abandoned, just repackaged.

The ostensible abandonment of armed struggle by the PLO was initially greeted with dismay by many of the inhabitants of the West Bank and Gaza Strip, who still nurtured the hope that Israel could be defeated on the battlefield and that a Palestinian state could be resurrected on its ashes. It appeared that the PLO, their instrument of national salvation, had finally given up. Feeling abandoned and betrayed, the Palestinians of the West Bank and Gaza arrived at the grim realization that no one else was going to deliver them from their predicament; if anything were to change, they would have to bring about that change themselves, with their own blood and suffering. The uprising, or Intifada, that began in December 1987 came to symbolize a last-ditch effort by Palestinians to recover their own national identity and homeland. Where the PLO had used guns and tanks, they fought with stones and slingshots. They confronted what they regarded as the Israeli occupiers of their land not for some vague Arab cause or even the PLO and its hidden agenda but for their own vision of a Palestinian state, a vision that owed more to Israel than to the PLO or any Arab state.

The uprisings in the occupied territories began spontaneously and spread rapidly throughout the Palestinian population. At the outset there was little question but that it was a genuine popular uprising against the Israeli occupation of the West Bank and Gaza, fed by deep-seated economic, social, and political frustrations. Day after day the world was treated to the spectacle of the Israeli military, so dominant on the battlefield, haplessly fending off attacking youths armed with stones and slingshots. Ever more draconian Israeli measures to suppress the disturbances seemed to have exactly the opposite effect. Arafat and the PLO leadership initially underestimated the seriousness of the Intifada and appeared genuinely surprised by both the magnitude of the disturbances and the persistence, even in the face of brutal Israeli repression, of the rioters. They were initially contemptuous of the slogan of the Intifada: The stones of our children are more powerful than all of the Arab cannons. However, as time wore on, they could no longer deny the success of the stone throwers.

What the Intifada demonstrated, in part, was how out of touch Arafat and the leadership of the PLO had become. Most of their political ties were to a generation on the West Bank whose time had passed. Twenty years of Israeli rule had eroded the old patriarchal society that once existed on the West Bank, and the region had, in the space of twenty years, been transformed from a predominantly rural to an urban society. The young Palestinian men and women of the West Bank were not only contemptuous of their elders but unwilling to follow blindly the distant and often aloof leadership of the PLO, which was alien to them and their immediate problems. Perhaps the greatest irony of the Intifada is that for the young Palestinians of the West Bank it is what they see next door in Israel—freedom, democracy, prosperity—that they want for themselves and are willing to die for. They are not moved by the example of the Arab despotisms that surround them or the pronouncements out of Tunis.

The high command of the PLO was also unprepared for the decision of King Hussein of Jordan to terminate his grandfather's annexation of the West Bank. Since 1948 all civil matters relating to such things as the registration of births, deaths, and marriages, as well as the provision of travel documents, were handled by the Jordanian government, and this did not change after 1967, despite the fact that the West Bank was under Israeli control. Jordan also paid the salaries of the eighteen thousand Palestinian teachers and civil servants who toiled on the West Bank under Israeli military occupation.

Once Arafat and his lieutenants realized the impact of the disturbances on both Israel and international public opinion, especially in the Arab world, they moved rapidly to exert some kind of control over the mobs of stone throwers and the spreading defiance of the Palestinian population to Israeli rule. Perhaps more than anything else, they feared the emergence of a new Palestinian leadership that might challenge their supremacy.

The PLO pumped money into the troubled areas to sustain those in the streets and the thousands of Palestinians engaged in strikes and work stoppages in solidarity with the rioters. PLO agitators slipped into the occupied territories to provide leadership and training to the troublemakers. As the uprising approached its one-year anniversary, on November 15, 1988, the Palestinian National Council (PNC), meeting in Algiers, declared an independent Palestinian state on the West Bank and Gaza. In addition, the Palestinian legislative body seemed implicitly to recognize the existence of the state of Israel.

Shortly afterward Arafat was invited to address the United Nations General Assembly in New York, but U.S. Secretary of State George Shultz, citing "associations with terrorism," refused to grant Arafat a visa to come to the United States. According to the statement issued by the U.S. Department of State:

The U.S. government has convincing evidence that PLO elements have engaged in terrorism against Americans and others. This evidence includes a series of operations undertaken by the Force 17 and Hawari organizations since the PLO claimed to forswear the use of terrorism in the Cairo Declaration of November 1985.

As chairman of the PLO, Mr. Arafat is responsible for actions of these organizations which are units of Fatah, an element of the PLO of which he is chairman and which is under his control. The most recent sign of Mr. Arafat's associations with terrorism was the presence at the Algiers session of the Palestine National Council (PNC) this month of Abu Abbas, a member of the executive committee of the PLO who has been convicted by the Italian judicial system of the murder of an American citizen, Mr. Leon Klinghoffer.[2]

The action provoked almost universal criticism of Shultz's decision, by U.S. allies and adversaries alike, and the General Assembly condemned the U.S. position on Arafat by a 151 to 2 margin. The General Assembly also voted to reconvene in Geneva to hear Arafat.

On December 7, 1988, following meetings with prominent U.S. Jews in Stockholm, Arafat, speaking on behalf of the PLO, accepted the right of Israel to exist. Six days later he reiterated his pledge in Geneva, before the UN General Assembly, and called on Israel to join in peace talks aimed at resolving outstanding differences. Arafat told the assembled UN delegates:

> The PLO will seek a comprehensive settlement among the parties concerned in the Arab-Israeli conflict, including the state of Palestine, Israel and other neighbors, within the framework of the international conference for peace in the Middle East on the basis of Resolutions 242 and 338 and so as to guarantee equality and the balance of interests, especially our people's rights in freedom, national independence, and respect the right to exist in peace and security for all.[3]

Under mounting international pressure, the United States had reversed its previous position and, through intermediaries, informed the PLO leadership that it was prepared for a substantive dialogue with the PLO if certain preconditions were met, including the renunciation of terrorism and the explicit recognition of the state of Israel. The United States had been assured that Arafat's address to the General Assembly would contain language approved by the State Department regarding the two key points, but the PLO chairman and his advisers changed the text at the last minute, and U.S. spokesmen made it clear that Arafat had not lived up to his end of the bargain and that there would be no dialogue. In a news conference the following day Arafat sought to clarify his statements before the General Assembly and articulate precisely, and without equivocation, the exact concessions sought by the United States. "In my speech also yesterday," said Arafat, "it was clear that we mean our people's rights to freedom and national independence, according to Resolution 181, and the right of all parties concerned in the Middle East conflict to exist in peace and security, and, as I have mentioned, including the state of Palestine, Israel and other neighbors, according to the Resolution 242 and 338."[4]

Thus, Arafat publicly accepted UN Security Council Resolutions 181, 242, and 338 without linking his acceptance to Palestinian self-determination. He also declared that the PLO "renounces" terrorism, rather than simply "condemns" it, long a point of contention and one particularly troublesome to Secretary of State Shultz and the United States. All ambiguities having been removed, the United States subsequently announced that all its preconditions had been met and that direct talks with the PLO could commence. U.S. Ambassador to Tunisia Robert H. Pelletreau, Jr., a former CIA official, was designated as the sole authorized channel for the dialogue.

With the stunning U.S. action, many observers proclaimed that a new chapter had been opened in the history of the Middle East conflict and that a lasting regional peace might finally be attainable. International opinion was overwhelmingly favorable; only in Israel were there shock and dismay over the U.S. decision, despite repeated reiterations of U.S. support for the Jewish state.

A Palestinian state, however, is still far from being a reality. Many major points of contention remain. Arafat has yet to demonstrate that he can police his own community and provide the kinds of assurances necessary for Israel to take him at his word. It is debatable whether a 2,336-square-mile Palestinian ministate, composed of the West Bank (2187.5 square miles, including Jerusalem) and Gaza (148.5 square miles), about the size of Delaware, would fulfill the aspirations of the PLO. It might turn out to be an even greater source of instability than the present stateless PLO, capable of undermining the security and stability of both Israel and Jordan.

There is little agreement, moreover, on what the boundaries of a potential Palestinian state would be. How can the problem of the forty-three-mile geographical gap between Gaza and the West Bank be solved? What would be its relationship with Jordan, which has a Palestinian majority? What kind of government would the new Palestinian state opt for: a representative democracy or an authoritarian system like most of the rest of the Middle East? Would its economy emphasize state planning or capitalism, or would it be some kind of mixed economy? Would it be a demilitarized state? If not, what kinds of military alliances would be permissible? Is the top leadership of the PLO ready to settle down and abandon its revolutionary pursuits for the hard work of nation building?

Even if Israel is ultimately compelled to accept some kind of accommodation with the PLO, the creation of a Palestinian state is not simply a Middle East issue; it has far-reaching implications for the United States and its allies. Indeed, the PLO has—since its inception—lined up politically and militarily with the enemies of the United States. Many of the PLO's top leaders are Marxists who gravitate naturally toward Moscow and to revolutionary regimes in the Third World. Despite public statements condemning terrorism for more than a decade, the PLO contains a number of terrorist organizations that have, in recent years, carried out attacks resulting in the loss of American lives. Arafat himself can be directly linked to the deaths of many Americans.

In the past the PLO and its apologists have used U.S. support of Israel to justify opposition to the United States and attacks on its citizens and interests. There is no assurance, however, that any eventual Israeli-Palestinian agreement will alleviate all sources of disagreement and tension between the United States and the PLO (or a PLO-dominated Palestinian state). Despite the publicity routinely accorded the PLO, there is little real understanding in the United States of its history, leadership, goals, and operations. This book is an attempt to correct that deficiency.

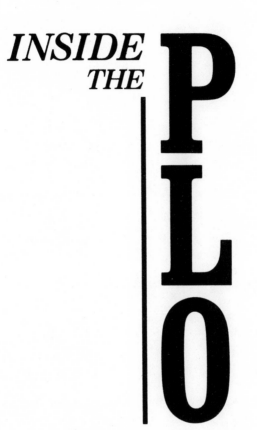

INSIDE THE
PLO

1 The Death of Abu Jihad

The Israeli Navy closely patrols its coastal waters to interdict would-be saboteurs and terrorists attempting to penetrate the country from the sea. In addition, helicopters skim up and down the beaches, reinforced by foot and Jeep patrols. Power plants and other high-consequence targets located near the shore are particularly well fortified and ringed with fences, sensors, bright lights, and other impediments to discourage terrorist attacks. The threat of attack from the sea has increased proportionally to the success the Israelis have had in sealing off their land borders with a sophisticated system of electronic fences and foot patrols.

Today it is Israel's coastline that represents its greatest vulnerability, and a number of recent terrorist attacks launched from the sea stand as a stark reminder of the need for constant vigilance by the Israel Defense Forces (IDF) regarding waterborne assaults. In March 1975 a Fatah squad landed on a Tel Aviv beach in two rubber dinghies, intent on attacking the Municipality Youth Center. However, a policeman raised the alarm, and the terrorists seized the nearest available target, the Hotel Savoy, in the city's red-light district. When it was all over, seven terrorists lay dead (one survived), along with three Israeli soldiers and eight hostages. Three years later, in March 1978, thirteen Fatah terrorists left a "mother ship" off Israel's coast in two large rubber rafts. They hit the coast about twenty miles south of Haifa near a kibbutz, where they murdered an American woman, the niece of U.S. Senator Abraham Ribicoff, walking alone on the beach. They subsequently hijacked a bus on the coastal highway. After killing some of the passengers, they sped toward Tel Aviv, crashing through hastily erected police roadblocks and firing indiscriminately at passing cars, buses, and pedestrians. The bus was finally halted just north of Tel Aviv and assaulted by Israeli police. Nine of the terrorists were killed, and two were apprehended; two others had drowned when they were swept overboard before the rafts reached shore. Forty-six people were killed, and at least eighty-five wounded in the incident.

It was precisely to guard against such incidents that, on the night of April 12, 1985, the Israeli Navy was put on alert after receiving an intelligence report that "terrorists are planning a landing on the shores of Tel Aviv." The report indicated that a ship had already set sail from the Algerian naval base at Annaba and was somewhere in the Mediterranean en route to Israel. On board the vessel, according to the report, were several squads of terrorists, who would be off-loaded into high-speed rubber rafts someplace beyond Israel's territorial waters. Their precise target was not known, but the terrorists were heavily armed and outfitted.[1]

Such reports often turned out to be false alarms, but this one was particularly detailed and compelling. It came from a highly reliable source. Thus, the decision was made at headquarters to place the Israeli Navy on a higher state of readiness in the event that the threat turned out to be real. The alert was still in effect nine days later, on April 21, as an Israeli SATIL, or missile boat, cruised at low speed in international waters, some hundred miles west of Israel's coast. It was another routine evening. The vessel was a fast attack craft (missile), or FAC(G), armed with four Gabriel and eight Harpoon sea-to-sea missiles (SSMs). Each Israeli SATIL, designated in Hebrew as a Sa'ar 4, also has ½-inch and 76-mm deck-mounted machine guns and a 20-mm Vulcan Gatling gun. Each with a crew of forty and with their CICs (command information centers) jammed with sophisticated electronic gear, the SATILs had often demonstrated their effectiveness, especially during the 1973 Middle East War, when they sank a number of Syrian naval vessels.

Sometime during the night of April 21, as the SATIL, which was patrolling in a box pattern, like two sister vessels some distance away, began to execute a turn, the radar operator suddenly saw a faint blip on his green screen. It was still far away. Initially it seemed to be heading for the Suez Canal, but a short time later its course began to shift in an easterly direction. The radar operator notified the captain of the SATIL. After examining the screen, the captain told his crew that it was probably just a navigational error on the part of the unidentified vessel, which would soon be corrected. But just the same, said the captain, let's keep an eye on it.

He ordered the SATIL to increase its speed to twenty knots. The seas were calm, and the SATIL glided along silently, its sharp bow cutting easily through the calm water. As the minutes ticked by, the blip on the radar screen grew stronger. It appeared to be a small vessel, not much larger than the SATIL, steaming at a speed of a little above ten knots in a northeasterly direction, which, if only slightly adjusted, would result in landfall at Tel Aviv.

Without hesitation, the captain ordered his crew to battle stations and informed the navy's headquarters in Tel Aviv. That done, he returned to the bridge and ordered a change of course and a further increase in speed so that he could interdict the errant vessel.

He had already made up his mind to take a look at the vessel in order to ascertain its intentions. He still regarded the vessel as what is known in navy slang as a skunk—that is, an unidentified ship. He knew by experience that it was probably a false alarm, but prudence dictated that every unidentified contact be checked out with the same caution and concentration that would be accorded a known hostile craft. The new course ordered by the captain would permit the SATIL to approach the skunk at a ninety-degree angle of attack, which would reveal the skunk's full profile, making identification easier, while only exposing the SATIL's narrow silhouette. If he was lucky, the captain knew, he might get within half a mile of the skunk before he was discovered.

Every few minutes the captain was provided with updated position reports from his vessel's command information center, which were further confirmed and verified by Naval Headquarters in Tel Aviv. Land-based fighters were also standing by in the event the captain needed additional firepower or support. As the SATIL closed rapidly on the skunk, the captain, eager to get the first glimpse of the potential intruder, scanned the dark waters of the Mediterranean through the night-vision telescope on the bridge.

The SATIL was almost on top of the skunk before the captain saw it, dead ahead. He ordered the engines cut, and the SATIL slid forward noiselessly, while the captain and crew tried, without success, to identify the vessel from its profile and markings. The captain then ordered the SATIL's searchlights turned on. Moments later a small freighter, with a displacement of about a thousand tons, lay directly in front of them, bathed in the brilliant white light. The SATIL fired a red flare to indicate to the skunk that it was required to stop to permit a check of its identity.

Suddenly there was a flash on the deck of the skunk. One of the lookouts yelled that someone on board the skunk had fired a rocket-propelled grenade (RPG) antitank weapon at them. The rocket missed the SATIL, but there was no longer any doubt about the unidentified vessel's identity; by its hostile action it had transformed itself from a skunk into a wolf, slang for an enemy ship. There was also small-arms fire coming from its deck. The captain gave the order to return fire, and the SATIL's 20 mm Vulcan Gatling gun cracked into action almost instantaneously, its six rotating barrels spewing fire at the wolf. At a rate of more than four thousand rounds a minute, the tracers being fed into the gun merged into a continuous stream of fire that linked the SATIL to its prey for several seconds. Then the target seemed to evaporate. The captain gave the cease-fire order. The smoking Vulcan, with its staggering firepower, recalled the line from *The Rubaiyat of Omar Khayyam:* "The Moving Finger writes; and, having writ, moves on. . . ." The wolf had disintegrated, almost everything above the waterline having been blasted away. For a few moments the hull lurched forward with the propeller still churning water. Then it, too, disappeared from sight.[2]

Silence descended over the scene, and the SATIL radioed its

report to Naval Headquarters and began the search for survivors. Within half an hour eight survivors and one body had been pulled from the water. Another SATIL had arrived at the site of the engagement and was standing off a short distance away in case it was needed.

The next morning the survivors were interrogated by Israeli intelligence officers. According to their testimony, there had been twenty-eight Palestinian commandos on board the ship. All were members of Fatah and had begun training at the Algerian naval base of Annaba in May 1984, in preparation for the operation. On April 12, shortly before they departed, they got a final briefing from Abu Jihad, the commander of Fatah's military forces.

The ship was the *Attavarious,* and it carried three high-speed rubber rafts with engines and a fiber glass dinghy with an outboard engine. The terrorists had been divided into three teams, all equipped with AK-47 assault rifles, RPGs, grenades, and explosives. The first team of seven commandos had been instructed to land on a relatively deserted beach near Tel Aviv, secure some kind of transport, and then fight its way to the Israeli defense complex in downtown Tel Aviv. Once inside the complex, the commandos were supposed to seize Israel's defense minister and as many high-ranking military officers as possible.

The second and third teams, each with seven commandos, had orders to land at Bat Yam, a southern suburb of Tel Aviv, and seize transport and hostages. Like the first team, they were then to converge on the defense complex with their hostages and rejoin their confederates. It was hoped the operation would disrupt Israel's thirty-seventh Independence Day observance on April 22, once again affirming the terrorists' affinity for timing their operations in conjunction with anniversaries and special dates.

Later that day, on April 22, twenty-four hours before the IDF officially went public with the *Attavarious* saga, an anonymous caller, who identified himself only as the spokesman for the "United Command of the Revolutionary Palestinian Forces," called a number of major news agencies in Beirut. He claimed that as he spoke, a major battle was being fought at Bat Yam. According to the caller, a ship had disgorged three boatloads of commandos at nine the previous evening. One boat had capsized, the caller said, but the other two had reached the beach and been engaged in a furious fire fight all night against the overwhelming forces of the IDF.[3]

Although few at the time understood the significance of the abortive Palestinian raid, a major threshold had been crossed. The *Attavarious* affair set into motion events that three years later, almost to the day, resulted in the death of Abu Jihad.

THE TARGET

Since the PLO relocated to Tunis, the once-peaceful nation of Tunisia has been drawn into the Middle East maelstrom and become a battleground in the war between the Israelis and the PLO. The most recent chapter in this struggle occurred after midnight on April 16, 1988, when a team of crack Israeli commandos slipped into Tunis and gunned down the number two man in the PLO, Khalil Ibrahim Machmud al-Wazir, better known by his nom de guerre, Abu Jihad. It was a daring but carefully planned and executed operation, sixteen hundred miles from Israel, which affirmed once again not only Israel's unparalleled special operations capability but also the ruthless extremes to which the embattled nation will go to protect its citizens and national interests.

As one of the raiding parties that would rendezvous at Tunis left Israel, the commander of a group of commandos turned to a companion and observed that it was the fifteenth anniversary of Operation Spring Youth. Spring Youth was the 1973 Israeli raid that, ironically, brought Abu Jihad to his position of prominence in the PLO by eliminating Black September leader Abu Yussef (Mohammed Yussef al-Najjar) and his deputy, Kamal Adwan, along with the Palestinian poet Kammal Nasser, the PLO's chief spokesman in Beirut.

During the night of April 9–10, 1973, approximately thirty Israeli commandos, members of the elite Sayaret Matkal and other special operations units, left missile boats in Zodiac rafts and landed on a beach near Beirut. The first two teams linked up with agents of Israel's foreign intelligence service, the Mossad (Ha-Mossad Le-Modeen Letafkidim Meyuchadim) who had slipped into the city earlier and climbed into vehicles that had been leased from Avis. One team sped toward the apartment house where Abu Yussef, Nasser, and Adwan lived, and gunned down the three men, while the other team blew up the headquarters of the Democratic Front for the Liberation of Palestine (DFLP). A third team, which had landed farther down the beach and was commanded by a former Israeli defense attaché in Washington, destroyed a Black September ordnance center, which included a car bomb workshop.

Several Israeli commandos were killed and wounded during the operation, and the retreating Israelis ran into heavy resistance as they raced back to the beach and the Zodiac rafts that would be used in their escape. Although the operation was supposed to be covert, hence deniable, the Israelis were forced to send in helicopters to evacuate the casualties and to drop spikes and caltrops on the roads to delay pursuit.[4]

Within weeks of the successful Israeli raid Abu Jihad was appointed chief of military operations of the PLO and commander in chief of the occupied West Bank and Gaza Strip, combining both portfolios of his dead predecessors. Abu Jihad was certainly not an unknown commodity to the Israelis. Born in 1936 into a well-to-do family that dwelled in the town of Ramle, on the Jaffa–Jerusalem road, he spent his formative years in the British mandate of Palestine. During the 1948 war, following the creation of the state of Israel, Abu Jihad's family was driven out of Ramle and took refuge in the town of Gaza, where Wazir completed his studies. At the age of twenty, Abu Jihad entered Cairo University, where he met Arafat and formed a relationship that lasted more than three decades.

Following graduation, he settled in Kuwait as a teacher and married his cousin Intisar Mustafa Machmud al-Wazir, who later became known as Um-Jihad and is head of the PLO's Martyrs' Fund. In Kuwait Abu Jihad established himself as a Palestinian activist, and following the creation of Fatah, he moved to Damascus to become the organization's financial chief. He also took the name Abu Jihad ("father of the holy war").[5] Together with Arafat, Abu Jihad planned the first Fatah attack against Israel, the operation described in Chapter Two involving an attempt to bomb a pumping station that was part of Israel's national irrigation system.

Although Fatah was launched with Syria's blessing, its leadership had no intention of becoming a handmaiden to Syrian policy. The independence demonstrated by Fatah soon brought Arafat and Abu Jihad into conflict with the Alawite minority that controls Syria, and they were accused of being involved in a failed coup attempt against the government. Abu Jihad was arrested, and in an act of mind-numbing brutality, thugs from the Syrian security service threw his young son Nidal from the balcony of the family's sixth-floor apartment to his death.

After his release from prison, Abu Jihad moved to Jordan, where he helped reestablish Fatah and preside over the dramatic growth of the PLO that followed.

In the early 1970's, after the PLO was driven from Jordan, Abu Jihad was given full command over all PLO military and terrorist operations and probably over those of certain groups outside the PLO umbrella that claim, for the record, to be independent elements of the Palestinian resistance. The list of terrorist operations personally planned and supervised by Abu Jihad is long. It includes the attack on the Israeli border town of Nahariyya in June 1974, which left four Israelis dead and six wounded; the hostage-taking episode at the Savoy Hotel; the hijacking of an Israeli bus in March 1978; the murder of two Israeli sailors in Barcelona, Spain, in September 1985; and, most recently, the seizure of a bus near the Dimona nuclear facility which left three Israelis dead and another three wounded.[6]

Indeed, far from being a "moderate" as he has been portrayed by many in the media, Abu Jihad was the architect of the terrorism that has held Israel in its grip for more than two decades. In one of his rare interviews he was quoted as saying: "The Kalashnikov [the Soviet-designed AK-47] is our only language until we free all of Palestine." In recent years he solidified his position in the PLO hierarchy and was widely regarded as Arafat's most likely successor. In this role he developed close ties to the military and intelligence organizations of many Arab governments—especially those in Syria, Libya, Jordan, and Algeria—and was generally viewed as the most cunning and resourceful PLO official by Arab leaders.

By contrast with Arafat, he was considered thoughtful and scholarly. He taught himself English and was a voracious reader, whose study was lined with books in French, English, and Arabic about Israel, especially its military and intelligence capabilities. He was consumed with a need to know every last shred of information about his adversary, as if he could somehow discover the clue that would seal Israel's destruction. He even read the daily Jerusalem *Post.* So fascinated was he by Israel that he once quipped that "when the war comes to an end, I will learn Hebrew."[7]

Highly secular in his world outlook, Abu Jihad was deeply influenced by Marxist thought, although it is hard to say whether he considered himself a Marxist. What is known is that he was an admirer of Mao Zedong and had received intelligence and military training in China during the early 1960's.

He had few vices. He chain-smoked, drank excessive amounts of black coffee, and loved nothing better than to linger over a meal with friends and family. While other PLO chieftains are frequently criticized by younger members of the PLO as "fat cats," addicted to luxury and pleasure, Abu Jihad lived modestly and was not known to maintain a mistress or bank accounts abroad. He was a devoted family man with five children, one of whom he named after his dead son Nidal. Yasir Arafat was his closest friend and treated Abu Jihad's children as though they were his own.

WAR IN THE SHADOWS

The Israeli war against the leadership of Black September and other Palestinian terrorist organizations began in earnest in 1972 after the slaughter of Israeli athletes at Munich and attacks on Israeli diplomats and supporters in Europe. Prime Minister Golda Meir summoned two of her top advisers—General Aharon Yariv, her personal adviser on terrorist activities, and General Zvi Zamir, head of the Mossad—and told them that what Israel had been doing to combat terrorism was not working and that new methods of fighting back were needed. After reflecting on the problem, Yariv and Zamir recommended that Israel carry the war to the terrorists and target the top leadership of Black September, not the rank and file but the people who actually planned and conducted the operations against Israel. Only by making the hunters the hunted, they reasoned, could Israel defend itself against the outrages of Black September and the PLO.

It was an agonizing decision for Meir, who worried that the decision to target individual terrorists might be morally corrosive or somehow antithetical to Israel's liberal traditions. Finally, however, she told Yariv and Zamir, "Send forth the boys."

In the months that followed, twelve top Black September operatives were eliminated by Mossad agents, known publicly as the Wrath of God, which was simply a cover in the event something ever went wrong. And something did go wrong, terribly wrong, on the thirteenth try. A team of Israeli agents gunned down a young Arab in Lillehammer, Norway, believing him to be the elusive Ali Hassan Salameh. He turned out to have been a Moroccan waiter, and six members of the Israeli hit team were captured and five sentenced to prison terms. In retrospect, it may well be that the Israelis were lured to Lillehammer by Black September operatives, who knew that they could bring international censure down on Israel, and perhaps neutralize the Mossad threat, by setting up a hit on the wrong man.

Although the Israeli government quietly passed the word that it was disbanding the Wrath of God teams, the war has continued up to the present day. But the war in the shadows has been far from one-sided. In addition to the constant drumbeat of terrorism and regular attacks on Israel by PLO infiltrators, a number of Mossad operatives have been killed by Palestinian hit squads. A top Mossad covert operator was assassinated in Madrid; another, wounded in Brussels. The Mossad's chief of station in France, Jacob Bar-Simantov, was killed on April 3, 1982.

HIT LIST

It has been the policy of every Israeli government since that headed by Golda Meir to give no quarter to those who plan and conduct terrorist operations against Israel. When the opportunity has presented itself, Israel has struck back with fury at its antagonists. Accordingly, the Israeli security services have maintained a list of those marked for death. First and foremost are the names of the few remaining perpetrators of the bloody attack on Israeli athletes at Munich in 1972, especially Abu Iyad. Others on the list include Abu Nidal; the commander of Force 17, Abu Tayeb; and the top leadership of the PLO infrastructure. From 1973 on the Israelis targeted Abu Jihad for death, and for much of that time he was the top name on the list. The bill of particulars against Abu Jihad was long. He personally briefed, and often bade farewell to, every terrorist team sent against Israel or an Israeli target, as he had in connection with the *Attavarious* affair. He often selected the targets himself, in an ongoing effort to locate Israel's soft underbelly. Although in private he reportedly had great respect for the Mossad and Israel's military prowess, in public Abu Jihad was contemptuous of Israel's ability to strike back at him. He openly commanded his terrorist squads and crowed over their "victories."

In September 1985 three Israelis were murdered on board a yacht anchored in Cyprus, the body of one woman left grotesquely slumped over a railing. It appears that they were innocent victims of mistaken identification by a team of PLO killers, which included a British gunman. Indeed, all were members of Force 17. In retaliation, the Israelis bombed the PLO compound at Hammam el-Shat in October 1985 (see Introduction). In carrying out the air strike on the PLO facility in Tunis, the Israelis relied in part on intelligence and planning that already had been done. Shortly after the PLO had relocated its "capital" to Tunisia, Israeli planners had prepared a comprehensive operation designed to destroy the organization's communications and operational infrastructure and thereby keep the PLO permanently on the defensive, rather than in an offensive posture.

Indeed, within days of the PLO's decision to relocate to Tunis, Israel's intelligence organizations began concentrating their attention on Tunisia. Information was gathered through public sources, as well as by stepped-up electronic surveillance and eavesdropping techniques. A converted Boeing 707, jammed with electronic gear, was often "parked" off the Tunisian coast to monitor Tunisian and PLO communications.[8] Once the size and scope of Palestinian activities in Tunis became clear, Israeli intelligence operatives initiated a crash program to recruit Tunisian agents. Some were recruited abroad; others, within Tunisia itself. When greed was used as an incentive, the Tunisian "assets" were told directly that they were working for Israeli intelligence. Some high-ranking Tunisian officials, who later were of invaluable help, were recruited under false pretenses, believing that they were working for various European intelligence services rather than the Israelis. Finally, some Tunisians, resentful of the PLO presence in their country, actually volunteered their services to the Israelis.

Efforts were even made to penetrate the various Palestinian groups themselves. In some instances Israeli agents pretended to be members of rival Palestinian groups. On other occasions money and other favors were used as incentives.

By mid-1985 the Israeli intelligence network in Tunisia was extensive and highly reliable. Israeli intelligence agents came and went at will, using forged or stolen passports, often disguised as Arab businessmen or European tourists. Members of Israel's elite navy commando unit, Flotilla 13, regularly infiltrated Tunisian territory, mapping beaches, inspecting potential landing strips, and generally getting to know the lay of the land. A local support network was established, safe houses were rented, weapons hidden in caches, and a clandestine communications system was put in place— all without incident. Most important of all, the Israelis developed an intimate knowledge of Tunis, which was to serve them well during the operation against Abu Jihad. So complete was the Israeli intelligence gathering that elements of the supersecret commando unit known until 1978 as General Headquarters Reconnaissance Unit 269 (it now has another numerical designation) and popularly called the Sayaret Matkal[9] even collected information about the residences of the various Palestinian leaders and thus were well prepared with precise information about Abu Jihad's villa when the order came to act.

THE DECISION TO KILL ABU JIHAD

The covert war between Israel and the PLO heated up once again in the fall of 1987. It did so for a number of reasons. The PLO had stepped up efforts to penetrate Israel and carry out attacks on Israeli territory. It was being assisted in this effort by a new alliance in southern Lebanon between the PLO and the Shiite terrorist organization Hizballah, which was a proxy of the late Ayatollah Khomeini's radical regime in Teheran. The emerging relationship between the two terrorist organizations spread alarm throughout the Israeli leadership. Finally, sometime during the early fall, Israeli intelligence came into possession of highly detailed information concerning the secret financial and logistic infrastructure of the PLO. As a result of all of these factors, it was decided in Jerusalem to take preemptive action against the PLO and its operational structure.

PLO and Fatah operatives were killed by the Mossad in Athens, in southern Lebanon, and on Cyprus. Meanwhile, consideration was given once again to mounting a major effort to assassinate Abu Jihad. Intelligence collection regarding Abu Jihad's habits and movements was intensified, and an old contingency plan to launch a commando attack against him at his residence near Tunis was dusted off and updated.

In early March 1988 Abu Jihad's fate was sealed at a fateful meeting between Israel's top military and intelligence officials and members of the so-called Prime Ministers' Club, composed of Israel's two former prime ministers, Defense Minister Yitzhak Rabin and Foreign Minister Shimon Peres, and the nation's current prime minister, Yitzhak Shamir. Israel's chief of staff, Lieutenant General Dan Shomron, who had commanded the 1976 Entebbe raid; his deputy and chief of operations, Major General Ehud Barak, a veteran of the Sayaret Matkal and the commander of Operation Spring Youth; Colonel Yigal Preseler, an antiterrorism adviser to the prime minister and also a veteran special forces operator; Chief of

Military Intelligence (AMAN) Major General Amnon Shahak; and the chief of the Mossad, Nachum Admoni, and his principal deputy, recommended that a major operation be put into motion to kill Abu Jihad.

In addition to his past transgressions, their recommendation was based on four factors. First, the *Attavarious* operation—though a failure—represented a violation of the unwritten code against targeting the top leadership of either side.[10] Since Abu Jihad was, for all intents and purposes, Rabin's counterpart, his involvement in the effort to penetrate the Israeli defense complex and either kill or take hostage Israel's top defense officials made him fair game for Israeli retaliation.

Second, there was deepening concern in Israel's intelligence community over the emerging alliance between the PLO and the radical Shiite terrorist organization Hizballah. In addition, the PLO had stepped up military operations against Israel itself, and the Israelis were looking for a way to strike back at the operational structure of the PLO.

Third, Abu Jihad's fate was sealed when it was learned that he was playing a crucial role in the West Bank and Gaza uprisings, the Intifada. The original uprising had begun spontaneously, without PLO involvement, but Abu Jihad had moved quickly to consolidate his control over events and to mobilize Palestinian discontent in the occupied territories. It was clear that he was in control of the insurrection, funneling money and instructions to operatives on the scene to sustain and nurture the violence. In this connection he had resisted any arming of the local Palestinian population, so as to cast Israel in the role of the "heavy." Day after day the world was treated to the spectacle of heavily armed Israelis beating and shooting stone-throwing Palestinians in a kind of reverse David and Goliath scenario. Ever the master tactician, Abu Jihad preferred to sacrifice Palestinian lives to win the world's sympathy and to pressure Israel on the issue of the occupied territories.

Israeli intelligence had discovered that Abu Jihad was personally directing his operatives on the West Bank and Gaza by placing international calls to them routed through international switchboards in Geneva and other European cities so as to disguise their origin. On a number of occasions he actually identified himself by name.

Abu Jihad, in short, was the link between the leadership of the Intifada and the PLO. He had been the PLO official in charge of the occupied territories for fifteen years and, virtually alone among the top leadership of the PLO, was aware of the changes taking place on the West Bank and Gaza. His wife, Um-Jihad, as head of the Martyrs' Fund, had looked after the families of those from the West Bank and Gaza whose breadwinners had been jailed, injured, or killed. Abu Jihad was respected by the young leadership of the Intifada because he had personally fought against the Israelis, unlike Arafat, Abu Iyad, Abu Lutf and the others.

According to Israeli intelligence sources, Abu Jihad was already planning the next, or third, stage of the revolt, which was the establishment of a shadow Palestinian government in the occupied territories that, in the view of most top Israeli officials, could make the West Bank and Gaza ungovernable.

Israel was also alarmed by the destruction of its informer network within the Palestinian community. All Palestinian collaborators with Israel simultaneously had been called to mosques and churches throughout the occupied territories and given the opportunity to end their ties to the Shin-Bet, Israel's internal security service. Each was offered mercy in exchange for turning in any weapons and swearing not to continue as an active informer. The alternative, of course, was death or banishment. What disturbed the Israeli intelligence community most about the action was the fact that virtually every collaborator and informer they had had had been fingered by Abu Jihad's seemingly all-knowing intelligence network.

Finally, there was simply the question of opportunity. In late February or early March an informant inside the PLO had provided the Israelis with specific information about Abu Jihad's movements. They knew exactly when he was expected to return to Tunis, and in the view of Israel's military and intelligence leaders, all that remained was to set the trap.

The members of the Prime Ministers' Club wasted little time in giving the operation a green light, and the March 7, 1988, Palestinian infiltration near Dimona, planned and orchestrated by Abu Jihad, simply reaffirmed their decision. It may well be that in arriving at the decision to kill Abu Jihad, Israel's political, military, and intelligence leaders were also motivated by additional factors. For example, the public esteem and credibility of Israel's military forces had been tarnished in recent years by the unpopular 1982 invasion of Lebanon. There had also been a storm of criticism over the army's failure to prevent recent Palestinian incursions into Israel, especially incidents involving a guerrilla who rode a hang glider over Israel's defenses and a terrorist squad that commandeered a car driven by three IDF (Israel Defense Forces) officers, who fled in terror rather than battle them. The Palestinian uprising in the occupied territories, moreover, had been met by confusion and brutality on the part of many Israeli soldiers, often in front of television cameras. Israel's military leaders, therefore, were eager for an opportunity to strike fear into the hearts of their enemies and to demonstrate that Israel could still carry out complex military operations far from its own borders. A dramatic success in Tunis, they reckoned, would do a great deal to rehabilitate the flagging prestige of the IDF.

For its part, Israel's intelligence community supported the mission to make up for its failure to predict the onset or severity of the Intifada. In addition, the six-year term of the director of the Mossad, Nachum Admoni, was to expire at the end of 1988, and it can be postulated that he, like all his predecessors, was eager to leave his post on the heels of a major success.

Israel's political leadership was certainly aware that a general election would be held before the end of 1988, and it must be speculated that each member of the Prime Ministers' Club sought to calculate the potential advantages and disadvantages inherent in such a mission. Also, despite their political differences, they worried about Abu Jihad's increasing effectiveness and power within the PLO. He was clearly emerging as the strongest potential successor to Arafat, whom the Israelis viewed as relatively complacent, self-indulgent, and uninspired. The thought of Abu Jihad's becoming chief of the PLO was a nightmare that no Israeli leader wanted to experience. Should he be eliminated, there was no successor on the horizon with his intelligence, shrewdness, and twenty-three years of operational experience.

THE PLAN

A number of key decisions that were taken at the outset shaped the essential nature of the operation against Abu Jihad and contributed greatly to its success. The operation was placed under the unified command of the military, including the collection of intelligence and other Mossad support activities. Mossad agents on the ground in Tunisia were charged with providing much of the operational intelligence and logistical support that was needed, but they were subordinated to the military and could not be tasked separately or act alone.

Four missile boats of corvette class, two Sa'ar 4.5's and two Sa'ar 4's, were assigned to the mission as mother ships, to transport the raiding party to Tunisia and evacuate it after the attack. The Sa'ar 4.5's, code-named Chochit, were each equipped with specially designed Bell 206 helicopters capable of evacuating casualties in the event of an emergency. One of the 4.5's was also equipped with a full hospital and surgical facility. To treat possible casualties, two of Israel's finest doctors—a surgeon and an anesthesiologist—were called back to active reserve duty to assist the army medical team that would be aboard the vessel. They participated in all the rehearsals and preraid exercises. The most serious medical problem they had to deal with, however, was the seasickness of some of the commandos on the long voyage to and from Tunisia.

Major General Barak was named overall commander of the operation, and one of the Sa'ar 4.5's was to serve as operational headquarters for the mission. With Barak in the command center would be the Mossad's deputy director of operations (who less than a year later rose to the top post in the Mossad) and Israel's chief of naval operations, who would be in direct command of the naval component.

The actual mission would be carried out by elements from the Sayaret Matkal and Flotilla 13. The naval commandos would be given the task of transporting the men of Sayaret Matkal to a rendezvous with Mossad agents on a beach near the ruins of Carthage and subsequently securing the beach-head and equipment. They would also evacuate the "hit" team back to the missile boats, once the mission was finished. The attack itself on Abu Jihad was to be carried out by a select team of commandos from the Sayaret Matkal, under the oper-ational command of its commander in chief.

Two Boeing 707's, one functioning as a flying headquarters and the other as an airborne reconnaissance and electronic warfare platform, would also be deployed. On board the head-quarters craft (identification number 4X-007) would be the chief of the Israeli Air Force, Major General Avihu Ben-Nun, who would coordinate all air activity with General Barak. The Mossad director and his military intelligence counterpart, Major General Shahak of the AMAN, would be aboard the other 707 (identification number 4X-497), coordinating the flow of the latest intelligence. Their RC-707 would also serve as a relay station, transmitting the action on the ground to the war room in the Israeli defense complex in Tel Aviv. In this way Tel Aviv would be in direct contact with the Sayaret Matkal commandos. Two flying tankers, also Boeing 707's, would be positioned over the Mediterranean to refuel the air-borne contingent, and four F-15 fighters would be in the vicin-ity to provide protection for the 707's and air support to the men on the ground in the event that trouble occurred.

Far from being a lone "jackal" with a silenced rifle, the hit team assigned to kill Abu Jihad was composed of hundreds of men and women, including most of Israel's senior military and intelligence officials, a small flotilla of naval vessels, and at least eight aircraft. The size of the contingent tasked with killing Abu Jihad was a reflection of the extraordinary prior-ity the Israelis attached to removing him from the scene and the lengths they were prepared to go to ensure that the mis-sion was successful.

THE "BOYS"

The men selected to carry out the Tunis raid represented the elite of Israel's most elite unit, the Sayaret Matkal. When the unit was formed in the early 1950's, its very existence was a closely guarded secret, and the unit still is wrapped in mystery and intrigue. The service records of those attached to the unit never reflect the time they spend in the Sayaret Matkal. Of regimental size, the unit also has a reserve component composed of men a few years older than the eighteen- to twenty-one-year-olds who are the norm in the IDF.

The unit is charged with conducting high-risk operations behind enemy lines, collecting tactical intelligence, and planting sensors and monitoring devices deep within enemy territory. It works closely with Israeli military intelligence and the Mossad. The Sayaret Matkal reports directly to the chief of staff and does not go through the chain of command. Accordingly, most of the unit's missions are determined by the chief of military intelligence, although the Mossad director can also task the unit directly.

The Sayaret Matkal is Israel's sharpest knife, used to carry out precision surgical operations where the slightest slip could result in disaster. It is deployed more often in peacetime than in war. Its men are cool, professional, and highly motivated. Stories of their heroism are legion, and the special character of the men of the Sayaret Matkal is illustrated by the story of a young member of the unit captured, along with four of his companions, during a deep-penetration mission in the 1950's near the Syrian town of Quneitra. The five were subjected to cruel torture during interrogation sessions until the young man reached the limits of his endurance and, unable to stand it any longer, committed suicide. When his corpse was returned to Israel, it was found that he had written a note between his toes, using the blackened end of burned matches. It read: "I have not betrayed."

Unlike those in the U.S. Delta Force, the British SAS, the West German GSG-9, or other elite special operations units, many of those who serve in the Sayaret Matkal come from the social, economic, and political elite of the country. The profile of the average Delta commando in the United States, by contrast, is decidedly blue-collar, and only rarely in this country does a former special operations man rise to the rank of general. In Israel the top echelons of the nation's defense establishment are dominated by former members of the Sayaret Matkal and other special operations units. The present chief of staff, General Dan Shomron, is a special operations veteran, as is the deputy chief of staff, Major General Ehud Barak, who commanded the Sayaret Matkal from 1969 to 1972. He proudly wears his nation's highest military decoration for a still-classified mission he conducted when he was with the unit. The IDF's current chief of planning and the chief of military intelligence (AMAN) are also veterans of Israel's special operations community. The commander of the unit until recently was the son of former Chief of Staff and cabinet member Chaim Bar-Lev.

It should also be recalled that Moshe Dayan once commanded a special operations battalion and that Ariel Sharon, who is a member of the Israeli Cabinet and has aspirations to be prime minister, was the founder of Israel's original special operations forces.

Ironically, many of the unit's recruits come from the political left. Few are the product of families identified with the Likud. Traditionally, most are kibbutzniks, from Israel's cooperative farms or from the ranks of the nation's intelligentsia. They tend to be idealists and, like their parents and grandparents, are motivated by the vision of a nation at peace with its Arab neighbors.

The men selected to go on the mission to Tunis were all in superb physical condition. None even smoked. Each was an expert in hand-to-hand combat, rappelling, and the use of various weapons. It had been drummed into each of them that the weapon—whether it was a pistol, rifle, or submachine gun—was an extension of the arm and, as such, an integral part of the body and brain. The unit is highly mission-oriented. Initiative is emphasized in the Sayaret Matkal, and every man is taught to take over and complete the mission in the event that his superiors are killed or incapacitated in battle.

During the raid the commandos would wear black fireproof coveralls, palladium boots, and lightweight utility vests made of bullet-resistant fabric. Each commando would be equipped with a miniature radio pack, with earphone and microphone, and an emergency location finder, in case he was captured or separated from his unit. The flying headquarters had sensors on board able to pinpoint an activated location finder and direct help to the individual in need. Each man also carried a first-aid kit, a knife, and extra ammo.

All the weapons used in the raid were Israeli-manufactured, in contrast with many special operations conducted by the Israelis that use captured Eastern bloc weapons to increase deniability. All the serial numbers and other markings, however, were removed. Similarly, all the ammunition was Israeli but bore no markings. Two of the squads involved in the mission, A and B teams, were outfitted with silenced Uzi submachine guns, and some carried .22 Beretta pistols, which were also suppressed. For added firepower, C and D teams carried Galil assault rifles and light machine guns. Most of the men also had stun grenades and numbers 24 and 26 fragmentation hand grenades slung from their utility vests.

In early April 1988 a final, full-dress rehearsal conducted near the Israeli port city of Haifa brought together all the operational elements of the mission. Israeli commandos landed on a beach in the vicinity of Haifa and made their way approximately the same distance as they would in Tunis to a mock-up of Abu Jihad's house, located on an Israeli Army ordnance base. In order to make the rehearsal as realistic as possible, the planners actually moved hangars and roads on the base, the better to simulate the approaches to the house. So that Soviet and American spy satellites would not recognize it, the final touches were added to the model and the exercise was conducted during a "window" when no satellites were overflying Israel. The commandos were divided into four teams, each composed of five or six men. Every member of A Team, the commando squad that would actually kill Abu Jihad, was issued a three-dimensional scale model of Abu Jihad's house to help familiarize them with the layout. During the rehearsal A Team "blew" the front door of the house, "killed" Abu Jihad, and exited the house in twenty-two seconds flat, well under the limit set by the mission planners. Unbelievably, during the actual raid they shaved nine seconds off their best rehearsal time. The final full-dress rehearsal was observed closely by the commander in chief of the IDF, General Shomron. Only after he had met with and been briefed by every team leader, talked with the rank and file, and reviewed the operational plan yet a final time did he give his final approval to the operation.

THE OPERATION IS
LAUNCHED

In late March the Mossad pulled all its agents out of Tunisia so as to avoid unnecessary risks or some accidental disclosure of the operation. During the second week of April the Mossad team that would function as part of the operation, composed of six men and one woman, entered the country, using a variety of carefully developed and nearly infallible cover identities. They quickly and efficiently set up their operational base and retrieved a number of weapons from a hidden depot for their own protection.

Meanwhile, under the cover of darkness, Zodiac rafts and other equipment were loaded aboard two of the missile boats, which set sail at dawn, ostensibly for the purpose of conducting naval maneuvers in the Mediterranean, in international waters south of Crete.

In order to get a firsthand look at Abu Jihad's residence in Sidi-bou-Said, east of Tunis, where many top PLO officials live, the commander of the Sayaret Matkal traveled to the Tunisian capital on a commercial flight from Rome, using a genuine passport and identity papers that would provide him with, at most, short-lived cover. He was met at the airport by the Mossad team leader and driven out to Abu Jihad's home, after which they traced the route to the sea and surveyed the landing site near Ras Carthage, long ago the port of the city of Carthage. The next time he traveled the same roads would be at night. The following day he left Tunis and arrived in Israel just in time to join his men aboard the second set of departing missile boats.

Once the little flotilla was at sea, three members of the Mossad team, using Lebanese passports, rented the vehicles that were to be used in the raid: a Peugeot 305 (license number 66TI2505) and two Volkswagen minibuses (license numbers

328TI48 and 8405TI53). The date was April 13, less than three days before the mission was scheduled to commence.

The other Mossad operatives maintained their surveillance of Abu Jihad's house to note any change in routine, observing the guards and the general traffic in and out of the neighborhood for the slightest sign of trouble. They reviewed the access and escape routes, checked and rechecked all the telephone lines in and out of the area to ensure that they had identified all the critical lines, and prepared to meet the commandos on the beach.

As the flotilla neared the Tunisian coast, startling new intelligence became available: Not only Abu Jihad but most of the PLO's other top leaders reportedly would be in Tunis on April 16, the day of the scheduled operation. The information was conveyed to General Barak on board the floating command vessel via secure and scrambled communications channels. He was consulted on whether the number of targets should be expanded but decided to proceed with the operation as planned. Only Abu Jihad would be "hit."

At the last minute Israeli intelligence also learned that the French had gotten wind of the operation and had conveyed an urgent warning to PLO headquarters that the Israelis were up to something. But Barak counted on PLO inertia and the unspecific nature of the French warning to prevent the PLO from taking any effective countermeasures that might jeopardize the operation. The operation continued as scheduled.

After nightfall on April 15 the Israeli flotilla converged at a designated point outside Tunisian territorial waters, just beyond the reach of the nation's coast radars. The RC-707, which had taken off from an air base in Israel a few hours earlier, was overhead to provide an electronic cloak for the missile boats. All was ready. The final order to go was given, and the two Sa'ar 4 missile boats with the commandos on board drew away, slicing through the choppy dark waters of the Mediterranean. They continued through the Gulf of Tunis until the coast of Tunisia loomed approximately sixteen to eighteen hundred meters away. The missile boats cut power, and two pairs of frogmen from Flotilla 13 slipped over the side of one of the vessels. Aided by swimmer delivery vehicles, known as pigs, they quickly made their way through the breaking waves to the deserted beach, where they were greeted by the Mossad team, which was waiting for them.

The RC-707 was in contact with the Mossad agents on the beach. However, the Zodiacs with the commandos were not launched until the frogmen actually met up with their Mossad counterparts on the beach, made positive identification, and sent back a coded signal to land the main force. Far behind the first RC-707 was the flying headquarters, which was relaying all communications from the operation back to Tel Aviv. Some distance away from the coast of Tunisia the low-flying formation of F-15's, already once refueled, were standing by to protect the 707's and to come to the assistance of the raiding party if needed.

The all-clear signal was transmitted to the missile boats, and within seconds five Zodiac rafts had hit the water. Their engines were cranked up, and loaded with heavily armed dark-clad commandos, they sped away through the breaking waves toward the beach. As they approached the sandy beach, the commandos jumped out of the Zodiacs, which returned to the missile boats. The missile boats then headed north into the Gulf of Tunis, just outside Tunisia's territorial waters, to await the next stage of the operation.

Back at the beach it was extremely quiet, the stillness of the night punctuated only by the rhythmical noise of the waves. The men of the Sayaret Matkal and the Mossad climbed into the three rented vehicles and sped away toward Tunis, passing along their route the ruins of Hannibal's ancient capital of Carthage, once mighty Rome's rival. Abu Jihad's home was located on a hill, above the sea, some five kilometers away.

ABU JIHAD'S RENDEZVOUS WITH DEATH

Shortly after 1:00 A.M., the raiders arrived at the house in Sidi-bou-Said, which the Mossad operatives had kept under constant surveillance. Everything was quiet. There was little traffic. Nevertheless, they knew that the neighborhood was crawling with PLO security personnel since the PLO's chief of intelligence, Abu al-Chol (Khalil Abdul Hamid), lived across the street from Abu Jihad, and Abu Mazan (Machmud Abbas), the PLO member responsible for the dialogue with the Israeli left, resided next door.

One last time a team of commandos, their faces hidden behind ski masks, checked their silenced weapons and the special tools they would use to breach the doors and then took up their positions around the house, melting into the darkness. Some members of the team had pulled on their night-vision goggles and were getting adjusted to them. Other commandos secured the escape route and the surrounding streets leading to the house. To prevent anyone in Abu Jihad's house or the immediate vicinity from sounding the alarm, the Mossad operatives tampered with the phone lines, allowing them to monitor all calls and block any they did not want to get through.

Abu Jihad, however, was not home. He was downtown attending a lengthy meeting with PLO external relations official Farouk Qadoumi regarding the controversial U.S. decision to close down the office of the PLO Mission to the United Nations. Anxiety set in as the commandos awaited his return. Tailed by Mossad agents, Abu Jihad finally arrived home around 1:30 A.M. Once his car was parked, his security detail took up their positions. An hour later, at 2:30 A.M., the lights went out in Abu Jihad's study on the first floor and subsequently were turned on in his bedroom on the second floor. The minutes ticked by with agonizing slowness. Finally, the bedroom lights were extinguished, and the house was enveloped in darkness. Nothing stirred in the neighborhood.

It was time to act.

After a brief pause the earphones of the commandos crackled with the order "Go!" A Team stealthily approached the front door, while B Team moved around to the rear entrance of the house. Members of C Team took up positions near both the front and back of the house to intervene in the event more firepower or other assistance was needed. D Team was farther from the house, ready to prevent anyone from coming to Abu Jihad's assistance.

A member of A Team slipped up next to Abu Jihad's car, where the driver was slumped over the wheel asleep. One shot from a silenced revolver ensured that he would never wake up from his slumber.

Both the front and back doors of the house were made of heavy wood with steel-reinforced plating. Using secret technology and tools, the commandos breached both doors with a minimum of sound and burst into the house. While B Team secured the entrances and the basement, A Team rushed up the stairs toward Abu Jihad's bedroom, killing a guard, Mustafa Ali al-Auwall, on the way. Another guard, Nabia Suleiman Crisaan, and a caretaker died at the hands of B Team.

A Team assembled momentarily outside the door to Abu Jihad's bedroom. Alerted by the muffled sounds coming from downstairs, he groggily raised his head from the pillow. But it was too late. In a split second the commandos were in the bedroom. Abu Jihad's wife was lying next to him. The darkness was punctuated by staccato bursts from the silenced submachine guns, which illuminated the room like the flashes of a strobe light, as the commandos riddled Abu Jihad's body, leaving his terrified wife unharmed.

The commandos withdrew as quickly as they came. The whole thing was over in thirteen seconds, the amount of time that elapsed from the breaching of the front door to the moment that the first members of A Team began to leave the house.

Slowly, deliberately, so as not to raise alarm if unseen eyes were watching, the commandos left the house and boarded the waiting vehicles. C Team secured the withdrawal, and once everyone had been accounted for, the drivers released the hand brakes in their vehicles, and they rolled noiselessly away, without starting their engines, down the long hill leading from the house. D Team was picked up on the way. Seconds later the commandos switched on the ignitions of their vehicles and raced toward the pickup site. At that moment the men from Flotilla 13 were speeding across the water to secure the beach at the pickup site, near the village of Gamarth, five kilometers north of Sidi-bou-Said, where they would rendezvous with the commandos.

Meanwhile, at the house, Um-Jihad, Abu Jihad's wife, turned on the lights and found her husband dead on the floor next to the bed, blood gushing from as many as seventy wounds. She grabbed the telephone, but the line was dead, so she ran outside and screamed from the veranda for help. But nobody responded. It was not until her daughter, Hannan, ran next door to the house of Abu Mazan that the alarm was raised.

As they sped toward Gamarth, the raiding party was served cold drinks, provided by a member of the Mossad team. While confusion reigned back at Abu Jihad's house, the commandos reached the pickup site and linked up again with their counterparts from Flotilla 13. The rented vehicles and the empty cans of Tunisian soda pop were abandoned on the beach, and the Zodiacs were back in the water within seconds and speeding toward their rendezvous with the missile boats. Once they had reached the missile boats, the 707's and their fighter escort turned abruptly eastward and flew through the gathering dawn toward Israel. The missile boats quickly left Tunisian waters and began their four-day voyage back to their home port, during which time they were under the constant protection of the Israeli Air Force.

Later that same morning four Mossad agents with ironclad cover identities, boarded four different flights and departed Tunisia. The other three Mossad agents had already departed with the raiding party.

AFTERMATH

Abu Jihad's death has set off a power struggle within the PLO that has yet to be resolved. The man who, according to most observers, benefited most from Abu Jihad's demise was Abu Iyad. However, as chief of both Fatah's and the PLO's intelligence and security organizations, Abu Iyad came under a good deal of fire from his colleagues regarding the breach of security and the failure of his intelligence system to detect the impending operation against Abu Jihad. In an interview with Radio Monte Carlo on April 22, 1988, Abu Iyad attempted to respond to some of the criticism. "For the past 20 years," he explained, "we have agreed that in view of the fact these leaders do not gather in one place but in different places, each leader should take measures to protect himself in consultation with the central security apparatus. As for Brother Abu Jihad, his basic post was in Baghdad and therefore, his visits to Tunis were brief."[11]

In the final analysis, the killing of Abu Jihad may have produced unintended consequences for Israel. While it removed the PLO's most gifted and effective military leader, it left a void that no other senior PLO leader is likely to fill, and it accelerated the shift toward political, rather than military, confrontation with Israel. Abu Iyad, Abu Tayeb, and Colonel Hawari, for example, all are covert operators and terrorists, not military leaders. Arafat, for his part, is a political leader, with little real military experience or skill. While Israel is a military superpower, by contrast with the PLO, and was never strategically threatened by the PLO's military operations, it is something less than a superpower in the political arena. Indeed, it may even be at a disadvantage vis-à-vis the PLO in terms of international perceptions and support. Thus, Israel may ultimately be more victimized by Abu Jihad in death than when he was alive.

2 | *The Rise of the PLO*

Early on the morning of Sunday, January 3, 1965, Aryeh Zizhik, an employee of Mekorot, Israel's national water company, discovered a suspicious object floating in a canal in the Beit Netofa Valley, part of the lower Galilee. The canal carried fresh water from the Jordan River more than two hundred miles to the Negev desert and was a vital element in Israel's program to "make the desert bloom." The diversion of the waters of the Jordan had been the main topic of debate at the 1964 Arab summit in Cairo and the target of bitter threats by the Arab governments, which vowed to destroy it.

Zizhik was ordered to close the canal gates and drain the water from a large section of the canal. A short time later explosives ordnance disposal (EOD) experts from Israel's border police arrived and approached the object, which turned out to be a plastic-covered rucksack, now lying on the bottom of the dry canal. Inside the rucksack were ten sticks of a powerful explosive known as gelignite and a detonator and batteries. The gelignite was Hungarian-made and of a type used frequently by regular units of the Syrian Army. The explosive device had not gone off because of flaws in its assembly, but had it done so, it would have caused considerable damage, especially if it had hit the canal locks or drifted downstream to the pumping stations.

Bedouin trackers quickly picked up the trail of the saboteurs, which led to the village of Araba and from there to the banks of the Jordan River, where the tracks stopped abruptly at the water's edge. The saboteurs had apparently crossed the river into Jordan, and it was assumed that they had probably entered Israel the same way.

Two days later a previously unknown organization called al-Fatah claimed credit for the operation. "It was," one PLO official later claimed, "the first salvo of the Palestinian revolution." Indeed, for both Israel and the stateless Palestinians seeking a homeland, life would never be the same again.

THE PALESTINIAN DIASPORA

There are approximately 5.5 million Palestinians in the world today. Their largest concentrations are in Jordan, Syria, Lebanon, Kuwait, Syria, and Israel (including the occupied West Bank and Gaza). In addition, significant Palestinian populations can be found in Saudi Arabia, Iraq, Egypt, the United Arab Emirates, Qatar, Libya, Tunisia, and Oman. Another half million Palestinians reside in the United States, Western Europe, and various developing countries.

The Palestinian diaspora occurred in the wake of the establishment of Israel in 1948 and the subsequent conflict between the newly created Jewish state and the nations of the Arab League. The causes of the Palestinian diaspora continue to be debated to this day. Many Palestinians simply fled their homes to avoid the fighting that broke out. Others were coerced by the Israelis to leave and, in some cases, forcibly expelled from Israel to create "security belts."[1] There is also little doubt that the massacre of Arab civilians at Deir Yassin by elements of the Irgun and Stern Group terrorized the Arab population and panicked many into leaving their homes for the relative safety of the surrounding Arab countries.[2] Thousands of Palestinians, moreover, left the country after being urged to do so by the grand mufti of Jerusalem and the Arab "confrontation" states—that is, those Arab countries engaged in direct military action against Israel. In his memoirs Abu Iyad describes how hundreds of thousands of Palestinians fled their homes under the mistaken assumption that they would soon be able to return in the wake of victorious Arab armies, after they had defeated the Jews. "In retrospect," writes Abu Iyad, "I think my compatriots were wrong to have believed the Arab regimes and in any case to have left the field open to the Jewish colonizers. They should have stood their ground, whatever the cost. The Zionists could never have exterminated them to the last man."[3]

In the aftermath of the population shift that occurred, more than a million Palestinians ended up in squalid refugee camps in Jordan, Lebanon, Egypt, and Syria, regarded as both a burden and a threat by the very states that had initially championed their cause. For those in the refugee camps, life was harsh and offered little hope. Other Palestinians, by contrast, fanned out throughout the Arab world and not only survived but, over time, excelled not just in the arts but as doctors, bankers, engineers, teachers, and journalists. In many Arab nations, especially some of the rich but technologically unsophisticated oil-producing states, the Palestinians form the backbone of the professional caste that keeps the oil flowing and the national infrastructures operating.

Throughout the 1950's and early 1960's most Palestinians looked to the various Arab confrontation governments to deliver them from their misery and to redeem their control over what had once been Palestine. Palestinians who wanted to fight Israel generally became incorporated into the conventional armies of the various confrontation states. However, with the crushing defeat by Israel of the Arab armies in the 1967 Six-Day War, Palestinians became increasingly disillusioned with the Arab states and vowed to take their future into their own hands. According to Abu Iyad, "We were convinced, for example, that the Palestinians could expect nothing from the Arab regimes, for the most part corrupt or tied to imperialism, and that they were wrong to bank on any of the political parties in the region. We believed that the Palestinians could rely only on themselves."[4]

Even before the Six-Day War, however, some young Palestinians had already embraced the notion of armed struggle as the road to self-determination. The founding fathers of the Palestinian Revolution had many things in common: Most grew up in Gaza; studied together in Cairo; became active members of the Moslem Brotherhood (a fundamentalist Islamic movement founded in 1928 in Egypt by Hassan al-Banna); enlisted in the Egyptian Army during the combined British-French attack on Port Said in the midst of the 1956 Suez crisis; and ultimately received Egyptian military or intelligence training. The central figure in this group was Yasir Arafat.

WHO IS YASIR ARAFAT?

Much of the information that appears in open sources about Yasir Arafat is contradictory and often erroneous, designed both to mythologize him and, in some cases, to hide his past from contemporary scrutiny. Mystery surrounds such details as the date and place of his birth, as well as why he changed his name.

Israeli intelligence files suggest that Arafat was born in 1928 in Cairo as Abed a-Rachman Abed a-Rauf Arafat al-Qudwah al-Husseini, although he has claimed on various occasions to have been born both in Gaza and in Jerusalem in a "house that was destroyed by the Jews." Alan Hart, Arafat's official biographer, also says that he was born in Cairo, but on August 24, 1929.[5] His mother was a member of the prominent Abu-Saud family, which owned a house in Jerusalem, near the Western ("Wailing") Wall, that was knocked down by the Israeli government in 1969 in order to make way for the Western Wall plaza.

Early in life Arafat dropped his last name and changed his first name to Yasir. Why Arafat wanted to distance himself from his illustrious relative the grand mufti of Jerusalem, Haj Amin al-Husseini, is not known. It is a surprising decision since al-Husseini was a direct descendant of Hussein, the grandchild of the Prophet Mohammed, and thus from one of the most celebrated families in all Islam. However, it may have something to do with the fact that al-Husseini had collaborated with Adolf Hitler during World War II.[6]

At various times later, after becoming a revolutionary, Arafat used sobriquets to conceal his real identity, such as Abu Amar, Abu Mohammed, the Doctor, Fauzi Arafat, and Dr. Husseini. The one he used most often was Abu Amar, which he subsequently adopted as his nom de guerre. He may have chosen Amar because in Arabic, *al-Amar* means "the command of God." There is a passage in the Koran (Sura 17:85) which says, "They put questions to you about the Spirit. Say: 'the Spirit is at my Lord's command (al-Amar).' " Most senior PLO members have taken on noms de guerre beginning with "Abu." Traditionally, in Arabic-speaking societies, when a man has his first son, his friends and neighbors thereafter refer to him as Abu (meaning "father of") and the name of the newborn child. If one is disgraced (in Arab societies) by having only daughters and no sons, he is often referred to behind his back as Abu al-Banat, meaning the "father of daughters." Although Arafat is not married and has no children and therefore is not the "father of" anyone, the name Abu served as a convenient means of portraying himself as a strong and virile man, which is greatly esteemed in his culture. The adoption of such names also serves to make it more difficult for foreign—initially Arab—intelligence services to keep track of various Palestinian figures, since noms de guerre create a good deal of confusion. For example, in the Arab world Musa and Daoud (David) are very common names; thus, the names Abu Musa and Abu Daoud told authorities very little about the real identities of the men. There are many Abu Amars in the Palestinian movement, including Jamel Suraani, who also serves on the PLO's Executive Committee with Arafat.

According to some sources, Arafat's father originally moved in the early 1920's to Cairo, where he lived off the comfortable income he received from the family properties in Egypt, Gaza, and Jerusalem. He had seven children from his first marriage: daughters Inam, Yosra, and Khadija and sons Gamal, Mustafa, Fatchi, and Yasir. In view of the date of his father's move, there is little doubt that Arafat was born in Cairo and attended elementary school there. Those who recall the family, however, say that they maintained their Palestinian identity and made little attempt to assimilate into Egyptian society.

There are unverified reports that Arafat's father and brother Gamal were members of the Moslem Brotherhood. What is known is that Arafat's family was highly politicized and that Yasir became immersed in Palestinian politics at a very early age. In 1946 Haj Amin al-Husseini, the former grand mufti, arrived in Cairo, from Berlin, with his cousin, Palestinian nationalist leader Abed al-Kader al-Husseini. Al-Husseini spent more than a year in Cairo rebuilding his Palestinian constituency, before moving in October 1947 to Beirut, where he lived until his death in 1974.

They met with Arafat's brother Gamal, who subsequently joined Abed al-Kader al-Husseini's forces during the 1947–1948 war. Gamal remained active in Palestinian politics and served as secretary of the "All-Palestinian Government," which was formed in Gaza on September 22, 1948, and headquartered in Cairo. He also served as personal secretary to the aging Palestinian "prime minister" Ahmed Hilmi, the manager of the Arab Bank in Jerusalem.

It is presumed that Arafat met with the two Palestinian leaders during their stay in Cairo, and there is a report that he subsequently became a personal aide to Abed al-Kader al-Husseini. Arafat also claims to have fought with al-Husseini's forces around Jerusalem in 1947–1948, but again there is no confirmation of this. What is known is that in 1951 he began studying engineering at Cairo's Fuad I University, where he rapidly became involved in student politics and was known as a Palestinian agitator.

Arafat reportedly paid little attention to his studies and spent much of his time training Egyptian and Palestinian students in irregular warfare tactics. It was in this context that he first met Salah Khalaf (Abu Iyad). Although Abu Iyad recalls that he didn't care for Arafat's Egyptian accent, "I was impressed by his obvious leadership qualities as I watched him training the students. He was very dynamic. Very tough. Very passionate."[7] The two men gradually formed a bond that has existed to this very day. Indeed, their roles really have not changed very much. Arafat remains the front man, the politician, the leader; Abu Iyad is the dark visage in the background, the tactician and "enforcer," the brooding intellectual.

Both men subsequently became active in the General Union of Palestinian Students (GUPS), and Arafat was elected president of the organization in 1952. It was as president of GUPS that Arafat first began to espouse publicly his notion of "an

independent Palestine liberation movement."[8] During this period Arafat and Abu Iyad drew around them other young
Palestinians, active in GUPS at Egyptian universities, who
were also committed to the notion of armed struggle as the
means of achieving self-determination and regaining their
homeland: Khalil al-Wazir (Abu Jihad), Mohammed Yussef
al-Najjar (Abu Yussef), Kamal Adwan, Machmud Abbas (Abu
Mazan), and Farouk Qadoumi. Together with Arafat and Abu
Iyad, these five men were to become the founding fathers of
Fatah and later were instrumental in the takeover of the PLO.

Three of the seven have already become casualties of the
struggle. Al-Wazir (Abu Jihad) was killed by Israeli commandos in Tunis on April 16, 1988, and Najjar and Adwan died in
an Israeli raid on Beirut on April 10, 1973.

Even in the early 1950's Arafat was an ascetic individual
who neither smoked nor drank and had little, if any, life
beyond "the struggle." He had no known liaisons with women
or other men and associated almost exclusively with other
Palestinian radicals. In 1956, on the eve of the Suez crisis, he
was graduated with a degree in civil engineering. A short time
later he and some of his Palestinian associates enrolled in an
Egyptian Army explosives ordnance disposal course, and
when he completed the instruction, he was made a second
lieutenant in the Egyptian Army. During the subsequent Suez
crisis Arafat was part of a commando battalion that saw some
limited action. However, he spent most of his time removing
mines at Port Said. For his part, Abu Iyad spent the war
guarding a bridge in the center of Cairo.

In late 1956 or early 1957 Arafat was arrested by Egyptian
security services as a political agitator, allegedly because of
his ties to the Moslem Brotherhood. He was released from jail
several months later and along with Qadoumi and Abu Jihad,
departed for Kuwait. Al-Najjar, Adwan, and Abbas went to
Qatar. Abu Iyad moved to Gaza, where he became a teacher.
They all agreed to rendezvous again in the future, when the
time was right, in order to form a revolutionary organization
dedicated to armed struggle against Israel.

During the late 1950's Arafat remained active as a student
leader, attending numerous international conferences as a
member of the Sudanese delegation. Short (five feet four
inches) and heavyset, Arafat wore cheap European suits and

lifts in his shoes. He had a small mustache and routinely wore dark glasses, which became something of his trademark. He was a fiery orator who thumped the podium and waved his arms when he spoke. At student conferences he routinely demanded the expulsion of the Israeli delegation if one was in attendance. During this time Arafat probably supported himself with payments from two intelligence services, the Egyptian Muchabarat and the Syrian Deuxième Bureau.[9]

It is believed that Arafat and his colleagues from their university days in Cairo were behind the establishment of a small monthly that appeared in Beirut in 1958 entitled *Falestinuna: Nada el-Chiat* ("Our Palestine: The Call of Life"), which was edited by Tufiq Khuri. The publication had some ties to the Moslem Brotherhood but was chiefly concerned with promoting the cause of an independent Palestinian state.

In 1959 Arafat, together with two partners, opened his own construction business in Kuwait. Their timing could not have been better. It was just at the beginning of the oil boom and at a time when the states around the Persian Gulf were starting to nationalize the oil companies in the region. Arafat's company secured Kuwaiti government contracts and built government facilities, roads, and housing. Arafat used his extensive ties within the Palestinian community to win still more contracts. In a relatively short period of time he was able to amass a modest personal fortune. Once he became fully involved in Palestinian nationalist politics, he sold his shares in the company to his partners and left Kuwait.

Fatah was born the same year Arafat started his business venture. Abu Iyad remembers the occasion:

On October 10, 1959, a small group of us met in a discreet house in Kuwait to hammer out the organizational structures of Fatah. More meetings with other participants took place over the following days, always in the greatest secrecy. There were fewer than twenty of us in all, representatives of underground groups from various Arab countries and beyond, coming together to centralize our activities for the first time. This limited congress marked the formal creation of what was to become the most powerful national liberation movement Palestine had ever known.[10]

The name Fatah is short for Harkat al-Tachrir al-Watanni al-Falestinia, or Palestine Liberation Movement; in reverse order its acronym is FATAH, which, in Arabic, means "conquest" or "victory." The word "Fatah" appears in a famous passage from the Koran (Sura 61:13): "Help from Allah and a speedy victory [Fatah]."

Arafat moved to Beirut the following year and divided his time between working as an engineer and revolutionary politics. In 1962 the FLN rebels in Algeria signed the Avignon Agreements, providing for the independence of Algeria. No event more captured the imagination of the young Palestinian revolutionaries than the defeat of the French in Algeria. Arafat, Abu Iyad, and the others all are steeped in the literature of the Algerian revolt. Revolutionary writers like black psychiatrist Franz Fanon, who spoke of the "liberating influence of violence," had a great impact on them. According to Abu Iyad, "Franz Fanon was one of my favorite authors. In his *Wretched of the Earth*, which I read and reread countless times, he said that only a people who doesn't fear the guns and tanks of the enemy is capable of fighting a revolution to the finish. By that he meant the Algerian nationalists would never have started anything if they had taken into account the balance of power at the time they launched their insurrection."[11] In addition to Fanon, Arafat and Abu Iyad embraced the works of Mao Zedong, Vietnamese General Vo Nguyen Giap, and Régis Debray, not to mention the mythology and symbolism that surrounded Che Guevara. Over the years they saw to it that the works of Mao, Giap, and Debray were translated into Arabic and regularly reprinted in Palestinian publications such as *Falistinuna* ("Our Palestine"), the official organ of Fatah, and *el-Thoura el-Falestinia* ("The Palestinian Revolution").

Nevertheless, while the example of Algeria served as an important beacon to Arafat and his lieutenants, they knew that there were substantial differences between the Algerian experience and their own unfolding struggle. Unlike French-dominated Algeria, Israel was not an outdated vestige of colonialism, but rather a young and energetic nation led by men and women who themselves had fought against and, for all intents and purposes, defeated a colonial power, in this case

Great Britain. Whereas the French colonizers of Algeria could always return to France, the Israelis had no place to retreat to; for them it would be a fight to the bitter end.

Fatah has been led, in effect, by Arafat since 1964, when he began to emerge as "first among equals," although it was not until April 15, 1968, that he was appointed by Fatah's Central Committee the "official spokesman and representative" of Fatah.

The Fatah operation to blow up the Israeli canal that was discovered on January 3, 1965, was the first independent guerrilla action taken against Israel by the Palestinians, and it rapidly established Fatah as the principal shock troops of the Palestinian Revolution.

GENESIS OF THE PLO

The Hotel Ambassador in Jerusalem, opposite the Turkish Wall, with high ceilings and potted palms, is a faded monument of the British colonial era. Once noted for its fine Middle Eastern cuisine, its rooftop dining room boasts a panoramic view of the city. Today one almost expects to see British General Sir Edmund Allenby or Sir John Bagot Glubb, better known as Glubb Pasha, striding through the lobby, and some of the aged staff members of the hotel actually recall waiting on both men.

The Palestine Liberation Organization (PLO) was founded at the first meeting of the Palestinian National Council, or PNC (in Arabic: al-Maglis al-Watani el-Falestini), at the Hotel Ambassador in what was then East Jerusalem, which lasted from May 28 through June 2, 1964.[12] A Palestinian lawyer, Ahmed Shukeiry, was named first chairman of the PLO Executive Committee. Shukeiry was a former Saudi Arabian ambassador to the United Nations. In addition to the creation of the PLO, the assembled delegates promulgated the Palestinian Covenant, or National Charter, which remained the PLO's guiding declaration of principles and goals until it was rewritten and renamed the Palestinian National Covenant at the fourth meeting of the PNC in 1968, held in Cairo. They also voted to create the Palestinian National Fund (PNF) to finance the operations of the PLO and other related activities. Finally, the PNC decided to establish the Palestine Liberation Army (PLA). Military camps, where young Palestinians would receive military training and be organized into an army capable of defeating Israel, were to be opened immediately in friendly Arab countries.

In addition to 388 Palestinian delegates at the meeting in East Jerusalem, there were representatives from the Arab League as well as all the Arab nations, with the exception of Saudi Arabia. It is not surprising, therefore, that the National Charter adopted by the PNC was strongly influenced, to the chagrin of many Palestinians, by the various Arab governments in attendance, which desired both to exert control over the fledgling Palestinian movement and to impose their own agendas on it. According to Israel's former director of military intelligence, Major General (ret.) Aharon Yariv, "The creation of the PLO was initiated by Gamal Abdel Nasser and the organization was established with the blessing of Nasser. The PLO was established in 1964 in order to offer a tool that would address the 'Israeli problem' without involving Egypt in a major war with Israel."[13]

There is a good deal of rhetoric of a pan-Arabist nature in the charter. Article 1, for example, asserts: "Palestine is the homeland of the Arab Palestinian people. It is an indivisible part of the Arab homeland and the Palestinian people are an integral part of the Arab nation."

The charter calls for the reestablishment of Palestine, consistent with the boundaries it enjoyed during the British mandate, and for the eradication of Israel. It implies the destruction of the Hashemite kingdom of Jordan, which was also viewed as an artificial entity imposed on the Arab world by Western imperialists. The drafters of the charter sought as well to place the Palestinian question in a larger geopolitical context, calling Israel "the instrument of the Zionist movement and a geographical base for world imperialism placed strategically in the midst of the Arab homeland to combat the hopes of the Arab nation for liberation, unity and progress" (Article 22). Thus, the drafters of the National Covenant were declaring, in effect, war not only on Israel but also on the United States and the other nations of the West, which they blamed for imposing Israel on the Arab world and for supporting conservative Arab regimes in their midst.

From its inception the PLO and its architects lined up squarely with the radical, anti-Western elements in the Arab world. While the PLO has undergone many changes in the intervening years, its opposition to the United States and most of the nations of Western Europe has never wavered; in fact, it has intensified.

GOVERNING STRUCTURE OF THE PLO

According to Alan Hart in his officially approved biography of Yasir Arafat, the Palestinian National Council (PNC) "is more or less the Palestinian parliament-in-exile. It is the highest Palestinian decision-making body and the P.L.O. is answerable to it."[14] Nevertheless, while the PNC ostensibly serves as the parliament of the PLO, in reality it acts more as a consultative organ than an actual legislative body. It includes, for example, many moderates, such as Palestinian professors and businessmen living in the West, whom many outside observers regard more as window dressing than as real players. The PNC not only provides the PLO with a democratic veneer that can be touted in the West but also is a propaganda platform for the PLO's leadership to communicate with the outside world and the Palestinian community at large. As but one yardstick of the actual influence wielded by the PNC, it is interesting to note that in Abu Iyad's 235-page memoir he mentions the PNC on only two separate occasions.[15]

Although the number frequently changes, at last count the PNC had 430 members, representing various segments of the Palestinian community, including armed militias and terrorist organizations. The PNC elects a Central Council (al-Maglis al-Markazi), with 60 or 70 members, which, because of its smaller size, is envisioned as meeting more often to formalize or ratify major decisions.[16] However, like the PNC, the PCC is really too large and unwieldy to be an effective administrative body and meets too infrequently to be a real decision-making unit. For a complete list of all PNC meetings to date, see Appendix One.

The PNC also elects the fifteen-man Executive Committee (al-Lagna el-Tanfizeyeh.) The Executive Committee is the PLO's Cabinet, with members assigned various portfolios. See Appendix Two for a list of those presently serving on the Executive Committee.

Although it was originally intended that the PNC meet every six months, it has met only nineteen times since its inception in 1964, or less than once a year. Thus, the Executive Committee oversees the routine operation of the PLO and is the repository of real power within the organization.

One other body of note is the Supreme Military Council (SMC), which was established during the PNC meeting in April 1972. It is chaired by the head of the Military Department of the PLO and has a representative from every political/military organization with membership on the Executive Committee. Although the SMC is supposed to coordinate the various aspects of the armed struggle, it remains more of a ceremonial body, and military action remains the prerogative of each constituent organization of the PLO.

Since the Executive Committee meets only every month or two, a great deal of power devolves to Chairman Arafat and his top aides, especially in view of the extraordinary financial resources they have amassed over the years. Their power, however, is not absolute, and on a number of occasions Arafat and his loyal supporters have been left with a "rump" organization when other component groups have chosen to "vote with their feet" and not attend key meetings. A good example was the 1983 PNC meeting in Algiers, where only Fatah and its chief components and supporters were in attendance. If enough component organizations sever their ties to the PLO or choose, for a period of time, not to recognize the leadership of the chairman and his allies, they can have a profound impact on the direction and policies of the PLO. Short of ousting the chairman and taking control of the PLO themselves, however, they have largely negative power; they are able to block initiatives but not necessarily initiate new policies.

THE CONSTITUENT
ELEMENTS OF THE PLO

The PLO, as noted, is an umbrella organization made up of various Palestinian groups dedicated to the creation of a Palestinian state. The PLO has approximately five thousand full-time employees, who are based in Tunis and throughout the Arab world.[17] Of course, the PLO does not publish a membership list. In this connection, it often resembles a floating crap game, with different players at different times. Various Palestinian groups, for example, have sworn allegiance to the PLO for a period of time, then left as a result of disputes and disagreements, only to return later and resume their places within the organization. We have assembled this list by investigating the attendance of different individuals and groups at meetings of the Palestinian National Council and utilizing data from foreign intelligence services. We have also included groups that have never been associated with the PLO, but are sometimes mistakenly included under its umbrella.

Fatah

Fatah, or the National Palestine Liberation Movement, is the largest single organization in the PLO. Established in 1959, it is headed by Yasir Arafat and headquartered at Hammam el-Shat, Tunisia. It is independent and financed by Arab governments, criminal activities, and profits from its extensive portfolio and other business activities. Fatah maintains offices throughout the Middle East, Europe, and Asia. It has approximately twelve thousand members.

Fatah/Force 17

Force 17 is a semiautonomous element of Fatah within the PLO. Led by Abu Tayeb, it serves as the Praetorian Guard of Chairman Yasir Arafat and carries out certain discreet tasks. Force 17 members, who generally operate under diplomatic cover, are stationed in every PLO embassy and with every PLO delegation around the world. The unit handles executive protection and physical security tasks, collects operational intelligence, and is responsible for certain internal security functions. Based at Hammam el-Shat, Tunisia, it has about eight hundred operators.

Fatah/Western Section

The Western Section of Fatah was headed, until April 1988, by Khalil Ibrahim Machmud al-Wazir (Abu Jihad). It is an operations body set up to promote armed struggle, or *ama-liyah fedayeeha*, in the occupied territories. Once headquartered in Amman, Jordan, today the unit is based at Hammam el-Shat, with a branch in Baghdad. It has about four hundred members. Since the death of Abu Jihad, Yasir Arafat has assumed full control of the Western Section.

Fatah/Special Operations Group (SOG)

The Special Operations Group, also known as the Colonel Hawari Force, was established to provide internal security within Fatah and to conduct covert international operations. It has about six hundred operators and makes its headquarters in Beirut, Lebanon.

Fatah/Intelligence and Security Apparatus (ISA)

Led by Abu Iyad (Salah Khalaf), this may be the most secret of all the major constituent elements of the PLO. ISA is the primary intelligence and counterintelligence arm of Fatah and the PLO and reportedly also has a covert "action" element. It maintains offices in Lebanon, Jordan, Egypt, Kuwait, Syria, and Saudi Arabia. There is no reliable estimate of its size.

Fatah Provisional Command (FPC)

The FPC, also known as Fatah—the Uprising, is pro-Syrian and led by Colonel Sa'id Musa Muragha (Abu Musa). Financed by Syria's defense establishment, the FPC was created in 1983 as the result of an uprising against Arafat's leadership. Owing to the fact that it was a breakaway element of Fatah, neither Abu Musa nor the FPC has attended any PNC meetings, and both are clearly outside the PLO umbrella. The FPC is headquartered in Damascus, Syria, with operations sites in Lebanon's Bekaa Valley. It has between three thousand and thirty-five hundred members.

Fatah Revolutionary Council (FRC)

Headed by the notorious Abu Nidal (Sabri Khalil al-Banna), the FRC was formed after he broke away from Fatah in 1973. Despite ostensible differences, Abu Nidal maintains relatively close ties to Abu Iyad, a relationship which amounts to a back door to the PLO. At the 1987 PNC meeting in Algiers, Abu Nidal opened negotiations regarding a formal rapprochement with the PLO, but no agreement was reached. The FRC finances its own operations, and according to a recent study published by the U.S. Department of Defense, it "may be one of the most economically viable of all terrorist organizations. The group is believed to draw one-third of its income from patron states, one-third from graft or blackmail, and one-third from its own network of business companies and front organizations."[18] Headquartered in Tripoli, Libya, and in Damascus, Syria, the FRC has some four to twelve hundred members.

Arab Revolutionary Brigades (ARB)

A covert instrument of Fatah, the ARB was formed in the early 1980's by Hassan Abdel Sater, a Lebanese from the village of Iaat, a suburb of Baalbek. From 1968 to 1979 Sater worked for the Jihaz el-Razd and later for the ISA, reporting to Abu Ali Ayad, one of Abu Iyad's deputies. In addition to serving as general secretary of the ARB, Sater owns a small printing shop in West Beirut that specializes in forged documents, especially fake Lebanese ID cards and passports. He resides in the Burj el-Barajni section of Beirut. Sometime after arriving in Beirut, Sater offered his services to the Libyan military attaché, Colonel Ben Abdel Rahman, and as a result has been financed ever since by the Libyan government. The ARB has played a role in numerous terrorist operations. Based in Beirut, the ARB has approximately two hundred members.

Al-Sa'iqa

Al-Sa'iqa, or Pioneers of the Popular War of Liberation, was established in 1968 by the Syrian Ba'ath party. It remains pro-Syrian and fought against Fatah in 1976 and in 1983 in Lebanon. It was a member of the PLO until 1983, when it broke with Arafat's leadership. It did not attend the Amman (1984) and Algiers (1987 and 1988) meetings of the PNC. Issam al-Qadi is the general secretary of the Damascus-based organization, which has an estimated one thousand to fourteen hundred members.

Popular Front for the Liberation of Palestine (PFLP)

The PFLP was formed in 1967 as a result of the merger of three other Palestinian groups: the Young Avengers, the Heroes of the Return, and Ahmed Jibril's Palestinian Liberation Front. Financially independent and headquartered in Damascus, the PFLP maintains close ties to Syria. Its political perspective is decidedly Marxist, reflecting the political orientation of its secretary-general, Dr. George Habash. The PFLP split from the PLO in 1983 but returned to the fold in 1987.

It has something in the neighborhood of seven to nine hundred members.

Popular Front for the Liberation of Palestine— General Command (PFLP—GC)

The PFLP-GC is a pro-Syrian group established in 1968 as a breakaway faction of the PFLP. Led by Captain Ahmed Jibril and funded by Syria, the PFLP-GC has not attended any PNC meetings since 1983. Headquartered in Damascus, the PFLP-GC has an estimated four to six hundred members.

Popular Front for the Liberation of Palestine— Special Command (PFLP—SC)

The PFLP-SC was founded by the late Wadia Haddad and was a breakaway faction of the PFLP. It is presently headed by Salim Abu Salim and has between 100 and 150 members. Its activities are financed by the funds left behind by Haddad. It has never been a member of the PLO.

Democratic Front for the Liberation of Palestine (DFLP)

Although basically independent, the DFLP is a pro-Soviet group with close ties to Syria. It was formed as a splinter faction of the PFLP in 1969 and is led by Naif Hawatmeh. Although the DFLP was estranged from the PLO's top leadership in the mid-1980's and did not send representatives to the 1984 PNC meeting in Amman, in 1987 it again became an active member of the PLO and was represented at the 1987 and 1988 Algiers PNC meetings. Today the DFLP has approximately five to seven hundred members, and is financially supported by Fatah. Its headquarters is in Damascus, and its main bases are in Lebanon's Bekaa Valley.

THE RISE OF THE PLO

Palestine Liberation Front
(PLF)/Abbas Faction

The PLF was established in 1977 by Mohammed Zaidan Abbas (Abu Abbas) after a split with Jibril's PFLP-GC. The PLF is strongly pro-Iraqi and maintains headquarters both in Baghdad and at Hammam el-Shat. It receives its financing from the government of Iraq, Fatah, and the PLO and probably doesn't have more than two hundred active members.

Palestine Liberation Front
(PLF)/Yaqub Faction

Tal'at Yaqub broke away from Abbas and the main PLF organization in 1983, after the Israeli invasion of Lebanon, and set up his own PLF faction. The Yaqub faction is also pro-Iraqi and financed chiefly by Saddam Hussein's government in Baghdad. While the Yaqub faction did not attend the 1984 Amman meeting of the PNC, it settled its differences with the PLO and attended the 1988 meeting of the PNC in Algiers. Yaqub died in 1988, and it is as yet unclear who will replace him. The group's headquarters is in the Bekaa Valley in Lebanon, and it has an estimated two hundred members.

Palestinian Liberation Front
(PLF)/Ghanem Faction

The Abed al-Fatah Ghanem faction of the PLF was also established in 1983. Based in Damascus, it has about a hundred members and is financed by the Libyan government and the Syrian intelligence community. It is pro-Syrian and was not in attendance at either the Amman or the Algiers PNC meeting.

Revolutionary Palestinian
Communist Party (RPCP)

The pro-Soviet RPCP is a significant element of the PLO, with representatives on all major committees, including the Executive Committee of the PLO. It is the successor organization to the Comintern PKP (Palestinian Communist party) and is headed by General Secretary Suleiman Najab. The RPCP has some five thousand members, most located in Lebanon, Syria, Jordan, and the occupied territories. It is financed by the Soviet Union.

Popular Struggle Front (PSF)

Led by Dr. Samir Ghusha, the PSF came into being in the occupied territories in the wake of the 1967 Middle East War. It subsequently moved to Lebanon and has an estimated six hundred members. Headquartered in Damascus, the PSF is financed by both the Iraqi and Libyan governments. Although it broke with the PLO in 1983, it returned to the fold at the 1988 PNC meeting in Algiers.

Popular Arab Liberation Movement (PALM)

Established in 1979 as a splinter group of Abu Nidal's FRC, PALM was headquartered in Baghdad until recently. The group was financed by both Fatah and the PFLP and headed by Naji Alush. However, it never numbered more than a hundred members and may have disintegrated in recent months.

Arab Liberation Front (ALF)

The pro-Iraq ALF is based in Baghdad and led by Secretary-General Abed el-Rahim Ahmed. It was established by Iraq's Ba'ath party in 1969 and is financed by the Iraqi government. It has some four hundred members and is part of the PLO.

Palestine Liberation Army (PLA)

The PLA was created during the founding meeting of the PLO in East Jerusalem in 1964. It was envisioned as the PLO's military arm. Although regarded as an independent fighting force, in reality the PLA brigades are attached to the regular armed forces of each Arab country on whose territory they are based. However, the PLA has in effect "lost" two of its brigades, the Qadasiyah and Hittin brigades, which have been "absorbed" by the Syrian armed forces. A large part of the Ein Jalot Brigade was sent to Lebanon before the 1982 Israeli invasion and remained under PLO control. The rest of the brigade was "absorbed" by the Egyptian Army. Another regiment of the PLA, which was stationed in Jordan, was also transferred to Lebanon prior to the Israeli invasion and remains, for the most part, there under the control of the PLO. Nevertheless, several units from the regiment are under the control of the Jordanian armed forces. The forces that remain under the PLO's control are financed chiefly by the PLO. The total strength of the elements under PLO control is approximately twelve to fourteen thousand men under arms. In 1983 the PLA was reorganized and officially renamed the National Palestinian Liberation Army, although it is still popularly referred to as the PLA.

Arab Organization of Fifteen May (May 15)

Although not previously a member of the PLO "family," since the mid-1980's May 15 has cooperated and conducted joint operations with the Fatah Special Operations Group, headed by Colonel Hawari. The operational chief of May 15 is Mohammed Amri (Abu Ibrahim), and the organization is headquartered in Baghdad. It has fewer than a hundred members and formerly financed its own operations by means of terrorist attacks and by providing technical services to other terrorist groups.

THE PLO AFTER THE 1967 SIX-DAY WAR

After the Israeli victory in the 1967 Middle East War, Fatah's leaders met in Damascus in late June 1967 and decided that they would carry the war to the Israelis in the newly Israeli-occupied West Bank and Gaza. They moved quickly to establish an underground network in the occupied territories (although most of the effort in 1967 was concentrated on the West Bank), consistent with Mao Zedong's revolutionary doctrine that "The people are like water and the army is like fish." In other words, Fatah would submerge itself among the 1.2 million Palestinians living under Israeli occupation, periodically venturing out to strike at Israeli targets. Arafat and his top lieutenants actually went underground themselves in the West Bank in order to oversee the progress. The effort, however, turned out to be one of Fatah's greatest failures, not so much because of Israeli efficiency in ferreting out the secret network as because of Palestinian apathy. At that point many Palestinians living on the West Bank were actually relieved to be out from under the often oppressive yoke of Jordanian rule and simply wanted to find some kind of accommodation with the Israelis.

Within months Arafat was forced to leave the West Bank on the run; he has reportedly not been back to Jerusalem since that time. His network was in shambles, and many of his closest confederates had been killed or captured. Once again safely ensconced in Jordan, Arafat returned to sending out Fatah squads to conduct hit-and-run terrorist attacks in Israel. The attacks were launched from Jordan, Syria, and Lebanon, but the Israelis struck back with retaliatory raids and hot-pursuit tactics that created a good deal of friction between Fatah and the host countries where its bases were located. Although in 1965 the Jordanians interdicted the Fatah squad—killing one member and capturing three—that planted the explosive charge in the Israeli canal, by the late 1960's the PLO was operating on Jordanian territory with impunity, a law unto itself.

In March 1968 the Israelis carried out their most dramatic raid against Fatah's main regional headquarters at Karameh, Jordan, in the process clashing with the Jordanian Army, which provided artillery and armor support to Fatah. Arafat and Abu Iyad only narrowly escaped. The Battle of Karameh cost Israel twenty-nine dead and more than sixty wounded, but Fatah losses exceeded a hundred dead and an unknown number of wounded. Even more damaging than the loss of some of its most able and experienced guerrillas, Fatah was forced to withdraw from its bases near the Israeli-Jordan border.

Initially, Arafat and the leadership of Fatah did not understand the full implications of their defeat. Indeed, they took perverse pride in the fact that they had stood up to the mighty Israeli Army and survived. Arafat, however, soon realized that the Battle of Karameh spelled the end of his dreams of ringing Israel with large hostile Palestinian military bases. Fearful of similar Israeli intervention, even Syria and Lebanon were imposing new restrictions on Fatah military operations originating on their territory. From now on Arafat and his fighters would have to pull back from the 1967 cease-fire lines, retreating into Jordan's mountains and to the Palestinian refugee camps ringing most of Jordan's major cities.

But while the Battle of Karameh had been a military disaster for Fatah, Arafat turned it into a political victory, by using the engagement to buttress his bid for the leadership of the PLO. Over the years the PLO's propaganda organs have even managed to turn the Battle of Karameh into a military "victory." Arafat has demonstrated repeatedly his ability to manipulate public perceptions in the Arab world, consistent with the old Arabic saying "The Arab soul is influenced more by words than by ideas, and more by ideas than by deeds." Shortly after Arafat became chairman of the PLO in 1969, friction with King Hussein began to increase dramatically as the Palestinians moved rapidly to create what, in effect, was an autonomous Palestinian entity within Jordan, maintained by force of arms. Palestinian fedayeen carried their weapons openly and routinely challenged the authority of the Jordanian police and military. The PLO established its own laws and regulations and administered justice within the refugee camps. PLO gunmen operated their own roadblocks and even "shook down" ordinary Jordanians for money.

The PFLP made two attempts to assassinate King Hussein in early September 1970. All in all, it added up to an intolerable affront to the king, who had to act or risk losing his throne.

During the struggle that began in September ("Black September") 1970 and continued until July 1971, when the last PLO stronghold at Irbid collapsed, some six to ten thousand

Palestinians lost their lives in fierce fighting with Hussein's Bedouin army. The PLO was ejected from Jordan and sought refuge in Lebanon. It was the end of the PLO "state within a state" in Jordan and the beginning of the PLO "state within a state" in Lebanon.

By contrast with Jordan, the lack of a strong central government in Lebanon made it an easy target of opportunity, and the secret 1969 Cairo Agreement, hammered out between representatives from Egypt and Lebanon, basically paved the way for the PLO to operate with impunity on Lebanese soil. The PLO was guaranteed the right to bear arms, unimpeded control over Palestinian refugee camps, and the use of Lebanese territory as a staging area for attacks on Israel. This was quite a contrast with the 1960's, when a stronger Lebanese central government arrested every Fatah squad on its territory.

In the early 1970's, as the PLO consolidated its power in Lebanon, Arafat and his lieutenants launched a covert terrorist war against Israel and the West, using Black September (see Chapter Three) and other deniable units. Black September's first targets were crude oil facilities in the Middle East and Europe, which were bombed. Even before the attack on Israeli athletes at Munich, Black September had assassinated Jordan's prime minister and wounded its ambassador to London. King Hussein of Jordan, the very symbol of Western influence in the Arab world, survived a total of at least seven Black September and other PLO assassination attempts.

For the PLO, the 1970's also were a period of establishing ties with the Soviet Union, Europe, the Third World, and the globe's terrorist organizations. Among the many groups that came to train at the PLO's terrorist camps in Lebanon were the German Red Army Faction (popularly known as the Baader-Meinhof Gang in the early 1970's), the Japanese Red Army, the Irish Republican Army, Italy's Red Brigades, the Turkish Liberation Army, the Armenian Secret Army for the Liberation of Armenia (ASALA), France's Direct Action, and a host of Latin American terrorists, including representatives from Colombia, El Salvador, and Nicaragua. Even Sandinista Interior Minister Tomás Borge spent a short time in a PLO training camp.

However, the October 1973 Middle East War and the subsequent oil crisis once again forced the PLO to take a back seat to the major Arab confrontation states, which managed to salvage honor they had lost in 1967. The PLO did win a significant political victory in 1974, when an Arab summit held at Rabat recognized the PLO as "the sole representative of the Palestinian people."

One year later tensions between Lebanon's ethnic and religious communities and the PLO exploded into open warfare, from which Lebanon has yet to recover. In the early 1970's the PLO began to play a major role in internal Lebanese politics. Supported and encouraged by the KGB's chief of station in Beirut, the PLO formed an alliance with the Lebanese left, and the combined forces moved to consolidate control over various ports, regions (especially in the southern Bekaa Valley), and installations, replacing the authority of the central government and carving out enclaves wholly under their jurisdiction. Even in the heart of the Lebanese capital, Beirut, the PLO established a kind of extraterritorial jurisdiction over the Fakhani section, where both Fatah and the PLO maintained their headquarters. Lebanese police and military units could not enter the area without engaging in an open military clash with the PLO and its allies. The PLO exerted the same kind of control over the Palestinian refugee camps on the edge of the city. Drunk with power, the PLO began to behave as though it were the real master of Lebanon, and this provoked the nation's religious and ethnic factions into a rapid expansion and arming of their traditional militias, as a way of protecting their communal members and interests. It was only a matter of time before Lebanon erupted in violence.

The resulting conflict enabled Syria to extend its influence over more than two thirds of the country, with Israel carving out a security zone north of its border. Wedged between the Syrians in the north and east and Israel in the south, the PLO read the handwriting on the wall and tried to build bridges to other communities in Lebanon's fractured political landscape, as well as to strengthen its military position in the country. This, in turn, led to confrontations with first the Christians, next the Syrians, then the Druze, and finally the Shiites.

Recognizing an opportunity in the collapse of the Lebanese state to destroy the PLO, the Israelis invaded the country in 1982, forcing Arafat and the PLO out of Beirut after laying siege to the city. Although Arafat described it once again as a "victory," he was compelled to withdraw to Tunisia. Gone was the terrorist state within a state that permitted the PLO almost unchecked freedom of movement, the ability to levy taxes, collect import duties, administer the law, and control a significant amount of the drug traffic flowing through Lebanon. With the loss of its training camps and operational bases and its membership spread across half a dozen nations, the PLO no longer could serve as a hostelry to international terrorism.

The reconstituted PLO camps in North Yemen, Algeria, Sudan, Iraq, and Tunisia had little in common with their predecessors. They were tightly controlled and supervised by local authorities. Only in Tunisia was the PLO afforded any freedom of movement, in the vacuum created by the rapidly deteriorating regime of Tunisia's aged leader, Habib Bourguiba.

Under heavy pressure from his followers, Arafat tried to orchestrate a return of the PLO to Lebanon in 1983 but was blocked by the Syrians, who had no intention of permitting him to come back to his former position of prominence. Syrian troops, assisted by rebellious Palestinian factions, drove the PLO from its last strongholds: the city of Tripoli and the refugee camps of Nahr al-Bard and Badawi.[19]

In a closed-door meeting after the PLO's evacuation of Tripoli, Arafat admitted to his top lieutenants that the political situation had changed dramatically for the PLO. According to his analysis, the PLO was about to enter the third phase of its existence. The first phase, from 1967 to 1974, said Arafat, involved shocking the world by means of brutal terrorist acts into recognizing the Palestinian issue and placing it at the front of world concerns. It was during this phase that the PLO began to fight the United States, which it viewed as an obstacle to realizing its goals. Continuing, Arafat said that during the second phase, which began in late 1974 or early 1975 and ended in 1983, the PLO gained international recognition and credibility and became a "legitimate" political organization. However, despite such successes, the PLO did not give up its armed struggle because he viewed it as necessary to keep the pressure on Israel and its allies, especially the United States. In the last phase, the one that was just beginning, concluded Arafat, the Palestinians would maintain their simultaneous diplomatic and military offensives, and in the end the Palestinian flag, he predicted, would be raised at the Haram Ash-Sharif (the Temple Mount in Jerusalem) and the Palestinian agony would come to an end. In other words, they were now entering the climactic phase of the Palestinian struggle, and deliverance was at hand.[20]

In short, Arafat was reaffirming his commitment to a strategy of presenting a generally moderate and accommodating political face to the world, while at the same time using proxies and secrecy, continuing the armed struggle against Israel and the West, and employing all the other methods at his disposal, including terrorism.

"MR. PALESTINE"

Whether he deserves such approbation or not, Yasir Arafat's name is today synonymous with the Palestinian struggle for dignity, respect, and independence. He is no less the embodiment of hope for the talented and educated Palestinian professionals engaged in the work of nation building for other Arabs who had the good fortune to be blessed rather than cursed by their geography than he is for hundreds of thousands of Palestinians, the "Shabab," who inhabit the foul and wretched refugee camps scattered around the Middle East. Professor Edward W. Said has called Arafat "Mr. Palestine," and in some respects Arafat has become a man of somewhat mythic proportions to both his advocates and his adversaries.

Without question, he has carefully cultivated his public image, or, as some would say, "images." In order to shed his image as a "terrorist," which was reinforced by his appearance in 1974 before the UN General Assembly wearing a pistol on his hip, Arafat has taken a number of steps to make his appearance more benign and statesmanlike. He no longer is ever photographed, if possible, with a weapon, and his public appearances and interviews are tightly controlled and in many cases carefully orchestrated. Even during the height of the Israeli bombardment of Beirut in 1982, Arafat's handlers were always careful to ensure that he looked the part of the victim, wandering among the ruins of the city, surrounded by children. As a sign of authority, he generally carried a small swagger stick instead of a gun, and his own heavily armed bodyguards were instructed, whenever possible, to remain far enough away to stay out of the photos.

At one point, in the early 1980's, Arafat even considered hiring a Washington, D.C., public relations firm to improve his image and that of the PLO in the United States. In 1983 Nabil Shaath, Arafat's chief financial adviser, traveled to Washington to meet with Robert Keith Gray, the chairman of Gray and Company Public Communications International, to discuss the possibility of a major PR campaign in the United States on behalf of the PLO. Gray had been the chairman of President Reagan's first inaugural and had been active in Republican politics for thirty years. At the time the overture was made, Gray was the most visible lobbyist in the nation's capital. He subsequently traveled to Tunis as a guest of the League of Arab States, ostensibly to deliver a speech on improving the image of Arabs in the United States. However, the speech had been arranged with the assistance of Shaath, who said that while in Tunis, Gray would meet secretly with Arafat to discuss the details of a possible PR campaign. Upon his return, Gray said that Arafat's bodyguards came to his hotel in Tunis late one night to escort him to a meeting with the chairman. But according to Gray, he had second thoughts about the meeting and refused the summons to meet with Arafat.[21]

Over the years Arafat has tried to serve many constituencies, often telling each what it wanted to hear, and damn the inconsistencies. He has projected a face of moderation to the world and one of confrontation and struggle to the Palestinian masses that adore him. Therefore, to understand Arafat, one must realize that above all else, he is first and foremost a politician, and a shrewd one at that. He has often been underestimated by his adversaries both within the Palestinian movement and throughout the Arab world, and while many of them have fallen by the wayside, Arafat is still here, perhaps stronger than ever before.

Much of the world views Arafat as a statesman, although twice in recent years Italy has issued a warrant for his arrest, which was later revoked. The first was issued by Italian magistrate Carlo Mastelloni on September 2, 1983, after members of Italy's Red Brigades terrorist group testified that they had—with Arafat's direct knowledge and complicity—received weapons from the PLO in the late 1970's. The warrant was subsequently dismissed on a technicality which was more a product of Italian political cowardice than any actual flaw in the legal procedures involved.[22] Indeed, the warrant had become a major embarrassment to Italy's Socialist prime minister, Bettino Craxi, who had met with Arafat on a number of occasions.

Mastelloni then issued a second warrant for Arafat on weapons-smuggling charges, this time adding Abu Iyad's name to it. According to the warrant, Abu Iyad, with Arafat's knowledge, provided weapons to the Red Brigades, including three surface-to-air missiles. The warrant for Arafat was upheld by an Italian court in October 1984 but quashed in June 1985 on the ground of insufficient evidence, although the arrest warrant for Abu Iyad remained in effect. A third warrant, for Abu Iyad but not Arafat, was issued in June 1988.

Other efforts have been made by various countries to charge Arafat with crimes against their citizens and interests, but all have failed. A 1985 effort, for example, by U.S. lawmakers and other interested groups and individuals to get the Justice Department to indict Arafat for the 1973 murders of U.S. diplomats in Khartoum also came up empty-handed, largely for political reasons.

Today, as chairman of the PLO, Yasir Arafat presides over a fractious and unwieldy organization. There is constant tension between the various constituent elements of the PLO and often intense competition for both resources and the hearts and minds of the Palestinian masses. Arafat can give orders to Fatah, but not to the other organizations that compose the PLO; he can only attempt to coordinate their activities and to impose on them a loose kind of discipline.[23] He cannot, for example, order Habash's PFLP to carry out a particular mission. Indeed, when a five-man combined PFLP/PLF (Abbas faction) force was interdicted by Israeli forces on February 5, 1989, only five miles from the Israeli border, it appeared to represent a violation of the PLO's pledge to renounce terrorism. Since both the PFLP and the PLF (Abbas faction) are members of the PLO, the raid into Israel's self-proclaimed "security zone" clearly was an embarrassment to Arafat and raised questions about exactly how much control he has even over the various constituent elements of his organization, much less over those Palestine groups that ostensibly reject the PLO's leadership.

Arafat's position atop the PLO is precarious, yet no real rivals are visible. It is full of frustrations and risks, yet he shows no sign of wanting to relinquish power or, after more than four decades of struggle, to retire to a quiet life in some Arab capital. He certainly has enough wealth to live out his days comfortably. Although for decades he described himself as a poor man, he has dropped the pretense of poverty in recent years. Yet, he denies that he is a millionaire. "No, I never was a millionaire," he said in a recent interview. "I was rich. In Kuwait I started three construction companies with partners. They were successful. When I left for Fatah and the P.L.O., my partners paid me for my shares and I left money behind, invested in companies that have become very successful. Let us say I have enough."[24] Despite his oft-repeated public declaration "I do not need possessions," most authoritative sources believe that Arafat is a multimillionaire, with a huge PLO discretionary fund available to him. Whenever he travels, says the former Fatah intelligence chief, Brigadier Atallah Atallah (Abu Zaim), Arafat carries a bag containing $200,000 in cash, which "he distributes . . . as he wishes."[25] There are also indications that he is no longer as austere a personality as he once was. In this connection more than $1.5 million was spent to upgrade the villa in Tunis provided him as his official residence by the Tunisian government.

Nevertheless, he is still a revolutionary, a man consumed by a mission, single-mindedly devoted to the struggle for a Palestinian homeland. Over the years, however, he has changed, some even say mellowed. Perhaps owing to his training as an engineer, Arafat is extremely methodical and patient, able to take the so-called long view of things. Unlike many of his contemporaries who rushed into the struggle ill prepared and without any real concept of a long-term strategy, and subsequently were chewed up by the Israelis or lost in the shifting sands of Arab politics, Arafat recognized at an early stage the need to build the necessary structure to sustain the struggle and to survive over time. He is less inclined to hyperbole as he grows older and more willing to see the world in realistic, if sometimes stark, terms. Unlike his youth, when he viewed the question of a Palestinian homeland as a zero-sum equation, he now appears ready to consider a Palestinian ministate composed of the Gaza and West Bank coexisting alongside Israel.

In this connection he is the ultimate pragmatist, some would say opportunist, able to shift allegiance abruptly or abandon an alliance at the drop of a hat. Throughout his long career, he has alternatively been at war against and an ally of virtually all the Arab confrontation states. He has battled for his very life against Syria's Assad and Jordan's Hussein and later embraced both men. There are even reports that his hated foe, Israel, has come to his rescue more than once rather than see him killed and replaced by a more radical or aggressive successor. By the same token, Israel, too, has actively sought his death on occasion, though not in recent years.

Arafat has remained alive through a combination of guile and shrewdness and the firm belief that there is no such thing as permanent friends or permanent enemies, only permanent interests. Indeed, above all else, Arafat is a survivor. He has managed to survive, and even to prosper, as a major player in one of the most violent and treacherous political arenas on earth, the Middle East.

He is obsessive about his security. Although in early 1989 he told followers that he anticipates direct negotiations with the Israelis and expects to see a Palestinian state erected on Palestinian soil within two years, he continues to be preoccupied with Israeli plots. Over the years he and his top aides have regularly proclaimed that the Israeli inner Cabinet just met to sign his death warrant. In view of the 1988 death of Abu Jihad at the hands of Israeli commandos, who can blame Arafat for being cautious? Arafat's paranoia also is fed by statements like that made by Israeli government minister Ariel "Arik" Sharon as recently as January 28, 1989, when he announced on a radio broadcast that "as long as Arafat is alive and roaming our surrounding vicinity there will never be peace."[26] On the other hand, the real threat to him is not from the Israelis; over the years he has escaped numerous assassination attempts orchestrated by Palestinian rivals and other Arab governments.

He is surrounded by a wall of bodyguards from Force 17,

most trained in the Eastern bloc, chiefly by the Romanians and East Germans. While they lack the subtleness and technological means of the U.S. Secret Service, they are nonetheless extremely loyal to Arafat, and few doubt that they wouldn't be willing to lay down their lives without hesitation in order to protect their leader. For his part, Arafat is also a great believer in luck and attributes some of his narrow escapes more to his own instincts and unpredictableness than to any evasive action by his protectors.

Arafat is nothing if not unpredictable. Always on the move, during a single month in 1988 he traveled to China and India, took two separate trips to Europe, and visited every Arab country but Syria twice. Much of his travel is spontaneous, with Arafat laying out his own itinerary at the last minute or even in midair. An effort to reconstruct his travel during the past year and a half suggests that he is on the road at least ten days a month. According to Abu Zaim, in one year, from mid-1983 to mid-1984, the PLO spent $7.2 million on air travel, accommodations, and entertainment, much of it by Arafat and his entourage. An Egyptian magazine, relying on documents from the PLO Supreme Military Council, estimated that Arafat alone annually spends $2.5 million on luxury suites in hotels, extra limousines, and related travel expenses, and this doesn't include the cost of his Learjet, which, Arafat claims, is picked up by the Saudis, or the heavily armored limousines that Force 17 maintains for his use in most of the Arab capitals that he regularly visits.

Arafat has no known life apart from the Revolution. He rarely goes to a restaurant and has not been to a movie or the theater for years, out of fear of establishing a pattern that his enemies could take advantage of by planning an attack on his life. He has few close friends, and the list is growing shorter all the time. Abu Jihad was, by all accounts, his best friend and confidant within the PLO, but he is buried at the Yarmuk refugee camp. Arafat is said to have loved Ali Hassan Salameh as a son and regarded him as a potential successor, but Salameh, too, lies in a martyr's graveyard.

There has always been a great deal of speculation about Arafat's personal life, especially his sexual preferences. For his part, Arafat has always dismissed the subject by saying, "I'm married to al-Fatah. Al-Fatah is my woman, my family, my life." There is considerable anecdotal evidence, however, that suggests that Arafat is a homosexual or at least bisexual. Lieutenant General Ion Mihai Pacepa, the former chief of the Romanian external intelligence service, the Departamentul de Informatii Externe (DIE), who defected to the West, reportedly brought with him audio and video tapes of Arafat's indiscretions with members of his protective detail that had been secretly made by Romanian security agents. In his recently published memoirs Pacepa describes one of Arafat's romps that was described to him by Constantin Munteanu, a Romanian general who worked with the PLO. Arafat was visiting Romania at the time, and his guesthouse, like that provided to any other official state guest, was routinely "bugged." According to Pacepa, Munteanu turned away in disgust after speaking with the agents monitoring Arafat, who was known by his code name, the Fedayee. "After the meeting with the Comrade [Romanian President Nicolae Ceauşescu]," Pacepa quotes Munteanu as saying, "he [Arafat] went directly to the guest house and had dinner. At this very moment the 'Fedayee' is in his bedroom making love to his bodyguard. The one I knew was his latest lover. He's playing tiger again. The officer monitoring his microphones connected me live with the bedroom, and the squawling almost broke my eardrums. Arafat was roaring like a tiger, and his lover yelping like a hyena."[27]

Arafat's apparent homosexuality, however, is tempered, in part, by an unusual story emanating out of London in 1987. On July 22, 1987, Ali Naji al-Adhami, a Palestinian cartoonist whose work was well known throughout the Arab world, was shot in the face, at point-blank range, on a London street outside the editorial offices of the publication he worked for, *Al Qabas*. He was rushed to surgery but died a short time later after being placed on a life-support system. According to two intelligence agents who were monitoring certain Palestinian activities in London, and were later expelled from Great Britain, the attack was planned and executed by members of Arafat's personal guard, Force 17, which maintains an extensive and very active network in Great Britain.

Al-Adhami, who was forty-two years old at the time, was a popular satirist and cartoonist whose works were syndicated throughout the Middle East. He had a rare gift for acerbic humor, and few public figures in the Arab world escaped his barbs and lampooning. He is remembered as particularly merciless when it came to members of his own community. In 1984 he described to an interviewer his satisfaction at being able to satirize "rich Palestinians who scream all day about the land and about sacrifices, when in fact they are more interested in their financial deals and private gains."

Al-Adhami had grown up in a Palestinian refugee camp in Lebanon and had become politically involved at an early age. His first drawings were completed in a Lebanese jail, after he had run afoul of local authorities because of his political activism. After his release he moved to Kuwait and started working as a cartoonist and political satirist. By 1985 he had so offended the PLO with his cartoons and pieces describing the organization's financial corruption that he was forced to flee to England, where he joined the staff of the Kuwaiti international paper *Al Qabas*. He had portrayed the leadership of the PLO as jet-setters who lived in luxury while millions of Palestinians still lived stateless and in misery. In a play upon words in Arabic, he dubbed Arafat "Father of the Lips" (Abu Shafaya), for the frequent photo opportunities of Arafat kissing children and world leaders.

In early 1987 al-Adhami focused on a new target: the personal morality of top PLO leaders. He created a cartoon character modeled on an ordinary Palestinian who asked provocative questions, usually alluded to only in private, about the individual rectitude and sexual probity of various Palestinian public figures. Among his cartoons were a number implying that Arafat had a relationship with a married Arab woman. It was allegedly for this transgression that Arafat ordered al-Adhami murdered.

The Western observer may wonder why Arafat, whatever his sexual proclivities, took such great offense at al-Adhami's cartoons. What difference does it make, after all, if Arafat is bisexual or a homosexual? Apparently the reason al-Adhami was killed is that he was delving too deeply and too persistently into the personal lives and habits, both financial and sexual, of the PLO's leadership, assaulting their elaborately developed public personas and holding them up to censure and ridicule. In Arafat's specific case, what counted was not so much the identity of his lover, male or female, as the fact that

Arafat was being portrayed as "unfaithful" to the Revolution; he was the man, after all, who was supposed to be "married" to Fatah.

If his relationships with other adults are often cynical and one-sided, Arafat is said to "melt" in the presence of children.

In recent years Arafat has worked to improve his appearance. Not only is he better tailored and groomed than a decade ago, but he has lost a good deal of weight and seems to be more physically fit than in the past. He is not known to be a gourmet and still abstains from smoking or drinking. His only known indulgence is honey, which he takes straight from the container or in his tea.

He is a restless man and often works well into the night, requiring only about four hours' sleep each day, supplemented by a few catnaps. Arafat is notorious for his short temper and fits of shouting and screaming when something doesn't go according to plan. He can be an emotional individual, who wears his emotions on his sleeve. Nevertheless, he appears to kill with little remorse and, sometimes, even on whim. Yet for all of the attention focused on him by the world's media and intelligence services, Arafat remains a mystery, even to those who know him best.

3

Covert Units
and Operations

I n the late morning of June 16, 1976, an armored black Cadillac limousine left the underground garage at the U.S. Embassy in West Beirut. The embassy was located in the predominantly Moslem section of the city, a few blocks west of the so-called green line dividing Christian East Beirut from Moslem West Beirut and only a block from the sandy beaches of the Mediterranean coast. The U.S. ambassador, Francis E. Meloy, who had arrived in the strife-torn country only a month earlier and was still getting acclimated to his dangerous new post, was about to pay a courtesy call on Lebanon's president-elect, Elias Sarkis. It was to be their first meeting, and it was scheduled to take place at Sarkis's residence in East Beirut. Accompanying Meloy were his economic counselor, Robert O. Waring, and the embassy's longtime chauffeur, Zohair Moughrabi. Four State Department security men followed close behind in a Ford station wagon.

As the car picked up speed, the American flags on the fender staffs unfurled and snapped in the breeze. It was a beautiful day, neither too hot nor too humid, with a light wind blowing off the Mediterranean, chasing away the haze of smoke and the stench that often settled over Beirut since the onset of factional strife. The Metn Mountains looming over the city looked green and lush in contrast with the gray and tortured city below, many of its once lovely buildings already shell-pocked and charred, the streets full of rubble and garbage. If one believed in omens, the weather was so lovely that it seemed to portend an auspicious day for the fifty-nine-year-old ambassador and his traveling companions.

The two-car convoy made its way quickly through the crowded streets, alive with residents eager to take advantage of the lull in the fighting to run errands and bask in the warm sunlight after spending so many hours in the gloom of their bomb shelters. The cars headed straight for the Museum checkpoint, near the city's racetrack and not far from the Lebanese parliament building, the only crossing point open into East Beirut.

Unknown to the ambassador and his companions, their progress was being carefully monitored by lookouts posted along the route, who reported via radio each leg of their journey. When they reached the militia checkpoint on the west side of the dividing line, the ambassador's limousine was given a cursory check and then waved on through. At this point the escort vehicle loaded with security men turned around and headed back to the embassy, as was its normal procedure since East Beirut was not considered "Indian country"—that is, hostile or dangerous territory.

What the security detail did not know was that after passing through the checkpoint and its six-foot-high sandbag chicane, the ambassador's limousine had been forced to stop again inside the narrow strip known as no-man's-land that ran between the two checkpoints. As armed men surrounded the vehicle, Moughrabi flipped the switch unlocking the doors and stepped out of the car. The men pushed their way into the limousine and turned off the car's two-band shortwave radio, although not before the chauffeur, Moughrabi, had transmitted a message to the embassy indicating that the ambassador had passed safely into East Beirut. Then, at gunpoint, Meloy and Waring were driven back into West Beirut, via a series of narrow back streets that ran behind the National Museum. Not a shot was fired, and apparently the militiamen manning the West Beirut checkpoint were totally unaware of the abduction that took place only a few dozen paces from their fortified position.

At the East Beirut checkpoint, however, Lebanese Forces sentries became suspicious when the ambassador's car, which they had been notified to expect, did not appear, and they contacted their headquarters inside the port of Beirut. About the same time, President-elect Sarkis contacted the U.S. Embassy to express concern over the ambassador's delay in reaching his residence.

Around 7:00 P.M. the bodies of Ambassador Meloy, Waring, and Moughrabi were found on the West Beirut waterfront, about a hundred yards from the residence of Charles Waterman, the CIA's chief of station. They all had been shot to death.

Few incidents better underscore the PLO's hidden involvement with terrorism and its use of proxy groups and covert units to achieve its aims than the brutal murder of the two American diplomats. Although the murderers were subsequently described as "unknown gunmen," there is little question who the perpetrators of the crime were. Indeed, the U.S. government engaged in a deliberate cover-up of the real facts in order to avoid public or congressional pressure to retaliate against those responsible for the murders. It was not the first time, and it wouldn't be the last.

The events leading up to the tragedy are complex.

During the Lebanese civil war, which began in 1975, the various elements of the Lebanese left formed a coalition known as the Lebanese National Movement (LNM). Composed of more than fifty different organizations, some large and powerful, others only tiny splinter groups, they had only one real thing in common, a hatred of the Lebanese right, embodied by the Christian community and its armed militia, the Lebanese Forces (Phalange). Among the organizations that composed the LNM were the PLO; Fatah; the Progressive Socialist party (PSP), headed first by Kamal, and later Walid, Jumblatt, its membership drawn mainly from the Druze community; the Syrian National Socialist party (PPS); the Lebanese Communist party (LCP); the Lebanese Ba'ath party; and the Socialist Arab Action party.

The professed goals of the LNM were to turn Lebanon into

a "pure" Arab state, to implement a "nonaligned" foreign policy, to dismantle the ethnic structure of the Lebanese political system, and to eliminate the Christian influence in the country. Shortly after its formation the LNM established a Joint Military Command of the Resistance to coordinate all leftist military activities in Lebanon. Since the PLO and Fatah were the best trained, equipped, and organized armed forces in embattled Lebanon, Yasir Arafat's and Abu Iyad's influence and practical control over the LNM were almost complete.

At the outset the LNM's hidden agenda was to assist Syria in implementing its policies in Lebanon. Arafat and his allies mistakenly believed that Syria would destroy the Lebanese Forces and the power of the Christian community, thus leaving Lebanon to the PLO and the Lebanese left, which would administer the country as caretakers for the Syrians.

In April 1976, however, the Syrians intervened in Lebanon to bring an end to the factional strife and, by doing so, to save the Lebanese Christian community from extinction at the hands of the LNM. Arafat and the LNM felt outraged and betrayed at this turn of events and threw their forces against the Syrians as they advanced toward Beirut. To deal with the situation, Syria's strong man, Hafez al-Assad, decided secretly to coordinate his military operations with Israel and the United States. This was done through a secret channel in London.

In April 1976 King Hussein, who was vacationing in London, met clandestinely with the Israeli ambassador to the Court of St. James's, Gideon Raphael. The meeting had been arranged, at Hussein's request, through the "good offices" of a Jewish physician, Emanuel Herbert, who served as the private doctor to the Hashemite royal family. The meeting, which took place late at night at Dr. Herbert's residence, was set up so that King Hussein could convey an urgent proposal regarding Lebanon from Syria's Assad to Israel's prime minister, Yitzhak Rabin.

A few days later, using the same channel, the Israelis—after conferring with the United States—indicated their acceptance of Assad's proposal, which, in effect, was to carve up Lebanon into zones of influence. The understanding that arose out of the secret meetings later came to be known as the Red Lines

Understanding. It permitted the Syrians to establish control over Lebanon north of the Litani River. The Syrians ceded the area south of the Litani River to Israel, as a security zone, and both sides undertook not to interfere with each other's forces.

The chief loser in this arrangement was obviously the PLO and its proxy, the LNM, which were not consulted by Syria. Arafat and his advisers immediately realized that they would have to take some kind of dramatic action to indicate their outrage and to make it clear to all that they did not feel bound by the agreement. Instead of retaliating against the actual parties to the agreement, at the direction of Abu Iyad, the Joint Military Command of the Resistance decided to strike at the United States, which it blamed for having, in effect, blessed the partition of Lebanon into spheres of influence. The chosen target was the American ambassador in Beirut, Francis Meloy.

The actual operation was assigned to a small leftist organization in the LNM known as the Socialist Arab Action party (SAAP), which, in the wilderness of mirrors that is Lebanon, was itself a covert extension of George Habash's Popular Front for the Liberation of Palestine (PFLP). SAAP boasted about 200 to 250 members and was ostensibly led by a Lebanese named Hashem Ali Hamdan. Some of the members of SAAP were also members of the PFLP and had terrorist operational skills and experience.

Ali Hassan Salameh, by then chief of Force 17, was also involved, according to sources within the CIA. One of Salameh's operatives, it turned out, was the son of the U.S. ambassador's driver, Zohair Moughrabi, a Lebanese national. Moughrabi's son, who also worked for the U.S. Embassy as part of the Lebanese support staff, approached his father, asking for his help in gathering some information about the ambassador's schedule, specifically at what time he would cross the green line. Moughrabi was told that there was a plan in effect to kidnap the ambassador for the purpose of extracting a large ransom from the United States. The son promised his father a chunk of the ransom money if he threw in with the "kidnappers."

Moughrabi was double-crossed by the terrorists, who killed him along with the American diplomats. The son has never resurfaced, and it is believed that he, too, may have been murdered, despite his key role in the success of the operation.

In his memoirs Abu Iyad calls the operation "a stupid and ignoble crime" and spends nearly two pages attempting to cover up his role in the Meloy affair.[1] Although he demonstrates an impressive knowledge of the episode, he claims never to have heard of the Socialist Arab Action party. In order to cultivate a "moderate" image to the outside world, he and Arafat publicly deplored the murders and subsequently claimed to have "arrested" eight individuals involved in the operation. Indeed, any public link to the murders outside Lebanon would have been devastating to the PLO, which was already striving for international respectability. Despite his promises, however, Arafat never turned over transcripts of the interrogation of the eight men to the Arab League delegation in Beirut, nor is there any evidence that the eight individuals were ever punished. The whole episode seems to have been an elaborate charade to distance Arafat, Abu Iyad, and the PLO from the operation.

The ambassador's Cadillac was later observed transporting members of Force 17 around southern Lebanon, especially the city of Sidon, yet the United States chose to ignore the outrage, as it had others in the past. President Gerald Ford was engaged in a tight race for election to a full term, and neither the country nor the administration was in any mood to undertake what would surely have been a highly controversial military action against the PLO and its allies. Unfortunately the U.S. failure to retaliate against the killers laid the groundwork for the subsequent deaths of other Americans in Lebanon during the 1980's, as terrorists—emboldened by American timidity in the face of repeated attacks—grew ever more aggressive.

THE PLO AND TERRORISM

After the humiliating defeat suffered by the Arab states in 1967 and the loss of the predominantly Palestinian-populated

West Bank and Gaza, as well as the Golan Heights and Sinai peninsula, Palestinians were agreed on the need to take their destiny into their own hands. But how? Armed struggle was the only answer, but they were clearly inferior as a military force to Israel, now the strongest military power in the region. Even a traditional insurgency seemed out of the question; Israel's borders were well defended, and the Israelis dealt mercilessly with guerrillas. It was clear to the Palestinians that they would have to develop bases near Israel where they could train and build an effective military force that could be used to carry out hit-and-run attacks. But this would take time, and there was pressure within the PLO to strike out at Israel in some way and demonstrate that unlike the defeated Arab armies, they—the Palestinians—had not capitulated. Indeed, for them the war was just beginning.

Within the PLO some, like George Habash of the Marxist Popular Front for the Liberation of Palestine (PFLP), argued that they should not lead to Israel's strength but instead hit them "where they were not." Habash embraced a campaign of striking soft targets and noncombatants, using terrorism to punish Israel and its allies, while at the same time keeping the Palestinian quest for a national home before an indifferent world. Similarly, as Abu Iyad wrote in his autobiography, after the PLO was driven from Jordan in 1970:

> Fatah's young men . . . unable to wage classic guerrilla warfare across Israel's borders . . . insisted on carrying out a revolutionary violence of another kind, commonly known elsewhere as "terrorism." They wanted to wreak vengeance not only on the Zionist enemy, but also on the Arab murderers and traitors who had made themselves Israel's accomplices. To keep the violence from taking an individualistic and anarchic form, there was no other way than to channel the wave of anger, to structure it and give it a political content.[2]

Initially, only a minority within Fatah and the PLO opposed the use of terrorism, fearing that it would alienate world public opinion and debase the righteousness of their struggle for a homeland. Some of those who opposed the use of terrorism themselves became victims of terrorism, as "moderates" within the Palestinian National Council were denounced, purged, and in some cases assassinated. A few factions, like the Marxist Democratic Front for the Liberation of Palestine (DFLP), headed by Naif Hawatmeh, have always rejected international terrorism in favor of traditional guerrilla tactics, confining their attacks to Israel proper. Although Israeli noncombatants have often been victims of the DFLP, it approaches being a legitimate insurgent organization.

By the mid-1970's it was becoming increasingly apparent to many within the PLO that the promiscuous use of terrorism by various Palestinian organizations, many of them under the PLO umbrella, had become more of a handicap to Palestinian ambitions than an advantage. Thus, Arafat and other PLO leaders began publicly to distance themselves from most terrorist acts, even those that they themselves were responsible for. As Arafat began to gain greater world stature, he openly deplored terrorism, at least to his Western audiences. It was, by contrast, a different story when he spoke to his Fatah commandos and to the Palestinian masses. Indeed, his rhetoric remained uncompromising, and he continued to hail various terrorists and their actions as "heroic," often speaking of the "martyrdom" of terrorists killed in action.

On numerous occasions Arafat has even made public pledges to "punish" those accused of terrorist crimes. In 1974, for example, in an interview given to *The New York Times,* Arafat disclosed that the PLO had "arrested" five Palestinian terrorists, members of the Arab Nationalist Youth Organization for the Liberation of Palestine, a Libyan-sponsored group, accused of an attack on a Pan Am plane in Rome that left thirty-one people dead, including fourteen Americans. However, the five terrorists were never punished; after spending a short time in a PLO jail in Lebanon, they were released and rejoined their former units.

In 1985 Arafat announced, in what became known as the Cairo Declaration, the PLO's "criticism and condemnation of all acts of terrorism." He said not only that the PLO was expressing its opposition to terrorism but that the organization would "take all measures to deter violators." Nevertheless, in the four years since the Cairo Declaration, not a single terrorist has been handed over by the PLO or any of its constituent elements to a government with a legitimate warrant for the terrorist's arrest or a pending request for the terrorist's extradition. There is no recorded case, moreover, of a terrorist being punished by the PLO, although the PLO has branded as "terrorists" a number of alleged spies for Israel who were subsequently executed. Indeed, Mohammed Abbas, the PLF leader responsible for the *Achille Lauro* seajacking and the cold-blooded murder of Leon Klinghoffer, an elderly American confined to a wheelchair, is still a member of the PLO's Executive Committee. Despite an even stronger renunciation of terrorism by Arafat on December 14, 1988, in Geneva, which opened the door for direct talks with the United States, there is no evidence that the PLO has really forsworn the use of terrorism. Even within its top echelons there is considerable disagreement over Arafat's renunciation of terrorism. More than a month after the Arafat's Geneva pledge, Habash openly criticized the PLO chairman's action. "Arafat could say: we are not terrorists, we are freedom fighters," observed Habash. "But when Arafat says that he denounces the previous stage of the Palestinian struggle, he is casting a slur on himself and he is also casting slurs on the struggle of the Palestinian people."[3]

THE SECRET PLO

The dark face behind the PLO's recent public mask of moderation is terrorism. Despite all its public pronouncements to the contrary, the PLO has never fully and effectively renounced the use of terrorism to achieve its goals, nor has it stopped conducting terrorist actions against the United States, Israel, and other nations. What it has done is to shift the responsibility for conducting the "armed struggle" against nations other than Israel to various "deniable" elements within the PLO or to "outside" organizations that ostensibly are part of a "rejectionist front" and beyond the control of the PLO. In this way Arafat and the leadership of the PLO can have it both ways. They can strive for diplomatic recognition and respect, while at the same time keeping the military pressure on Israel and the West.

Virtually every Palestinian organization that subscribes to

the PLO umbrella, no matter the degree to which it is involved in the political arena, has a clandestine/operational side. The clandestine/operational element of each organization not only is dedicated to promoting the "armed struggle" but is charged with intelligence collection, the security of the organization's leadership, and maintaining the organization's influence in the constant struggle for money, power, and prestige with rival Palestinian groups. Most units also engage in a certain amount of counterintelligence work, designed to prevent infiltration by Israeli, other Arab, or various Western intelligence organizations. According to a high-ranking Israeli intelligence source, while Arafat continues to issue statements denouncing terrorism and committing the PLO solely to political struggle beyond Israel's borders, "the rank and file of those [clandestine/operational] organizations continue to collect intelligence for operations, continue to plan, to line up operators and establish ad hoc alignments and terror squads for future operations."[4]

In the mid-1980's the PLO maintained, or could regularly call on the services of, at least five clandestine units to carry out covert operations, including terrorist acts. These units were Fatah's one-time intelligence section, the Jihaz el-Razd; Arafat's Praetorian Guard, Force 17, under the command of Colonel Mohammed Natour (Abu Tayeb); the Special Operations Group of Colonel Hawari (Abdullah Abed al-Hamid Labib); the so-called Western Section, headed until his death in 1988 by Abu Jihad (Khalil Ibrahim Machmud al-Wazir); and Black June (June 15 Movement), also known as the Fatah Revolutionary Council (FRC), led by Abu Nidal (Sabri Khalil al-Banna).

BLACK SEPTEMBER

Black September was the first of the PLO's deniable covert units. It took its name from the bloody military defeat suffered by the Palestinians in September 1970, when King Hussein drove the PLO, which had openly challenged his rule, from Jordan.

Black September's most dramatic attack, code-named Ikrit and Biram, occurred at the Munich Olympics. Just before dawn on the morning of July 18, 1972, eight Black September terrorists slipped into the Olympic Village and made their way to an apartment block at Connollystrasse 31, where the Israeli Olympic team was quartered. The terrorists, led by a Libyan named Mohammed Masalhad, forced their way into the apartments occupied by the Israelis, killing 2 team members—a coach and a weight lifter—in the process. The terrorists took 9 Israelis hostage and, in exchange for their safety, demanded the release of 234 Arab prisoners incarcerated by the Israeli government and of West German terrorist leaders Andreas Baader and Ulrike Meinhof, who had recently been captured and imprisoned in a Frankfurt jail.

What the West German government had dubbed the "Games of Peace and Joy" had suddenly been transformed into a nightmare reminiscent of the nation's Nazi past. Jews were once again locked in a drama for survival on German soil. Ironically, the West German government intentionally had minimized security in Munich in order to avoid comparisons with the 1936 Berlin Olympics, known as "Hitler's Games," which had been characterized by military pageantry and omnipresent security.

The seventeen-hour standoff between authorities and the terrorists rapidly became a media extravaganza without modern parallel. More than a half billion people reportedly tuned in on their television sets to watch the real-life drama unfolding at the Olympics. Without question, the most powerful and enduring image of the games was that of the ski-masked Black September terrorist on the balcony of the squat concrete apartment block at Connollystrasse 31, which changed the popular image of a Palestinian from a "refugee" to a "terrorist."

The terrorists and their nine hostages ultimately were transported to the German air base at Fürstenfeldbruck, fifteen miles away, where a 727 jetliner was ostensibly standing by to fly them to Cairo. The German government had positioned five snipers at the airfield to take out the terrorists, but in the melee that occurred five terrorists and all nine hostages were killed. Israel went into national mourning.

The Munich Massacre was not the only operation, only the

most dramatic one, carried out by Black September. The organization had burst onto the international stage in November 1971, when four terrorists murdered Jordan's Prime Minister Wasfi Tell in the foyer of Cairo's Sheraton Hotel.[5] It was 1:25 P.M. and Tell was just returning to the hotel after a luncheon meeting of the Arab Defense Council, without his usual complement of bodyguards. The assassin, Ezzat Rabah, stepped out of the crowd and pumped five rounds into Tell in front of dozens of horrified European and American tourists. Then, one of his confederates, Monzer Khalifa, bent down and lapped the mortally wounded Tell's blood from the floor. His shocking action was a clear statement to the world that these were terrorists unlike any ever seen before.

As Rabah, Khalifa, and their two companions—Ziad Khelou and Jawa Khalil Baghdadi—were bundled away by police and security forces, they held up their fingers in a victory salute and cried out, "We are members of Black September."[6] Later, during his interrogation, Rabah told authorities, "We wanted to eat him [Tell] for breakfast, but we got him for lunch."

In the months that followed, Black September carried out attacks on the Jordanian ambassador to the United Kingdom and various European supporters of the state of Israel. Other targets included Jordanian intelligence agents in Bonn, a Sabena jet hijacked in May 1972, oil storage facilities in West Germany and the Netherlands, and a West German industrial concern singled out because it supplied electrical motors to Israel.[7]

The PLO disavowed any connection to Black September, and this myth has been perpetuated in dozens of supposedly authoritative Western texts on terrorism. According to John Richard Thackrah's *Encyclopedia of Terrorism and Political Violence,* for example, Black September allegedly "broke away from Al-Fatah because it disagreed with the latter's emphasis on the need for political action as a national liberation movement. The Black September group belonged to the minority group of 'avenging' Palestinians, members of which committed individual acts of violence."[8]

In reality, Black September was the covert arm of Jihaz el-Razd, the intelligence and reconnaissance department of Fatah, the largest constituent element under the umbrella of the PLO and the one headed by Yasir Arafat.[9] The commander in chief of Black September was Abu Iyad, who delegated operational control of the unit to Mohammed Yussef al-Najjar, chief of the Jihaz el-Razd, and a darkly handsome young Palestinian by the name of Ali Hassan Salameh. Later code-named the Red Prince by the Israelis, who hunted him relentlessly until finally killing him in Beirut in 1979, the black-clad Salameh was known for his intelligence, expensive tastes, marriage to a former Miss Universe, and his utter ruthlessness.[10]

In his book *My Home, My Land,* no less a figure than Salah Khalaf, better known as Abu Iyad, admits, "Its [Black September's] members always insisted that they had no organic tie with Fatah or the PLO. But I knew a number of them and I can assure you that most of them belonged to various Fedayeen organizations."[11] Abu Daoud, a top Black September operator involved in the Munich Massacre, goes even further. Captured in Jordan in February 1972, Abu Daoud told interrogators: "There is no such organization called Black September. Fatah announces its own operations under this name so that Fatah will not appear as the direct executor of the operation. What is called Black September is only the intelligence apparatus, Jihaz el-Razd."[12]

INTELLIGENCE UNITS

After the Israelis killed its first chief, Mohammed Yussef al-Najjar, in Beirut on April 10, 1973, as a part of Operation Spring Youth, Ali Hassan Salameh took over the Jihaz el-Razd, under the overall command of Abu Iyad. When Salameh left to lead Force 17, he was succeeded by Brigadier Atallah Atallah (Abu Zaim), who later defected to Jordan in the mid-1980's. According to a senior Israeli counterintelligence official, the Jihaz el-Razd was a competent intelligence unit that was both resented and feared within the PLO structure, at least in part because it was so successful. "They were doing a good job," recalls the official. "They knew a great deal and came up with the right conclusions."[13] Sometime in the mid-1970's, however, the Jihaz el-Razd was succeeded by the Intelligence and Security Apparatus as Fatah's chief intelligence unit, responsible for the collection, analysis, and trading of intelligence. However, the ISA has few, if any, operational responsibilities, and some Western intelligence organizations believe that the Jihaz el-Razd continues to exist as a deniable covert arm of Fatah's intelligence community. Its present activities, they maintain, are cloaked in mystery. Historically the unit was absolutely loyal to Abu Iyad, and there are suggestions that it has been kept intact to serve his hidden agenda, which has more to do with internal struggles within the PLO than with carrying out external operations.

In recent years the Western Section has also been in eclipse. Under the tight control of Abu Jihad, the unit was widely criticized for its lack of success in conducting various terrorist and military operations against Israel. The Israelis regularly preempted Abu Jihad's operations or intercepted terrorist squads before they could reach Israel's borders. The younger generation of Palestinian terrorist leaders like Abu Tayeb (Colonel Natour) and Colonel Hawari were trying to push aside Arafat's old comrade-in-arms Abu Jihad and usurp responsibility for conducting the war against Israel and its allies. They favored more ruthless and aggressive tactics, which they maintained would produce more tangible results.

The leadership of Fatah is basically divided into two age-groups. First and foremost are the founding fathers, who met in Cairo and Kuwait in the 1950's and launched the organization. Nearly all are in their late fifties and early sixties. This group includes Arafat, Khalaf (Abu Iyad), Qadoumi, Machmud Abbas, and a few others who are still alive.

The second group is composed of the combat and operational commanders who joined Fatah in the years immediately preceding the Six-Day War (1967). By contrast with the founding fathers, the combat commanders are in their forties and early fifties, and all can be described as survivors since their ranks have been depleted by battlefield losses, Israeli assassination squads, and internal disputes within the PLO. Some no longer belong to Fatah, and instead head their own breakaway factions. Members of the second group include Abu Tayeb (Colonel Natour), Colonel Hawari, Salah Ta'amri, Abu Musa, Abu Nidal, and Haj Ismayel.

FORCE 17

The covert unit most loyal to Arafat and the old-line leadership of the PLO is Force 17, which serves both as Arafat's personal bodyguard and as the "enforcer" of his will. Charged with "the security of the Revolution," Force 17 has a mandate that extends far beyond traditional executive protection, and today it serves as the chief covert "action arm" of Fatah. The unit traces its origins back to an incident that occurred on March 21, 1968, when an Israeli armored brigade and two paratroop battalions, supported by reconnaissance units and artillery, attacked the largest Fatah base, located at Karameh in the Jordan Valley. It was the first such raid directed against Palestinian guerrilla forces in the wake of the Six-Day War the year before. During the protracted battle, in which Jordanian armored units joined in to support Fatah, the organization's main headquarters in Jordan was destroyed. Yasir Arafat was forced to flee his besieged headquarters on a motorcycle, dressed as a woman. Abu Iyad was also nearly captured but took refuge among some nearby rocks, hiding out until Israeli search parties gave up the hunt for him.

Arafat reportedly was terrified by his close brush with death, and it was clear to him and his top lieutenants that they needed their own Praetorian Guard, which could provide them with loyal and effective personal protection. In addition to the Israelis, both Egypt and Jordan were increasingly opposed to Fatah's leadership—the Egyptians because they had lost control over the organization and the Jordanians because they feared the growing influence of the PLO in their country—and therefore represented a serious threat to the survival of Arafat and his lieutenants. Indeed, in a few instances Israeli and Arab agents actually cooperated in their attempts to get Arafat and his closest advisers.

As a direct result of the Battle of Karameh and a number of unsuccessful assassination attempts directed at Arafat by various Arab and Israeli agents, as well as by Palestinian rivals, a special section within Fatah's intelligence section, the Jihaz el-Razd, was established to provide Fatah's leaders with personal security. In addition, the Jihaz el-Razd was tasked with gathering intelligence crucial for their personal safety and with ferreting out and destroying enemy agents who managed to penetrate the PLO/Fatah.

After the PLO was driven out of Jordan in 1970 and resettled in Lebanon, Force 17 was formed within the Jihaz el-Razd to carry out the security function. Sometime in 1972–73 it became operationally independent from the Jihaz el-Razd, although its mission and responsibilities initially were tightly circumscribed and concentrated almost entirely on protection of the PLO chairman and the unit's commander in chief. Only later was Force 17's mission expanded to include the protection of other senior PLO officials and the collection of intelligence data. It was later, too, that protection came to embrace the destruction of Arafat's rivals and other special tasks directed by the chairman.

The first commander of Force 17 was the former operational chief of Black September, Ali Hassan Salameh (Abu Hassan). Salameh had learned a great deal during his days with Black September, and he drew on that experience in recruiting operatives and developing the infrastructure of Force 17. The chief criterion for selecting operatives was absolute and unequivocal loyalty to Salameh and Arafat. Although the initial recruits were all Palestinian, in time Salameh reached out to draw into the unit many non-Palestinians, including Lebanese Christians, Lebanese Shiites, and even a number of Western Europeans. Although the recruitment of non-Palestinians meant that most of Force 17's members were not interested or involved in the internal disputes and bickering that characterized the PLO, it also meant that the unit was more vulnerable to penetration by foreign intelligence organizations. In time the United States, the Israelis, and even the Lebanese Christian Phalange had agents within Force 17.

In addition to protecting Arafat, the unit provided a multilayered security blanket around Salameh, who, because of his involvement in the Munich Massacre and his role with Black September, was the top Palestinian target of the Israelis. At the outset the unit was relatively small, but in time it gradually added to both its numbers and missions, and by 1975 it reportedly had grown to more than four hundred men.

Salameh had little practical knowledge of executive protection, so he turned to the East German HVA (Hauptverwaltung für Aufklärung) and the Romanian DIE for assistance. Under the tutelage of the Eastern European intelligence services, Force 17 rapidly evolved into a competent and ruthless executive protection unit. The unit took its orders directly from Arafat and no one else in the top ranks of the PLO. Because of their loyalty, Arafat saw to it that his protégé, Salameh, and his deputy, Mohammed Natour (Abu Tayeb), were gradually admitted to the senior leadership circles of the PLO.

Because of his Western tastes and habits and his reputation as a womanizer and playboy, Salameh was a natural target of various foreign intelligence services. Few people in the PLO had as much access to the organization's secrets as Salameh, and he clearly had the chairman's ear. Since his death in 1979 there has been a great deal of speculation that Salameh may have been a CIA asset. There is little question that he cooperated, when it served his purposes, with a number of foreign intelligence services, including the CIA. According to a former Lebanese intelligence official, Salameh was "a golden source of information. He used his contacts with Bashir Gemayel in order to convey information to the Lebanese Christian Forces and to the CIA."[14]

Salameh worked closely with former CIA official Robert Ames, who died in 1983 in the bomb blast that destroyed the U.S. Embassy in Beirut. Whether Salameh was actually "run" by Ames or regarded as a CIA asset is still open to question, but it is clear that Ames established a discreet back channel to Salameh that was cloaked in secrecy because of Secretary of State Henry Kissinger's agreement with the Israelis not to deal directly with the PLO. Ames, who first met Salameh in Kuwait, is quoted by a colleague as saying, "I was the one that established contact with Ali Hassan Salameh." There is evidence that Ames, in the aftermath of the 1973 Khartoum incident, in which two American diplomats were murdered by the PLO, reached an "understanding" with Salameh whereby the United States provided the PLO with an annual payment for the "protection" of the embassy in Lebanon and other U.S. facilities in the Middle East. In addition, Salameh reportedly shared a great deal of intelligence data collected by and about the PLO with Ames.

Just prior to Ambassador Meloy's murder, Salameh reportedly asked Ames for CIA funds to support the moderate wing of Fatah in its internal struggle with more radical elements. Ames passed the request along to his superiors at CIA headquarters in Langley, Virginia, with a positive recommendation, but Kissinger was totally opposed to the idea, and nothing ever happened.

In October 1976 Salameh approached Charles Waterman, the CIA chief of station in Beirut, and told him that "the Soviets have asked us [Fatah] to pick you up and hand you over to them for interrogation." Salameh said that the best way to deal with the problem was for his men to go through the motions of grabbing Waterman and interrogating him, but "without any Soviet involvement." CIA headquarters was outraged by the proposition since it violated the "gentleman's agreement" between the CIA and KGB not to target each other's operatives. Waterman was ordered to refuse Salameh's overture, and within a week he had packed up and left Beirut for several months to let things cool off. Nevertheless, in December 1976, while Waterman was out of city, the U.S. government decided to reward Salameh for his efforts to "protect" Waterman and the CIA station. The CIA arranged for him to fly to the United States with his girl friend, Georgina Rizak, who later became his second wife. Upon his arrival he was greeted by Ames and spent a week in New Orleans before traveling on to Los Angeles, where he met Waterman. From there he flew to Honolulu with Georgina.

According to a former Ames deputy, not long afterward Israeli intelligence officials approached the CIA chief of station in Paris, Alan Wolf, and informed him, "We are going to blow Salameh. Unless you tell us he's your man, we are going ahead with our plans." The Israelis' blunt warning created a dilemma for the CIA. It didn't know whether it was simply a ploy by the Israelis to "smoke out" the truth about Salameh and discover if he was a CIA asset or they really intended to "hit" him. If the CIA disclosed its relationship with Salameh, it would amount to an admission that it was violating the U.S. pledge to Israel made by Henry Kissinger that the United States would not deal with the PLO unless it renounced terrorism, recognized Israel, and accepted, unconditionally, United Nations Resolutions 242 and 338. On the other hand, if it didn't tell the Israelis, it might lose one of its top sources in the region. Ultimately Wolf told the Israelis—presumably at Ames's direction since Ames was the Middle East national intelligence officer (NIO)—that Salameh was *not* a CIA asset. Then Wolf dropped the subject without further discussion.

According to Ames's former deputy at the time, the Israelis knew that Salameh was a CIA asset and therefore should never have touched him. Indeed, Wolf should have taken more extensive steps to protect Salameh, contends the CIA officer. Ironically, the 1983 car bomb that destroyed the U.S. Embassy in Beirut and killed Ames was fabricated by a former Salameh disciple who learned his craft under the tutelage of the late leader of Force 17.

For their part, the Israelis deny that they ever warned the CIA or Wolf about their intentions with respect to Salameh. "It is not our habit to inform the CIA or the U.S. government in advance about operations we intend to carry out," says a former Israeli intelligence official who was deeply involved in conducting covert operations. Even within the CIA there is skepticism about the nature of Ames's relationship with Salameh, although there is no effort to deny the existence of the relationship. According to a former CIA official involved in Middle East operations, Salameh "jerked us around. On the one hand, he offered help and protection, but on the other hand, he was deeply involved in operations that caused the death of American citizens and diplomats."[15]

After Salameh was killed by the Israelis in January 1979, his deputy, Abu Tayeb (Colonel Mohammed Natour) assumed control of Force 17. However, lacking Salameh's stature, Tayeb initially had to be content with simply providing executive protection to Arafat. The special missions once performed at Arafat's behest were delegated to others. It took Abu Tayeb almost three years to ingratiate himself to Arafat and Abu Iyad (Salah Khalaf) and reach the level of trust and importance enjoyed by Salameh. It was a turbulent time in Beirut: Most of Lebanon was engulfed in civil war; old loyalties and alliances were breaking down; no one was safe from betrayal. Only after the PLO was forced out of Lebanon did Force 17 once again become a covert arm of the PLO.

As an outgrowth of the PLO reversals, Force 17 underwent certain structural changes, reflecting the new realities out-

Colonel Abu Tayeb (Mohammed Natour), the commander in chief of Force 17, Arafat's Praetorian Guards. Force 17 has carried out deniable terrorist operations on behalf of the PLO's leadership. *From the authors' personal collection*

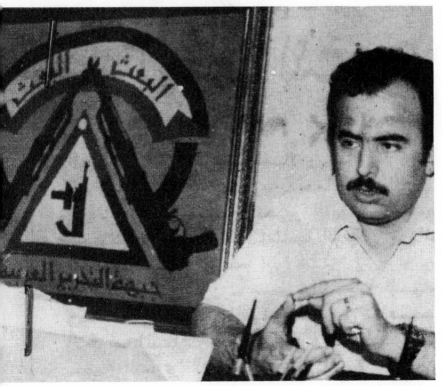

Abd al-Rahim Ahmed, leader of the pro-Iraqi Arab Liberation Front, a member organization of the PLO *From the authors' personal collection*

Funeral of U.S. Ambassador to the Sudan Cleo A. Noel and former Chargé
d'Affaires G. Curtis Moore, who were murdered by PLO terrorists under the
direct command of Yasir Arafat and Abu Iyad   *AP/Wide World Photos*

Funeral of Abu Jihad, number-two man in the PLO. He was killed by Israeli commandos in Tunisia on April 15, 1988. *AP/Wide World Photos*

Wreckage of Pan Am Flight 103, which was destroyed by a bomb on December 21, 1988. The bombing was carried out by the Popular Front for the Liberation of Palestine-General Command at the behest of the Iranian government. *AP/Wide World Photos*

The Italian cruise ship *Achille Lauro,* which was seized on October 7, 1985, by Palestinian terrorists belonging to the Palestine Liberation Front-Abbas Faction, which is part of the PLO   *AP/Wide World Photos*

The PLO evacuation from Beirut in 1982, as Israeli troops closed in on the beleaguered city *AP/Wide World Photos*

Yasir Arafat's famous speech at the United Nations on November 13, 1974. He wore a sidearm on his hip and was accompanied by three of the terrorists involved in the actual murder of the two American diplomats in Khartoum. *AP/Wide World Photos*

The "Red Prince," Ali Hassan Salameh, who was the operational chief of Black September and later the commander of Force 17. He was killed by the Israelis in 1979. *AP/Wide World Photos*

Abu Iyad, the second most powerful man in the PLO, circa 1985–86. He heads the Intelligence and Security Apparatus of Fatah and the PLO. *From the authors' personal collection*

lined by Arafat. The unit and its commander, Abu Tayeb, were placed under Arafat's direct command, even though Abu Iyad would continue to provide some supervision over its activities as "coordinator" of Force 17. Abu Iyad, for example, would continue to oversee operational details involving Force 17, while Arafat was given exclusive control over the unit's finances, which were handled directly by him and Abu Tayeb. Nevertheless, like other PLO organizational charts, rigid structures and lines of authority rarely lasted for long. Force 17 was no exception. Within months Arafat had delegated certain financial details to Abu Iyad. Abu Iyad, in return, often involved Arafat in matters pertaining to the operational side of the unit.[16] According to PLO operatives later captured by the Israelis and interrogated, on at least one occasion Abu Tayeb told his lieutenants during a briefing regarding a terrorist operation against a Western target in the Middle East that he "had the blessing of Abu Amar [Yasir Arafat] for the operation."

Today Force 17 maintains cadres in Tunisia, mostly around its headquarters near Tunis, in North Yemen (in and around the capital of Sana), and in Lebanon (nearly all in three locations: West Beirut, Sidon, and Tyre) and a small unit in Iraq. It also has operational squads and support networks in Western Europe: Spain (Madrid), Great Britain (London), West Germany (Berlin, Munich, and Bonn), and France (Marseilles). The European arm of Force 17 has its own operational commander, financial officer, and intelligence apparatus. It operates a series of safe houses throughout Europe, one of which serves as the regional command center. Couriers shuttle between the different elements, and arms and false documentation are stockpiled for use in actual missions.

Force 17 personnel also are attached to every PLO embassy and mission throughout the world. In the larger embassies there are usually eight to ten Force 17 members, most operating under diplomatic cover. They provide security for the facility and the members of the delegation and handle internal security as well. In addition to their security-related tasks, members of Force 17 are generally clandestine collectors of intelligence and recruiters of local Palestinians as part of the covert infrastructure of international terrorism.

Under Abu Tayeb, Force 17 continues to recruit foreigners rather than Palestinians, whose loyalty can be compromised. In 1988 some of Arafat's personal bodyguards were Germans and Scandinavians. In the 1985 attack on the Israeli yacht in the harbor of Nicosia, Cyprus, that left three dead, a British national, who was later captured and tried, was one of the gunmen. Similarly, in a series of attacks on the British air base at Akrotiri, Cyprus, Force 17 employed both Cypriot and French nationals.

THE COLONEL HAWARI FORCE (SPECIAL OPERATIONS GROUP)

In 1981 Western intelligence noted the emergence of a new unit within Fatah called the Special Operations Group (SOG). "It is possible that the group was established earlier, but we were first able to detect its existence only in 1981," asserts a high-ranking European intelligence official. Today the SOG is responsible for all internal security matters and active counterintelligence activities within Fatah and the PLO. The origins of the Special Operations Group, perhaps the most secret of all Fatah/PLO units, and of its commander, Colonel Hawari, are obscure.

Yasir Arafat and Abu Jihad visited Algiers in December 1962, less than six months after Algeria had won its independence, to meet with Algerian President Mohammed Ben Bella and his minister of defense, Colonel Houari Boumedienne. The young Palestinian revolutionaries were thrilled by the Algerian success and anxious to obtain Algerian support for their own revolution. As a result of the meeting, Fatah was permitted to open an official office on the Rue Victor Hugo in Algiers, the so-called Palestine Office. In addition, a small group of Fatah recruits was sent to Algeria in 1963 to receive military training at a military academy called Cherchel.[17] Among the recruits was an intense young Palestinian by the name of Abdullah abed al-Hamid Labib, known today as Colonel Hawari.

Born forty-seven or forty-eight years ago in the Gaza Strip, Labib belongs to the second generation of fighters, who joined Fatah in the early or mid-1960's. He reportedly adopted his nom de guerre, Colonel Hawari, while training in Algeria, as a tribute to Fatah's benefactor, Colonel—later President—Houari Boumedienne. Little is known about Labib's activities until he surfaced nearly a decade later as an intelligence operator with the Jihaz el-Razd. According to some reports, he was among the first el-Razd operators to join Black September, and he is described as one of those "who helped bring the Black September organization into being."[18]

Labib apparently is a protégé of Abu Iyad, who was Black September's overall commander in chief and commander of the Jihaz el-Razd and who today heads Fatah's Intelligence and Security Apparatus. Nevertheless, Labib also has a reputation for dogged loyalty to Yasir Arafat. In recognition of his loyalty, when the Special Operations Group of Fatah (Aman al-Rais, or "Security Organization of the Leaders") was established, Labib (now Colonel Hawari) was chosen as its first commander. Hawari reports directly to Arafat and to his old mentor, Abu Iyad, and appears to run the unit with ironfisted control, allowing no detail to escape his attention. While the unit has a deputy commander, he appears to deal only with administrative matters. So complete and pervasive is Hawari's control that the Special Operations Group has generally become known as the Colonel Hawari Force.

The unit was initially charged with operating covertly against the Syrian intelligence services and their forces stationed in Lebanon. By 1983 it had also been ordered to conduct operations against dissident Fatah rebels like Abu Musa. The Special Operations Group of Fatah specialized in hitting Syrian targets in Lebanon with vehicle bombs, conducting ambushes against Syrian convoys, killing Syrian soldiers in sniper attacks, and attacking Syrian roadblocks. During 1983 and 1984 the unit carried out successful vehicle bomb attacks in Damascus and against Abu Musa's headquarters at Chatura in Lebanon's Bekaa Valley. Elements of the SOG are based in Lebanon, Tunis, Iraq, and Western Europe.

In late 1984 or early 1985 the Special Operations Group began to conduct serious operations in Europe. On April 1, 1985, a bomb exploded at the Syrian Airways office in Rome. While no group claimed responsibility, intelligence reports suggest that this was Hawari's first operation outside the Middle East. Later that same month, on April 26, more bombs went off in Geneva. The Libyan Arab Airways sales office was the target of the first, the second destroyed the car of a Syrian diplomat, who was wounded in the attack, and the third, also wired to the car of a Syrian diplomat, was discovered and defused by local authorities. Two Palestinians arrested in the aftermath of the attacks claimed to be members of the Martyrs of Tel e-Zatar, a cover name for the Hawari group.

The following month two Romanian bomb disposal experts were killed trying to defuse a Hawari bomb, although details regarding the intended target of the attack have yet to be revealed. On June 2 another attack occurred in Geneva, this one a bomb that exploded at a railway station. An Arab newspaper in London received an anonymous call from a man claiming responsibility for the action in the name of the Martyrs of Tel e-Zatar.

The next day British authorities defused a bomb located outside the Syrian Embassy in London. It was learned that the bomb had been planted by a Hawari operator known only as Mutran, and a month later, on July 2, Italian authorities arrested him and charged him with carrying forged documents. (He was later extradited to Great Britain, where, in June 1988, he was sentenced to eighteen years in prison for the attempted bombing.)

In mid-July Spanish police discovered a Hawari safe house in Madrid and arrested two Palestinians. Following the reversal in Spain, little was heard from Hawari and the Special Operations Group for nearly nine months. Then, on April 3, 1986, a bomb exploded aboard TWA Flight 840 en route to Athens from Cairo. Four Americans were killed, and nine other passengers, including five Americans, were injured in the blast. The four fatalities, one of whom was an infant, were sucked out through a hole in the side of the 727. The explosive device contained approximately one pound of the Czech-made plastic explosive Semtex and had been placed aboard the plane by a Lebanese operative of the Hawari group, May Elias Mansur. Although she admitted that she was a member of the National Syrian Socialist party, Mansur denied any complicity in the attack and is currently believed to be in Lebanon.[19]

That summer the Hawari group launched operations against a number of American targets in Western Europe, but all were aborted because of increased U.S. security precautions and awareness. In August two Palestinians and two Tunisian women were arrested in Casablanca, Morocco, with unassembled bombs in their possession. The bombs had been constructed by the Special Operations Group's master bomb maker, Abed al-Qadir Ayyash, from the May 15 Organization and were supposed to be planted in a number of public places and at a synagogue.

In March 1987 seven people were arrested by French police after arms and explosives were discovered in a basement storage room in Paris. One of those taken into custody later admitted to working for Colonel Hawari. During the past three years Hawari's operators have carried out a campaign of terrorist attacks against Syrian targets, in retaliation for Syria's ongoing effort to destroy every last vestige of the PLO presence in Lebanon and its support of anti-Arafat organizations like Ahmed Jibril's Popular Front for the Liberation of Palestine—General Command and Abu Musa's Fatah Provisional Command. Although Hawari's organization was still active in Lebanon in early 1989, its operations are difficult to track because of the clandestine nature of the unit and the lack of publicity accorded its successful attacks by the tightly controlled state-run press in Syria. Another issue which has created some confusion is that the Special Operations Group is known to have absorbed a number of key operatives who formerly belonged to the May 15 movement (Arab Organization of May 15), which takes its name from the date the state of Israel was established in 1948.[20] In this connection there is some question of which May 15 operators joined the Hawari organization and which did not and, therefore, of which terrorist actions involving current or former members of the May 15 movement have been sanctioned by Hawari.

THE MAY 15 MOVEMENT

Virtually all of the members of May 15 had been followers of Wadia Haddad, who had at one time been George Habash's deputy and chief of operations of the PFLP. Haddad may well have been the most effective Palestinian terrorist leader in history. He was the mastermind behind countless terrorist operations, including the 1970 hijacking, and later destruction, of four jetliners in one of the most ambitious terrorist operations of all time. George Rosie, in *The Directory of International Terrorism,* calls the multiple hijackings "One of the most significant terrorist events in postwar history."[21] Three of the captured planes were flown to Jordan's Dawson's Field (Zarqa) and blown up, and another aircraft was hijacked to Cairo, where it was later destroyed. A fifth hijacking was attempted against an El Al jetliner but failed.

During his lifetime Wadia Haddad was feared and respected by every intelligence service, in both the Middle East and the West. Few people even knew what Haddad looked like, and Western intelligence services identified a variety of photos of different men as Haddad, one of the most elusive terrorists in the world. Amazingly, no photo likeness of Wadia Haddad has ever been authoritatively authenticated, and he remains the man without a face.

Haddad was rarely ideological, and if he had a creed, it was the power of violence. Above all else, he was an operator with a love of the clandestine. In mid-1975, when George Habash began to mellow and consider accommodation with Arafat, Haddad broke with his old mentor and medical partner and created the PFLP—Special Command, also referred to as the PFLP—Special Operations Group. According to some accounts, Libya's Muammar Qaddafi facilitated the break by providing Haddad with a large sum of money because he wanted to see the creation of a more aggressive Palestinian terrorist organization. In contrast with the PFLP, which was headquartered in Damascus, the PFLP-SC established its base of operations in Iraq, including training camps and a small headquarters facility in Baghdad. Another training camp was established near Aden, in the capital of the People's Democratic Republic of Yemen (South Yemen), and a small office-residential facility was maintained in Aden.

The PFLP-SC's most sensational terrorist action was the hijacking of an Air France A-300B Airbus by a transnational terrorist force that included two West Germans, one Iranian, and a Palestinian. The plane was ultimately diverted to Entebbe, Uganda, where the passengers were rescued by Israeli commandos in a dramatic raid on July 4, 1976. Although the Israeli rescue was a watershed event in the war against terrorism and a clear defeat for the terrorists involved, not to mention Uganda's strong man Idi Amin, who had provided support and assistance to the terrorists, Haddad nonetheless clearly demonstrated the power of terrorism and, for a period of days, managed to dominate the world's headlines.

During the next year and a half the PFLP-SC was the most active and imaginative Palestinian terrorist organization, responsible for dozens of attacks that left dozens dead and injured. However, it appears that by 1977 Haddad knew he was terminally ill with cancer, and he moved quickly to select and train the next generation of leadership of the PFLP-SC. In early 1978 Haddad entered a sanatorium in East Germany, from which he never reemerged.

Within three years of Haddad's death on April 28, 1978, and burial in Iraq, the PFLP—Special Command fragmented into three separate organizations: the Arab Organization of May 15, the PFLP—Special Command, and the Lebanese Armed Revolutionary Faction.

May 15 rapidly developed a reputation for effective attacks against aviation-related targets (jetliners and airports) with highly sophisticated explosive devices. Among the former Wadia Haddad disciples who gravitated to the organization was his former chief of operations, Abu Ibrahim, a Syrian citizen of Palestinian descent who received his original terrorist education as a member of the Syrian Deuxième Bureau. Abu Ibrahim was joined by the brilliant bomb engineer Mohammed Rashid and his Moroccan wife, Khadija. Rashid had been a Palestinian student in West Germany when he had been recruited into the ranks of international terrorism by Hanni al-Hassan, the former president of the General Union of Palestinian Students (GUPS) in West Germany. After an apprenticeship as a bomb maker with the Baader-Meinhof

Gang, Rashid had received additional training in explosives and special operations in Syria, East Germany, and Bulgaria. (Of Haddad's principal deputies, only Salim Abu Salim, his chief planner and tactician, failed to join May 15.)

The May 15 Organization announced its presence to the world on January 17, 1980, when a powerful bomb went off on the fifth floor of London's Mount Royal Hotel, causing extensive damage to six hotel rooms. Three German hotel guests were injured in the explosion, and a twenty-two-year-old Arab man was killed. It was later determined that the Arab, who was traveling on a phony passport from Bahrain, was in actuality a Palestinian by the name of Hassan Elias Badr and a member of the May 15 movement. Apparently he had been fabricating two bombs when one of them had detonated prematurely. The second bomb, which was undetected, detonated five hours later in the rubble, injuring a policeman. A typed statement later delivered to a Beirut-based news agency claimed that the explosion was in commemoration of the "martyrdom of al-Haj Jaber [Fawaz Rahmin Jaber]," one of the terrorists killed by the Israelis at Entebbe. The statement also maintained that several Israeli intelligence agents staying at the hotel and Jewish immigrants on their way to "occupied Palestine" had been killed or wounded in the incident, a claim wholly without foundation.

Six months later, on July 27, 1980, two hand grenades were thrown into a group of Jewish teenagers waiting for a bus to transport them to summer camp in front of the Antwerp Agudath Israel cultural center. One youth was killed, and twenty others were injured. The attacker, Naser Said Abdel Wahib, was arrested by Dutch authorities, and later discovered to be a member of the May 15 Organization.[22]

On December 31, 1980, a New Year's Eve party at the Norfolk Hotel in Nairobi, Kenya, was bombed, leaving sixteen dead and eighty-seven injured. One American was among the dead, and eight others were among the injured. Eight hours before the blast the bomber, a Moroccan by the name of Qaddura Mohammed Abed al-Hamid, who was traveling on a Maltese passport, slipped out of Kenya on a Kenya Airways flight to Saudi Arabia. A former member of Fatah and the PFLP, al-Hamid was believed to have joined the May 15 movement subsequently. The hotel was owned by the Block family, a prominent Jewish family with close ties to Israel.

In 1981 May 15 carried out attacks against El Al offices in Rome (May 15 and August 10), the building housing the Israeli diplomatic delegation in Athens (August 9), the Israeli Embassy in Vienna (August 10), and the Greek passenger liner *Orion,* as it was approaching the Israeli port of Haifa (December 20). All the attacks used explosive devices. The following year, May 15 bombed the El Al office in Istanbul (January 9), the Mifgash-Israel Restaurant in West Berlin (January 15), and the Israeli Consulate and a Jewish club in Sydney, Australia (December 23). Although Israel accused the PFLP of carrying out the Sydney attacks, a Lebanese immigrant by the name of Mohammed Ali Beydoun, with suspected links to May 15, was arrested in February 1983 and charged with the bombings. May 15 also claimed credit in 1982 for two operations against Pan Am planes. On August 11 a bomb exploded under the seat of a Japanese teenager named Toro Ozawa, who was traveling on a Pan Am 747 from Tokyo to Honolulu. Ozawa was killed, and sixteen other passengers were injured. Mohammed Rashid was later arrested by Greek authorities on an unrelated charge, but the United States demanded Rashid's extradition and said that it had conclusive proof linking Rashid to the attack. On August 25 a bomb was discovered in Rio de Janeiro underneath a seat on another Pan Am flight that had arrived from Miami. The explosive device was almost identical to the one that killed Ozawa.

In the early 1980's a number of highly sophisticated suitcase bombs began to appear in connection with terrorist operations against Western targets, which were subsequently linked to the May 15 Organization and its leader, Abu Ibrahim. Indeed, such suitcase bombs virtually became the trademark of the May 15 Organization. Many of the suitcases bore the brand name Valigeria and came in a variety of different colors, shapes, and sizes. The explosives used were the Czech-made plastic explosive Semtex; PETN, a British-manufactured explosive from World War II; and Gelatine Donarit from Austria.[23] Plastic explosives can be rolled out in thin sheets (as little as a quarter of an inch thick) and secreted in the lining of a bag. The detonator and batteries were most often hidden in the handle of the bag and were all but invisible to most X-ray scanning.

In the mid-1980's, as their bomb-manufacturing techniques became even more refined, May 15's bomb makers switched to soft-sided bags constructed of canvas fabric and vinyl. Most of the bags were small enough to pass as carry-on luggage (nineteen by twenty-eight by seven inches), and a number were blue and brown in color and bore the brand name Creation Beumas, Paris on the outside. As in the hard-sided suitcases, the explosive material was hidden in the bag's lining, and the batteries and detonator were disguised in the bag's handle or in consumer electronics items in the bag. Some of the explosive devices had both a barometric detonator and a time-delay fuse, making them all the more difficult to detect.

A number of May 15 suitcase bombs similar to the ones described above were discovered by Western authorities before any damage could be done. On April 16, 1984, for example, Greek authorities arrested a Jordanian national named Fuad Hussein Shara at the Athens airport. They were acting on intelligence information linking Shara to a number of suitcase bomb incidents, as well as to the assassinations of British and American diplomats. During the investigation the authorities called on Diane Codling, a British woman residing in Athens who had been Shara's partner in importing religious artifacts from the Middle East. In Codling's apartment authorities found a suitcase that she had checked on a flight from Athens to Tel Aviv. Inside the lining was a high-altitude explosive device (barometically triggered) which had failed to explode. Despite the fact that she had returned from Tel Aviv via London, before finally reaching Athens again, none of the security checks and X-ray scanners had detected the bomb.

Authorities were later able to piece together what had happened. Apparently the suitcase Codling carried to Tel Aviv contained the bomb, but the device was not activated because she was flying on Olympic Airlines and the terrorists did not want to bring down a Greek jetliner. Once in Tel Aviv, she phoned a number that had been given to her by her partner and identified herself. The man on the other end of the line said he wanted to meet with her, and a time and place were agreed upon. At the meeting the man asked to see her suitcase and excused himself for a short time. When he returned, he indicated that she could leave the country, and the following day she boarded an El Al flight to London. But nothing happened. After spending several days in London, she flew back to Athens.

According to authorities, a defect in the device had prevented it from going off. Since Shara had used Codling as an unwitting accomplice, intending that she die in the explosion, no charges were ever filed against her. The Israelis discovered that the man Codling met with in Tel Aviv had long since left the country. Because of their failure to detect the bomb, the director of security at Ben-Gurion Airport and all his deputies were fired, along with the entire shift that was on duty when Codling checked in for the flight to London. In late June 1984 Shara was released by Greek authorities and permitted to board an aircraft for Algiers, where he disappeared.

Similarly, Western intelligence sources learned that on May 7, 1984, a dark brown suitcase had been couriered from the Middle East to Eastern Europe, en route to its final destination, West Berlin. The courier was described as a light-skinned man, about twenty-two years of age, using a passport from the United Arab Emirates in the name of Jamail Khalid al-Kadri Aka al-Badri. Six weeks later, on June 25, West Berlin police raided an apartment in the U.S. sector and found two suitcases, each containing approximately two pounds of explosives secreted in its linings, that matched the description of the bag that had reached Eastern Europe on May 7. Two Arabs found in the apartment were taken into custody: thirty-seven-year-old Abdel Ali Darwish and forty-year-old Yussef Hassan Sa'id. Although they were discovered to be members of the May 15 Organization, both men were later expelled from the country rather than held for trial.

A MARRIAGE MADE IN BAGHDAD

Sometime in 1983 or 1984 Colonel Hawari, who was based in Baghdad and running operations against the Syrians, met

Abu Ibrahim. He subsequently recruited most of the May 15 network and, for all intents and purposes, absorbed it into his own Special Operations Group. The May 15 movement was receptive to his offer because of a series of internal disputes that had left it broke, leaderless, and unable to conduct operations. It needed a patron, and Hawari offered money and the protection and infrastructure of his organization and, by implication, those of Fatah and the PLO. From Hawari's point of view, it was a great coup. He had acquired an organization with years of collective operational experience, as well as the finest bomb craftsmen in the world. In addition to Abu Ibrahim and Rashid, Hawari gained the services of the beautiful and deadly May Elias Mansur. Among the other operatives who made the transition was one later arrested in Casablanca in conjunction with the plot to bomb a number of targets.

The Special Operations Group has enjoyed close relations with Iraq for several years. After Abu Nidal was expelled from Baghdad to Damascus as part of Iraq's bargain with the United States for improved relations, Colonel Hawari moved his headquarters to Iraq. Indeed, Saddam Hussein's Ba'athist regime embraced Hawari and his followers with open arms because of the bloody attacks they had carried out, often at the behest of Baghdad and with Iraqi funding, against Syrian forces in Lebanon. The Iraqis regard Syria as one of its two principal adversaries, both for historical reasons and because of President Assad's support of Iran in the Iran-Iraq War. By supporting Hawari as an Iraqi proxy, Saddam Hussein was able to continue the fight covertly against Syria at the same time his government was engaged militarily in a war against Iran.

Despite his close relationship with the Iraqi regime, however, Hawari always clears every operation in advance with Arafat. According to an Israeli intelligence officer, Hawari has "always operated under Arafat's umbrella. He is much less independent, if this is the right description, than Force 17 and Abu Tayeb."[24] Sometime around 1986, Hawari relocated his principal headquarters to Beirut, while still maintaining offices in Baghdad.

A current matter of concern to the Hawari organization is the arrest of Mohammed Rashid by Greek authorities. The United States has formally requested the extradition of Rashid to stand trial for the August 1982 bombing of a Pan Am flight just before it landed in Hawaii. One person was killed and fifteen were injured in the explosion, which failed to bring the plane down. Although the attack occurred prior to the absorption of May 15 by the Special Operations Group, the PLO diplomatic mission in Athens has paid Rashid's legal fees and provided him with an interpreter. The PLO's deputy chief of mission has also been present in the courtroom for each hearing involving the extradition request.

ABU IYAD: THE DARK VISAGE IN THE SHADOWS

Through the years Abu Iyad, né Salah Khalaf, has been one of Arafat's closest collaborators and supporters; he has also been one of his most persistent critics. Where Arafat is often viewed as an accommodationist, Abu Iyad is the chief spokesman of the confrontationalist faction within the PLO. By the same token, he has a reputation for being a pragmatist; for example, he doesn't dismiss out of hand the notion of a Palestinian ministate composed of the West Bank and Gaza. Indeed, in his book *My Home, My Land,* he recalls that he was among the first to raise the notion of any kind of coexistence with the Jews of Israel. "At a press conference held October 10, 1968," he writes, "I announced that our strategic objective was to work toward the creation of a democratic state in which Arabs and Jews would live together harmoniously as fully equal citizens in the whole of Palestine."[25]

He is the PLO's spymaster, the leader of its security and covert apparatus, and the principal link to so-called rejection front elements, like Abu Nidal. He directly oversees the PLO's internal security, including Force 17, the Special Operations Group, and the Intelligence and Security Apparatus. He was the commander in chief of Black September and personally involved in the planning and execution of the Munich Massacre. He directed the 1973 seizure of the Saudi Embassy in Khartoum and the murders of the U.S. ambassador and deputy chief of mission (DCM) and the Belgian chargé d'affaires (see Chapter Eleven). He played a key role in the assassination of the U.S. ambassador to Lebanon, Francis Meloy, in 1976 and in dozens of other terrorist operations, although the full extent of his operational role within the PLO is a matter of some debate within the international intelligence community.

He has never openly acknowledged his role with Black September, perhaps because of the terrible vengeance the Israelis have inflicted on all connected with the organization. Nevertheless, as noted earlier, he dismisses the claims of Black Septembrists that they had nothing to do with the PLO. He is generally ranked as the second most powerful man in the PLO, especially after the death of Abu Jihad in 1988, and enjoys a unique independence of action accorded no other senior figure within the PLO. A few informed observers in foreign intelligence services even believe that Abu Iyad may, in fact, be more powerful than Arafat. What is known is that everyone in the PLO who underestimated Abu Iyad's power came to regret it. The quiet man in the background for a quarter century, Abu Iyad embodies the dark side of the PLO and is the last of the organization's original operational leaders (from the combat echelon) not buried in a PLO martyrs' cemetery.

Like the biographies of other top PLO leaders, that of Abu Iyad is full of contradictions and omissions. He was born in Jaffa, near Tel Aviv, in 1933. His family left Jaffa one day before Israel's declaration of independence, when he was fifteen years old. By his own account, he still harbors great hatred against the British, for their colonial domination of Palestine and for their policies that drove "a wedge between Arabs and Jews."[26] In his memoirs Abu Iyad describes how the British used a strategy of divide and conquer that pitted the Jews and Arabs against each other in order to rule over Palestine.

From Jaffa, Abu Iyad and his family moved to Gaza, his father's hometown, to await the inevitable Arab victory that would permit them to return to their home. They left nearly everything behind, taking with them only the bare necessities. "I can still see my father," writes Abu Iyad, "clutching our apartment keys in his hand, telling us reassuringly that it wouldn't be long before we could move back. Thirty years have passed, and I have never again seen the house where I was born."[27] But instead of being condemned to live in a tin-roofed hut or tent in a refugee camp, Abu Iyad's family was relatively fortunate and was taken in by relatives. Nevertheless, they were still poor, and Abu Iyad remembers living in a single room for two years before they could afford more comfortable circumstances. During this period he and his parents and four siblings slept on mattresses laid over the floor.

After finishing high school in a refugee camp in Gaza, Abu Iyad went on to study in Cairo, where, as noted earlier, he became active in Palestinian student politics. He studied to be a teacher and even wrote two plays. It was during his university days that he met and married his wife, the daughter of a wealthy Palestinian businessman. He repeatedly found himself at odds with local authorities because of his political activities and at one point was locked up for thirty-five days "in the prostitute section of the Abdin prison [in Cairo]."[28] As mentioned before, it was also in Cairo that he first met Yasir Arafat, and they became fast allies. While he and Arafat have remained close collaborators for more than a quarter of a century in the cause of Palestinian self-determination, it appears to be a relationship based on mutual need and respect rather than on any close personal bond. Intelligence observers suggest that their personal friendship disappeared long ago and that their meetings are marked by a correct and business-like, if sometimes formal, attitude.

Today Abu Iyad is a man of fifty-six or fifty-seven, heavyset and balding, his upper lip hidden behind a bushy mustache that has remained black, even while his hair has begun to turn gray. He is five feet eight or nine inches tall and hides his increasingly obese body beneath well-tailored Lebanese-made safari suits. Twenty years ago his face lacked the puffiness that characterizes it today, and his fingers were not discolored from chain-smoking. With a full head of hair and a well-set jaw, which has now disappeared beneath a double chin, he was almost handsome, perhaps the best-looking of the revolutionaries who founded the PLO. However, if age has taken its toll, one feature remains that indelibly links the Abu Iyad of today with the Abu Iyad of the past: the dark, burning eyes that miss nothing, that seem to penetrate everywhere and have a magnetic, almost hypnotic, quality.

It is this quality of being able to take in everything around him that most unnerves those who have met with him. Abu Iyad, they report, can sit during negotiations for hours like a sphinx, barely moving except to draw on a cigarette, participating only with his eyes. Although a relatively sedentary and unexcitable man, without the sense of frenetic movement around him that one associates with Arafat, Abu Iyad is capable of decisive, even brutal action when the circumstances call for it. Indeed, he has not hesitated to order the executions of those suspected of collaborating with the enemy.

He has a steel-trap mind and the ability to cut through rhetoric and peripheral matters to the heart of a problem. Though hardly voluble, he is a captivating conversationalist when the spirit moves him and reportedly even enjoys a good joke now and then. His sense of humor, however, does not extend to himself, the PLO, or the Palestinian struggle, maintain those who have spent a good deal of time in his presence. About these topics he is deadly serious.

Despite being a man of few words, Abu Iyad is generally regarded as the most articulate of the senior PLO leaders, able to electrify a crowd with his rhetoric or move a small group of decision makers to action with the persuasiveness of his arguments.

He projects a cold and distant demeanor, as befits someone with a love of the clandestine, but associates report that his eyes have been known to mist over with tears at the description of some very sad or tragic event. Nevertheless, Abu Iyad claims that he has cried only once since he reached manhood, when he was but seventeen and beaten by his father for some forgotten transgression.

Although described as a devoted family man, he rarely sees his family, which still resides in Cairo. During the period in the early 1970's when he directed the activities of Black September, he was so concerned about his family's security that he visited only once or twice a year. Even today he takes great pains to shelter them from the limelight and to maintain their anonymity. He has been married for more than thirty years and has three sons and three daughters, whose ages range between eighteen and twenty-eight. He reportedly is especially close to a daughter, Jihan, who is confined to a wheelchair because of polio. He has relatives who live in Kuwait and has maintained a house in the oil-rich sheikhdom ever since he worked there as a teacher. He also keeps a simple bedroom in the PLO compound at Hammam el-Shat.

Abu Iyad's life is configured by security considerations. Like Arafat, he is always on the move, never sleeping in the same bed two nights in a row. According to Eric Rouleau, "he lives the life of a hounded man."[29] He rarely visits public places or eats in restaurants for fear of assassination and is always accompanied by bodyguards from Force 17. He is protected around the clock, by three shifts of no fewer than four bodyguards per detail. Nevertheless, he is a fatalist who has told Rouleau that "any man is capable of assassinating whomever he likes so long as he is prepared to die doing it."[30]

4 | *The PLO's Complex Foreign Relations*

A t the time of the nineteenth PNC meeting in November 1988 in Algiers, the PLO had official representatives in 105 countries. These included twenty-five embassies, twenty-three diplomatic missions, nineteen information bureaus, and representatives in thirty-eight other countries. According to Arafat, as of the end of January 1989, ninety-four of the these countries had already "sent me papers of recognition of the the Palestinian state and consequently we expect the coming period to witness the opening of new embassies for us in many countries."[1] The PLO also has three observer positions with the United Nations, one each at the UN headquarters in New York, the UN offices in Geneva, and UNESCO in Paris. It also has observer status at the Organization for African Unity (OAU), the Non-aligned Movement, and the Islamic Conference Organization (ICO). What this list demonstrates is the remarkable degree to which the PLO has won diplomatic acceptance and forged links to other governments and international organizations. The broad recognition accorded the PLO has served to isolate Israel and contributed to the promotion of punitive measures against the Jewish state, like the infamous "Zionism is racism" resolution at the United Nations.

In terms of its foreign relations, moreover, Yasir Arafat and the PLO have, over the years, lined up against the United States on virtually every major foreign policy and national security issue. They have made common cause with America's enemies and undermined its friends. Today the PLO is part of a subversive network that extends around the world, including ties to the Soviet Union and Eastern bloc countries, virtually every radical regime in the Third World, and a majority of the globe's terrorist groups.

The PLO's foreign policy is shaped and executed chiefly by Yasir Arafat, Abu Iyad, and the two al-Hassan brothers, Hanni and Khaled. Much of Arafat's diplomacy is conducted in the open, with an endless succession of ceremonial visits and photo opportunities, whereas Abu Iyad and Hanni al-Hassan operate on a more covert level, meeting regularly with military and intelligence officials from the Arab countries, the Third World, and the Communist bloc.

THE SOVIET BLOC

The PLO has enjoyed a close relationship with the USSR for two decades. The Soviets provide the PLO with arms, training, intelligence, and documentation. Prior to 1982 they transferred to the PLO great quantities of weapons, including such things as a battalion of tanks from Hungary; but since the PLO was driven out of Lebanon, Soviet arms transfers have been far more modest. The PLO can also generally count on Soviet support at international meetings and in organizations like the United Nations. In addition, Arafat and his top deputies meet with Soviet officials on a regular basis. It is estimated that Arafat has traveled to the Soviet Union at least twenty-seven times, twice on official visits when he was received by the general secretary of the Communist party. Arafat's chief contact in the USSR is Vladimir Buljakov, head of the Soviet Foreign Ministry's Middle East Department. On January 17, 1989, for example, Buljakov delivered a personal message to Arafat in Tunis from General Secretary of the Communist Party Mikhail Gorbachev, reaffirming Soviet support for the

"just national rights of the Palestinian people" and the establishment of "an independent Palestinian state."

While there is no control room in the basement of the Krem-
lin that coordinates every act of Palestinian terrorism, the
Soviets have long served as quartermaster to the PLO and to
the radical Arab states that also provide the PLO with political and military assistance. Moscow can harbor no illusions
about the use to which some of its matériel and training is
being put. Not only is that support finding its way, directly or
indirectly, to various Palestinian terrorist organizations, but
the PLO and its constituent elements also serve as a further
disseminator of hardware and training to other terrorist
groups around the world.

According to the PLO's UN representative, Zehdi Terzi,
"Our boys go to the Soviet Union. They go everywhere for
their training, for their education; there is no secret about
that."[2] A majority of all PLO officers have received at least
some military training in the Soviet Union or other Communist country. For example, out of 22 officers of the September
Martyrs Battalion (part of the Castle Brigade of the PLA), 21
had attended military schools in the USSR and other Eastern
bloc countries. A typical PLO military delegation of 194 officers and NCOs arrived at a Soviet military facility at Simferopol, in the Crimea, on September 1, 1980, to receive
advanced training. The delegation included representatives
from Fatah, the PLF, the PFLP, the DFLP, the PFLP-GC, the
ALF, and al-Sa'iqa. They spent four months at the facility and
received nine different course offerings.[3] Representative of the
kind of training they received, a combat engineering course at
the Simferopol military academy provided instruction in such
things as "the production of incendiary devices; the preparation of electrical charges; bridge destruction; and atomic and
chemical warfare."[4] Another course emphasized "river cross-
ings and all types of sabotage."[5]

Recently, however, Soviet support of the PLO has become
more discreet and less visible. Efforts have been made to insu-
late Moscow from direct involvement with the terrorist elements of the PLO. Most of the sabotage and terrorist training
has been farmed out to Moscow's Eastern bloc allies and Soviet proxies like Syria and Cuba. Although relations have
cooled slightly since the Gorbachev era began, Moscow re-

mains the PLO's most important foreign ally and the source, indirectly, of most of its military hardware and training.

In return for Soviet support, Arafat and the PLO regularly back Moscow's policies—including some of its more unpopular and ill-considered policies—in their public statements and at international meetings. Indeed, the PLO broke ranks with the rest of the Arab world to applaud the Soviet invasion of Afghanistan, a position reaffirmed on April 4, 1988, by PLO Executive Committee member Suleiman Najab. According to Najab, in a statement carried on Soviet television, "the position held by the Soviet government creates all conditions necessary for solving the Afghan problem since it corresponds to the interests of those who desire peace and at the same time puts a barrier in the path of those who would like the conflict in the region to continue."[6] According to a top intelligence official, most important of all was the fact that the PLO connection helped the Soviets "penetrate the Arab world" and its support of the Palestinian cause served as an entrée to Arab regimes traditionally hostile to the Soviet Union.[7] For years Soviet propaganda regularly contrasted Moscow's support of the PLO with U.S. military and economic aid to Israel, drawing the obvious distinction that only the Soviets were the "real friends" of the Arabs.

Among the Soviet Union's satellites, East Germany (DDR) remains the PLO's closest ally. The East German intelligence service provides technical support to the PLO and is known to have conducted joint covert operations with PLO intelligence elements. Force 17 has received training and other assistance from East Germany. In addition to East Germany, the PLO cultivates close relations with Bulgaria, Albania, and Romania.

Cuba also cooperates extensively with the PLO. For a number of years Castro's Cuba enjoyed cordial relations with Israel, but this began to change in the mid-1960's. In 1965 a Fatah delegation arrived in Havana under the cover of the Palestinian student organization GUPS to attend the nonaligned youth festival. It was the first of many such contacts between the PLO and Cuba, including ten to fifteen trips by Arafat to Havana over the years. By 1972 the relationship had developed to the point that Cuba severed its diplomatic ties with Israel and gave its embassy to the PLO. Many of the PLO fighters captured by the Israelis during the 1982 invasion of Lebanon had been provided with advanced training in Cuba, including various special operations and demolitions courses.

THE ARAB WORLD

Both Fatah and, later, the PLO were set up to serve the hidden agendas of Egypt and Syria, not only to keep the pressure on Israel but as a way of channeling Palestinian revolutionary frustrations away from the governments in Cairo and Damascus. Initially, Fatah's chief patrons in Syria were General Hafez al-Assad, who was commander of Syria's air force before becoming president of Syria in 1971, and Colonel Ahmed Suwaydani, the nation's top intelligence official. Suwaydani had served as Syria's military attaché in Beijing and, like Arafat and Abu Iyad, had been deeply influenced by the works of Mao and General Giap. He was eager to put their theories into practice in the Middle East and was instrumental in providing Fatah with its first two bases in Syria in 1964.

Over the years, however, Arafat and the PLO gradually moved out of the direct orbit of the Arab states that sought to use the Palestinians for their own purposes, often by playing them off one against the other. While some Palestinian resistance groups remain under the direct domination of various intelligence services, especially the Syrians, the PLO has attempted to steer a neutral course between the competing Arab states, openly fighting them and their proxies whenever it was necessary to preserve its own independence and freedom of action.

The PLO has, at one time or another, been in open military conflict with three Arab states: Jordan, Lebanon, and Syria. In addition, at least eight other Arab states have had serious political clashes with the PLO, resulting in the arrest and expulsion of PLO members and an open break in relations: Libya, Egypt, Iraq, Sudan, South Yemen, North Yemen, Oman, and Morocco. Only the oil-rich Arab countries that the PLO depends on heavily for funding have enjoyed relatively smooth and uninterrupted relations with the PLO, often mediating its disputes and in some cases "buying off" its adversaries. Nevertheless, in the past some of the more radical and internationalist elements in the Palestinian community, such as the PFLP, have actively targeted Saudi Arabia and the Persian Gulf states.

In many respects the PLO has had a more negative impact on the rest of the Arab world than on Israel, its ultimate enemy. Eric Rouleau reports that Abu Iyad once described, in allegorical fashion, this unintended consequence of the PLO's struggle before an audience of Arab diplomats: " 'A man vigorously shook a tree in order to make a splendid orange fall to the ground; but while the fruit he wanted remained solidly attached, all the others—thirteen in all—fell one after the other.' The rotten oranges, the Fatah leader explained, represented the 13 members of the Arab League, while the one that wasn't ripe enough symbolized the Zionist state."[8]

Today Syria is far and away the chief military sponsor of Palestinian terrorism, with close operational ties to many of the Palestinian organizations under the PLO umbrella as well as to those like Abu Nidal's FRC and Ahmed Jibril's PFLP-GC that are ostensibly outside the PLO's dominion. In addition to weapons, Syria provides various Palestinian units with safe haven, training, intelligence, and such things as false documents and technical assistance. Damascus serves as a major transit point for Palestinian terrorists of every ilk as well as the city of choice as a location for their headquarters. Like the Soviets, the Syrians are more wary today than in the past about their territory's being used as a staging area for Palestinian terrorist attacks and raids. Therefore, Palestinian terrorist organizations have been encouraged to transfer such activities to bases in Lebanon in areas under the Syrian control. There is also ample evidence that some Palestinian groups are directly tasked by the Syrians to carry out terrorist attacks, in payment for the support provided to them by the government in Damascus. A good example was the episode involving Nizar Hindawi, an Abu Nidal operative, who deceived his unsuspecting pregnant girl friend into attempting to board an El Al flight on April 17, 1986, with a suitcase bomb. It turned out that Hindawi had been trained at one of Abu Nidal's camps at Duma, east of Damascus. Upon completion of his training, he was sent from Damascus to London, accompanied by his case officer, a Syrian major in the air force's intelligence service. Hindawi entered Britain on an official Syrian passport. He was told to befriend a local girl and ultimately to use her as a way of secreting explosives on board an Israeli jetliner; of course, the girl would be sacrificed in the operation. The same case officer turned the bomb over to Hindawi, and once the operation failed Hindawi was given temporary shelter at the Syrian Embassy in London.

Britain temporarily broke relations with Syria and imposed sanctions on the Syrians over the incident, after stating that there was "conclusive evidence of official Syrian involvement" in the attempt to blow up the El Al jumbo jet. Despite Great Britain's outrage over the incident, the European reaction was, at best, tepid. Ten of the eleven European Community (EC) partners agreed to place limited sanctions on Syria. Greece, however, broke ranks with the other members of the EC and wouldn't even support limited sanctions, not surprising considering the openly anti-Semitic and anti-American nature of the Papandreou government. During Papandreou's administration, Greece not only looked the other way but actually cooperated, on an intelligence level, with Syria and a number of Palestinian terrorist organizations, including Abu Nidal's FRC. In late 1986 the Greek government gave or sold to Palestinian terrorists ten to twenty blank passports, which presumably were used to facilitate terrorist operations.

Similarly, Hindawi's brother, Ahmed Nawaf Mansour Hazi, and two confederates, Farouk Salameh and Faiz Sawana, also were recruited by the Abu Nidal organization and trained by Syrian specialists at the Duma camp. The three men subsequently were sent to Europe to carry out several bombing attacks, the best known being the La Belle disco bombing on April 5, 1986, that later served as a pretext for the April 14, 1986, U.S. bombing raid on Libya. According to the West Berlin interrogation of the suspects, the three later admitted that they had been provided with the explosives used in the La Belle bombing by the Syrian Embassy in East Berlin. They also indicated that they were given the operational intelligence for the bombing by the Libyan Embassy in East Berlin.

Syria's support of Palestinian terrorists, however, is less a matter of philosophical commitment than the desire to use them as proxies to achieve Syrian policy objectives. Most

Palestinians have few illusions about Syria's assistance and are well acquainted with Hafez al-Assad's ruthlessness. In October 1988 Abu Iyad, for example, complained openly about "4000 Palestinian detainees in Syria's oppressive prisons."[9]

Libya's assistance to Palestinian terrorists is also extensive and well documented. Muammar Qaddafi's government provides money, safe haven, some training, and logistical support to various Palestinian terrorist organizations, although Qaddafi himself is generally regarded as erratic and unstable by most Palestinian terrorist leaders. During the Israeli invasion of Lebanon and earlier, when the PLO was locked in combat with the Lebanese Christian community, Qaddafi showered arms on the PLO. Like Syria, Libya has often "hired" Palestinian terrorist organizations affiliated with the PLO to carry out terrorist strikes against Israel, the United States, and other "enemies." Qaddafi turned to the PLO, for example, when he wanted to strike back at Israel for downing a Libyan passenger plane in 1973. Libya also contracted with the PLO to eliminate certain opponents of Qaddafi's rule living in Europe.

There were at least twenty terrorist training camps on Libyan soil in 1986, including the nine listed below:

1. The 7th of April camp, located near Jardinah. The Sandinista terrorist Patrick Argüello, who was killed trying to hijack an El Al plane with Leila Khaled of the PFLP, was trained at this camp. The camp specializes in a six-month course that teaches terrorists to use small arms, explosives, and shoulder-fired missiles, as well as the finer points of hijacking and planning and executing other kinds of terrorist attacks.
2. Camp "476," located at the Gialo Oasis (Wahat Yalu) south of Benghazi. Trains Africans and the Islamic Legion.
3. A camp near the village of Sinawen.
4. Camp at Bir ad Dawim for the training of the Irish Republican Army (IRA).
5. A camp near Tobruk.
6. A camp near al-Beda for Egyptian and Sudanese terrorists.

7. A camp at al-Aziziyah, which is reserved chiefly for Tunisian, Moroccan, and Sudanese terrorists.
8. A camp at Ma'tan Bisharah near the Kufra Oasis.
9. A camp in the town of Zuwarah.

In 1985 the Libyan government became even more brazen in its efforts to incite and foment terrorist actions, going so far as to publish and distribute posters and handbills around Lebanon—in some cases plastering Palestinian refugee camps with them—offering incentive payments to anyone who would carry out an act of terrorism against Israel or the United States. The "bonuses," denominated in Lebanese pounds, that would be paid for various actions were as follows:

For planting an explosive charge	10,000 LP ($2,500)[10]
For throwing a grenade	20,000 LP ($5,000)
For a shooting incident	30,000 LP ($7,500)
For a suicide operation (paid to the family of the "hero")	30,000 LP ($7,500)
For conducting an operation against American installations in Europe	200,000 LP ($50,000)

After the precipitous decline of the Lebanese pound that began the following year, the Libyans were forced to recast their offer in U.S. dollars. So far did the value of the Lebanese pound plunge, in fact, that planting an explosive charge would have been worth less than $35 to the terrorist by the late 1980's. Various captured terrorists have also described Libyan promises to insure them for as much as $250,000, payable to their families, if they were killed carrying out an operation.

There is no information on whether the Libyan incentive plan actually stimulated acts of violence against the United States or Israel. It may well be that the offer was another of the flamboyant public relations gestures that Colonel Qaddafi is so adept at making, which garner him acclaim from the Arab masses and headlines in the West. Nevertheless, over the years Libya has paid out millions of dollars in bonuses to terrorist groups for particularly bloody or dramatic terrorist operations. For example, it reportedly paid the infamous

PFLP terrorist "Carlos the Jackal" two million dollars for the 1985 takeover of OPEC's headquarters in Vienna. In the early 1970's Libya—for both political and operational reasons—actually decided to form its own Palestinian terrorist group rather than just sponsor outside organizations. Libyan agents recruited disenchanted members of the PFLP and the PFLP-GC and established something called the Arab Nationalist Youth Organization for the Liberation of Palestine, with the unwieldy acronym of ANYOLP. Headed by Maruan Haddad, the ANYOLP was entirely financed by and trained in Libya. The virtually unlimited support provided by the Libyans gave the ANYOLP operators extraordinary latitude in carrying out terrorist operations. Among the organization's major operations were an attack on the Israeli ambassador's residence in Cyprus and the attempted hijacking of an Israeli ARKIA airliner (April 9, 1973); an attack in Athens on a TWA flight arriving from Tel Aviv that left four dead and fifty-four injured (August 5, 1973); a murderous assault at Rome's Fiumicino (Leonardo da Vinci) Airport that left thirty-one dead and more than forty injured (December 17, 1973); the hijacking and later destruction on the ground of a British Overseas Airways Corporation (BOAC) flight from Beirut to Amsterdam (March 3, 1974); and the bombing of a TWA flight en route from Tel Aviv to New York, after a stopover in Athens, that killed all eighty-eight passengers and crew (September 8, 1974). The group seemed to fizzle out in the mid-1970's, and Israeli intelligence reports suggest that most of the members of ANYOLP rejoined the Habash and Jibril organizations. There was speculation that some of the members of ANYOLP never had actually cut their ties to their old organizations anyway.

Iraq and South Yemen also provide safe haven, training, and some military support to Palestinian terrorists, although Iraq's support of terrorist groups has diminished to some extent as a result of its efforts to cultivate international support during the Iran-Iraq War. Jordan, Algeria, Tunisia, and Egypt are service hubs for the PLO, used for banking, international meetings, the housing of family members, educating children, air travel links, meetings with the international media, and rest and relaxation. For Egypt and Algeria, this represents a vast improvement over their past behavior, when they openly provided extensive military support and training to Palestinian terrorists. Algeria still gives the PLO some military and financial assistance, but certainly far less than in the past.

As noted earlier, the oil-rich Arab states, especially Saudi Arabia and Kuwait, are the chief financial backers of the PLO. However, the PLO is not above occasional efforts to intimidate both states in order to remind them of their vulnerabilities. Following the 1979 seizure of the Grand Mosque in Mecca, for example, Fatah contrived to ensure that information reached the Saudis that four truckloads of PLO weapons were going to be smuggled into Saudi Arabia. The Saudis, already paranoid over the incident at the Grand Mosque, reacted with alarm and, for weeks, mobilized every available resource to search each truck, plane, and ship arriving in the country. The Saudis, who got the message, have been extremely solicitous of Palestinian sensitivities ever since and have never been late in paying the PLO its regular stipend.

The Sudan is too preoccupied with its civil war to take an active role in supporting the Palestinians at the present time. The PLO was deeply embarrassed in the Sudan a few years ago during the airlift of Falasha Jews from the country by the United States and Israel. One of Arafat's cousins was the PLO representative in the country, and he willingly took a bribe from the Israelis to "look the other way" during the operation. When his calumny became known, he was quickly pulled out of the Sudan and sent elsewhere.

Morocco, on the other hand, has attempted to maintain good relations with both the PLO and Israel and has succeeded for the most part. Morocco, and especially King Hassan II, remains the only trustworthy channel of communication between the PLO and Israel. Morocco, for example, served as the location of the secret negotiations between Egypt and Israel that led to Anwar el-Sadat's trip to Jerusalem. If and when the Israelis enter any direct negotiations with the PLO, they are likely to be facilitated by Morocco. The Moroccans, however, had been deeply distressed by the PLO's support of the guerrillas of the Polisario (Popular Front for the Liberation of the Western Sahara), who are engaged in a military struggle with Morocco over the future of what was formerly known as Spanish Sahara.

Lebanon is something of a special case. The PLO's power in

Lebanon has been greatly diminished since its expulsion in the early 1980's, although Arafat has worked hard to reestablish a presence in the country. It is too early to tell what, if any, success he will ultimately have since both Syria and Israel oppose any restoration of the PLO's state within a state.

In summary, all the Arab states give nominal support as well as a good deal of lip service to the PLO. No Arab leader can publicly challenge the premise on which the PLO is predicated—that is, the "right" of Palestinians to a homeland—and all have formally recognized the PLO as the sole representative of the Palestinian people. As an example of the unique position the PLO enjoys in the Arab world, at the present time no Arab country requires that Arafat use a passport, and he crosses national frontiers without such formalities, explaining, "My keffiyah is my passport." Interestingly, the last passport Arafat possessed was Algerian, and it has expired.

For all of the talk of Arab unity during the past quarter century, the Arab world is more riven by factionalism and discord than any other region of the world. Many Arab nations enjoy closer relations and greater commonality with allies and trading partners outside the region than with their Arab brethren. Their opposition to Israel has been the only issue that has served, at times, to promote unity, and even that opposition began to crumble with the Camp David accords. Arafat and the PLO have no permanent allies and no permanent enemies in the Arab world, a reality that they have learned through bitter experience.

As one illustration of the vicissitudes of the Arab world, the story of Colonel Abu Musa (Sa'id Musa Muragha), head of the Fatah Provisional Command (FPC), is both interesting and informative. In 1976 he was serving as commander in chief of all PLO/Fatah forces in southern Lebanon. The Syrian Army had pushed deep into Lebanon, and the Palestinian forces that formerly stood in its way had been massacred at Tel e-Zatar by the Lebanese Forces (Christian Phalange) militia. PLO leaders reached the conclusion that any resistance against the Syrians would be futile.

Abu Musa, however, refused to accept their decision. While agreeing that the PLO did not have the forces to stop the Syrian advance into Beirut, he vowed to block the Syrians from moving into southern Lebanon. In July 1976 Syrian troops were ordered south to Sidon. With a small group of Fatah fighters Abu Musa ambushed the Syrian armored convoy just outside Sidon, destroying four tanks and several armored personnel carriers, inflicting a number of casualties on the Syrians. Although he failed to keep them from their objective, the Syrians wouldn't soon forget Abu Musa's brazen act of defiance.

Two years later, in 1978, while he was crossing the street opposite his home in Sidon, two Syrian agents opened fire on Abu Musa. He was found a short time later by Zalah Ta'amri, a high-ranking Fatah military commander, lying in the street, blood oozing from multiple gunshot wounds, and was rushed to a local hospital in critical condition. It took him more than a year to recover from his close brush with death; his former vitality is gone, and he walks only with the assistance of two canes.

Ironically, four years later old enemies became allies when the Syrians supported Abu Musa's revolt against Arafat and the entrenched leadership of Fatah and the PLO. Only a short time before they had tried to kill him, and now the Syrians were publicly embracing him and supporting his claim to the leadership of Fatah. In 1983 Abu Musa's Fatah Provisional Command (FPC) fought side by side with the Syrians to drive Arafat's forces from Tripoli, their last foothold in Lebanon. Today the FPC is still funded by the Syrian defense establishment and Abu Musa spends a good deal of time in Damascus.

IRAN

In the mid-1960's opponents of the shah's rule in Iran formed linkages to the PLO. Ayatollah Khomeini had recently arrived in the Iraqi city of Najaf, one of the two spiritual centers of the Shiite religion, the other being Qom, Iran. He had been jailed by the shah after criticizing his regime, and the shah had responded by banishing him to Turkey, whence he had made his way to Najaf.

While he was exiled in Najaf, Khomeini established contacts with Arafat and the PLO. There is evidence that PFLP leader George Habash and his deputy, Wadia Haddad, attempted to follow suit but were rebuffed, most likely because of their Marxist leanings and identification with atheistic Soviet communism, which Khomeini traditionally viewed as antithetical to his devout Moslem beliefs. Habash ultimately managed to form close ties with the Marxist Mujahedeen el-Halq. In 1976 a letter from Habash to Hamid Ashraf, leader of the Mujahedeen el-Halq, fell into the hands of the shah's hated secret police, SAVAK (Sazeman-e Ettela't va Amniyat-e Keshvar). The letter, which was deemed authentic by Western intelligence organizations, outlined various forms of cooperation between the PFLP and the Mujahedeen el-Halq.

In a sense, both Khomeini's revolution and that represented today by the PLO were born at the same time, and they marched hand in hand for almost two decades. Since Israel maintained close ties to SAVAK and had been granted, in effect, de facto recognition by the shah's government, it was perceived as an archenemy by the mullahs, the Mujahedeen el-Halq, and other opponents of the Peacock Throne in the bazaar. Not only is Israel regarded by the fundamentalists as an outpost of the Crusader state that intruded on the Islamic world nearly a millennium ago, but Jews are regarded as beyond redemption and as "eternal schemer[s] against God."[11] As such, in the ayatollah's cosmology they represent one of the principal threats to Islam. The PLO's anti-Americanism was also appreciated by the mullahs, who viewed the United States as the cornerstone of the shah's power. The ayatollah also hoped that the PLO would serve as a bridge to the Persian Gulf Arab states, which he sought at one time to enlist in his campaign against the shah. Thus, the ayatollah and his supporters saw the PLO as a natural ally, one that could provide them with entrée to other terrorist and revolutionary organizations around the globe.

The PLO attempted, on a number of occasions, to carry out terrorist operations against Israeli targets in Iran. Officially, Israel and Iran maintained no diplomatic relations, only interest sections in other embassies. However, the reality was that Israel had a major diplomatic mission in Teheran. On August 6, 1969, for example, Palestinian terrorists tried to mount an operation to attack the building housing the Israeli mission, but the attack was foiled by the Mossad and SAVAK.

Four months later, in December 1969, when the shah met Yasir Arafat for the first time at the Arab summit in Rabat, Morocco, he complained about the PLO's support of Iranian revolutionaries. Arafat apparently refused to respond to the shah's accusations or to provide the Iranian monarch with any assurances that the ties would be suspended in the future. As a result, the shah developed a strong enmity for Arafat and the PLO that lasted until his death.

The shah's failure to mollify Arafat and other Palestinian terrorist leaders resulted in a continuation of the violence against Iranian targets. On June 9, 1970, three Iranian terrorists—all graduates of the Fatah/PFLP training camp at Nahr al-Bard—hijacked an Iranian National Airlines 727 en route from Teheran to Kuwait, with a stop in Abadan. It was forced to land in Iraq, where the passengers and plane were released.[12] The Iraqis detained the trio for a short time and then released them.

The following year, in June 1971, acting on information received from a source working at Iran's oil terminal on Kharg Island, the PFLP attempted to sink an Israeli-owned Liberian-registered tanker, *Coral Sea,* transporting Iranian oil to the Israeli port of Eilat. Ten bazooka shells were fired at the tanker from a speedboat as it was passing through the Strait of Bab el Mandeb at the entrance to the Red Sea, but they caused only minor damage and several fires that were quickly extinguished.

Arafat and the Palestinian movement continued to view the shah as an enemy, despite the shah's statements of support for their cause. Typical of such statements, on December 13, 1974, the shah told an interviewer that "despite the fact that some Palestinian terror groups have trained Iranian saboteurs, that have penetrated our country in order to kill people and destroy facilities, Iran has always stood, and will continue to stand in support of the Palestinians."[13] Indeed, on the diplomatic front the shah's government maintained its public support for the PLO, nearly always voting with the Arab bloc on UN resolutions regarding the Palestinian question, including the resolution that granted the PLO observer status at the UN headquarters in New York. Palestinian leaders like Arafat, however, complained that the shah's support was more symbolic than tangible, that what really counted were actions, and in this category Iran was both a collaborator with and supporter of Israel. In addition, the shah's support of his fellow monarch King Hussein during his battle with the PLO in September 1970 only served to increase PLO suspicions of the shah and his government.

Faced with what he regarded as intractable opposition from the PLO, the shah grew less reluctant to criticize Arafat and the organization openly. He blamed the PLO and the Palestinians for much of the violence that overtook Lebanon in the 1970's, as well as for their support of international terrorism. In a September 1976 meeting with Israeli Defense Minister Shimon Peres, the shah told his visitor: "We recently captured a hundred terrorists and I have no intention of surrendering to blackmail. The Palestinians are poisoning all the wells and are busy carrying out subversive acts against the pro-Western regimes of the region."[14] Until the shah's fall in January 1979, there was no abatement in efforts by Palestinian terrorists to strike at Israeli targets in Iran, although SAVAK was very effective in preempting such operations. Indeed, as the shah's regime began to totter in 1978, there was an increase in Palestinian activity in Iran, and several successful operations were carried out against Israeli targets, including two attacks against El Al offices in Teheran.

The PLO clearly left its imprint on Khomeini's revolution. Beginning in 1969 and continuing throughout the 1970's, Iranian revolutionaries received training in PLO camps in Lebanon, Syria, Iraq, and Libya. Many future members of Ayatollah Khomeini's regime passed through the camps, including Mustafa Ali Tzamran, defense minister under Mehdi Bazargan, the ayatollah's first prime minister. Tzamran had been among the first Iranian graduates of the Palestinian terrorist training camps in Lebanon. He subsequently became the main coordinator for training other Iranian revolutionaries at camps in the Bekaa Valley. Iranian Foreign Minister Sadegh Ghotbzadeh, who was later executed by his political enemies in the Khomeini regime, also received training in Lebanon and in the early 1970's relocated to Syria, where he liaised with both the PLO and Libya.

Accompanied by a special Libyan emissary, PLO official Farouk Qadoumi (Abu Lutf) traveled to France on November 22, 1978, to meet with Khomeini, just prior to the ayatollah's triumphant return to Iran. While the substance of their discussions is not known, within days of the meeting Libyan radio began transmitting coded messages to the Iranian clergy in Iran and broadcasting the ayatollah's religious addresses.

Khomeini returned to Iran on February 1, 1979, and he and his followers moved rapidly to consolidate power and destroy any centers of opposition. Little more than two weeks later, on February 17, Arafat journeyed to Teheran and, the following day, raised the Palestinian flag over the building that had previously served as the Israeli mission. According to a beaming Arafat, eager to claim his share of the triumph, the "PLO trained within its camps 10,000 Iranians." He also said that "the PLO gave the Iranian revolutionaries more than 10,000 Kalashnikovs" and had provided Palestinian "volunteers" to the Iranian Revolution. He concluded by saying that he hoped that Iranian "volunteers" would now participate in the Palestinian Revolution.

Khomeini subsequently responded by thanking the PLO for its help and promising that Iranian volunteers would assist in the liberation of Jerusalem and the elimination of the Zionist state. Hanni al-Hassan was named the PLO's representative in Teheran and for the next year and a half regularly met with Khomeini, as well as with Iran's intelligence apparatus. In a show of revolutionary solidarity, Arafat publicly announced that he would send a PLO squad to kidnap or kill the shah during his exile in the Bahamas. While there is no evidence that the PLO mounted any operation against the shah, on July 17, 1980, five gunmen attempted to kill exiled Iranian Premier Shahpour Bakhtiar at his Paris apartment. Although Bakhtiar was unhurt, two people were killed and three wounded in the attack. Two of the terrorists were also wounded by French police, and all five were ultimately captured. The leader of the group was a Palestinian, Anis Naqqash (Abu Mazam), who used numerous names during his interrogation and trial. Naqqash claimed to be a Fatah intelligence officer and said that Arafat had personally ordered the attack. An Israeli intelligence report links Naqqash to either Force 17 or Colonel Hawari's Special Operations Group. Naqqash and three of his companions were ultimately tried, convicted, and sentenced to life imprisonment. The remaining member of the group received a twenty-year sentence.

However, the honeymoon didn't last very long. Within two years Hanni al-Hassan returned to Lebanon. While some of the reasons for the souring of the relationship are known, others remain a mystery.

On November 4, 1979, the U.S. Embassy in Teheran was seized by a howling mob and more than sixty Americans were taken hostage. It was the second time that the embassy had been stormed. Earlier, on February 14, 1979, militants—many of them wearing the red-and-white checkered keffiyahs of the Palestinian fedayeen—took over the residence and laid siege to the chancery before the situation was brought under control. Former U.S. ambassador William Sullivan expressed his belief that the keffiyahs were indicative of the fact that many members of the mob were *agents provocateurs* who had been trained by George Habash and the PFLP, although he offered no hard evidence to support his accusation.[15]

Arafat was instrumental in the release of thirteen of the American hostages seized in the November takeover.[16] All were either female or black. Ironically, a number of those released in this simpleminded gesture of solidarity against what was perceived as a white, male-dominated American power structure were, in reality, U.S. intelligence agents. The hostage takers deceived themselves by believing their own simplistic stereotypical view of the United States. To Arafat the hostage crisis represented an extraordinary opportunity. He was confident that if he could successfully mediate the crisis and secure the release of the remaining Americans, the United States, and especially the faltering Carter administration, would be deeply in his debt. By coming to his rescue, Arafat hoped to wring concessions out of an eternally grateful Jimmy Carter, who, he believed, would then place tremendous pressure on the Israeli government to negotiate a favorable settlement with the PLO. When Khomeini refused to go along with his efforts to resolve the crisis, thus denying the PLO its golden opportunity, Arafat was outraged, and relations between the PLO and Teheran began to deteriorate rapidly.

A second reason underlying the PLO's disengagement with Iran involved the advent of the Iran-Iraq War in September 1980. With the exception of Syria and, to a lesser extent Libya, Iraq received the support of the rest of the Arab world. Because of a need to show unity with its Arab brothers and because of the deteriorating state of its relations with Syria in Lebanon, the PLO lined up with Iraq, further irritating its relations with the revolutionary government in Iran.

Today the PLO remains estranged from the late Ayatollah Khomeini's Iran, although it does maintain significant ties to Iranian proxy groups in Lebanon.

THIRD WORLD

For the past two decades the PLO has actively courted Third World countries for support, especially those with revolutionary traditions of their own. In currying favor, the PLO has extended the offer of military training, weapons, and even economic aid. Arafat's largess to African leaders is well known. On one recent extended swing through sub-Saharan Africa, he reportedly doled out five million dollars in cash to each African head of state he met with as a way of showing his gratitude for their support. Most, if not all, of the money undoubtedly found its way into Swiss bank accounts.

Moreover, in some cases, oil-rich Arab governments like Libya and Saudi Arabia have agreed to provide substantial economic subsidies to corrupt and impoverished Third World despotisms in return for their support of the PLO in international organizations. Illustrative of such inducements was the case of Uganda under Idi Amin's brutal dictatorship. In 1975 Libya pledged money to Amin if he would sever his ties with Israel and recognize the PLO. Not one to stand on principle, Amin quickly agreed, especially since he was angry at the Israelis for refusing to sell him, on liberal credit terms, a dozen F-4 Phantom jet fighters. Once the Israelis were expelled, Amin handed over their embassy to the PLO. During the hijacking of the Air France jetliner to Entebbe the following year, the hijackers used the building as their operations headquarters.

Similarly, after the Somoza regime collapsed in Nicaragua, the Marxist-oriented Sandinistas, in one of their first official acts in power, broke relations with Israel and turned over the

Israeli Embassy to Yasir Arafat and the PLO. Arafat was one of the first foreign leaders to journey to Managua after the Sandinista victory, and his visit was the culmination of a decade of support and assistance provided by the PLO to the Sandinistas. Indeed, more than two hundred Sandinistas had received training in PLO/PFLP camps in first Jordan and later Lebanon. After the PLO had established ties with Cuba in the late 1960's, Fidel Castro brought the Palestinians together with the FSLN (Frente Sandinista de Liberación Nacional) in the belief that the PLO could provide the Central American revolutionaries with weapons and training. By using the PLO as a proxy, Cuba could further disguise its extensive collaboration with the FSLN.

The PLO has provided much support to the Sandinista government in Nicaragua, including arms shipments, training, advisers, and funds. PLO advisers have assisted Nicaragua in its war against the contras and served in combat with the EPS (Ejército Popular Sandinista) counterinsurgency battalions. The PLO has trained Nicaraguan intelligence officers and was instrumental in facilitating Libyan arms shipments to the Sandinista military. There is reason to believe that the shipment of a hundred tons of arms destined for Nicaragua and being transported in four Libyan aircraft, which were seized in 1983 during a refueling stop in Brazil, may have been arranged by the PLO. PLO pilots—trained in Syria, South Yemen, Libya, North Korea, and other countries—have flown with the Nicaraguan Air Force, largely to gain needed experience, and have also supplemented the depleted ranks of Aeronica, the country's national airline.

Through the Sandinistas the PLO made contact with the leftist guerrillas in El Salvador, a fact emphasized by Yasir Arafat in a 1982 speech: "We [the PLO] have connections with all revolutionary movements throughout the world, in Salvador, Nicaragua—and I reiterate Salvador—and elsewhere in the world."[17] Approximately fifty Salvadoran guerrillas passed through PLO training camps in Lebanon, and the deputy commander of the FMLN (Frente Farabundo Martí de Liberación Nacional), Shafik Handal, was sighted on several occasions meeting with PLO officials in the Middle East. At least one top FMLN military leader also traveled to the Middle East to observe his men training with the PLO and even visited Palestinian fortifications at Beaufort Castle in southern Lebanon, near the Israeli border.

The PLO maintains ties to virtually all the other major terrorist/guerrilla movements in Latin America. While the governments of Argentina, Uruguay, and Peru have supported the PLO at the United Nations and in Third World convocations, the PLO has shown its gratitude by training antigovernment guerrillas from those same countries.

Guerrillas from Mali, Eritrea, Rhodesia (Zimbabwe), and the African National Congress (ANC) have also received training from the PLO. While the precise number is unknown, it is believed that the total number of Africans trained by the PLO/Fatah is around five hundred. Most African guerrillas, however, have been sent by their revolutionary movements to Libya, rather than the PLO, for instruction. In the case of Rhodesia, the PLO actually sent military advisers to assist the guerrillas in their war against the white settler government of Ian Smith, and today the PLO maintains close relations with the successor government of Zimbabwe.

THE UNITED STATES AND WESTERN EUROPE

Despite the fact that for more than two decades the PLO and its constituent groups have carried out countless attacks against U.S. citizens, property, and interests, as well as those of Western Europe, the PLO simultaneously has pursued an active diplomatic offensive designed to secure recognition and support of its claims and to put pressure on Israel. PLO representatives meet routinely with European intelligence officials to discuss issues of mutual concern and even to trade intelligence material. In January 1989, for example, Abu Iyad held talks with unnamed French "officials" regarding "security issues of interest to both sides" and Arafat's forthcoming meeting with French President François Mitterrand. Rarely a week goes by, moreover, without Arafat and the senior leadership of the PLO hosting a visiting delegation of European parliamentarians. Similarly, Arafat has held numerous meetings with members of the U.S. Congress and delegations composed of prominent American citizens, including representatives of the U.S. Jewish community. He is readily accessible to the Western media, having long ago recognized their influence on public attitudes in the Western democracies.

In his meetings with Western officials and reporters, Arafat is unfailingly courteous and always makes an attempt to come across as a reasonable and rational individual eager to find a peaceful solution to the Palestinian question. However, such appearances belie the PLO's record as a terrorist organization and Arafat's own long-standing hostility toward the United States and the West. Over the years he has made hundreds of threats and statements calling for violence against the United States and its allies in the Middle East. On a Voice of Palestine radio broadcast in 1979, for example, he exhorted Palestinians to "adopt the most violent means against the U.S. and its interests in the region."[18] Arafat also called on Arab countries to "boycott the United States economically if they cannot boycott it politically."[19] He has alleged that the United States, not Israel, is the real enemy of the Palestinian people and declared that Israel is a U.S. puppet and a "bridgehead" for U.S. "imperialism."[20] He has accused the United States of wanting "to subjugate and humiliate the Arab nation" and of "aggression" against Palestine and the Arab nation."[21]

Responding to accusations of PLO terrorism, Arafat maintains that the United States is a terrorist nation, that former President Ronald Reagan "declared his blessing to kill me," and that the PLO stands "with Libya against any aggression against it by Israel or the United States."[22] In a broadcast to Libya, following the downing of two Libyan fighters by U.S. war planes, he said he was "prepared to send men from our joint forces in order to fight, together with you, in sister Libya against this aggression."[23] Referring to the bombing of the U.S. Marine barracks in Beirut, with the loss of 241 American servicemen, he taunted the United States for the "shameful withdrawal of their navy and marines from Beirut because of the courage and unity of the Palestinians," as if to take credit for the attack.[24] Outraged by the midair interception by U.S. war planes of an Egyptair jetliner carrying the murderers of Leon Klinghoffer to safety, Arafat described it as a "crazy" action and alleged that it was an outrage against the entire Arab world.[25] When asked if he would hand over to the United States Mohammed Abbas (Abu Abbas), the leader of the PLF and mastermind of the *Achille Lauro* episode, he laughed and responded that Abbas "is free, of course, and he is a member of the PLO Executive Committee. I do not think we will do what Reagan says."[26]

In short, Arafat is both ideologically and militarily opposed to the United States and its policies, and he has made little secret of his feelings over the years. It may be that he doesn't believe that anyone in the West actually reads his statements and listens to his broadcasts, but they certainly provide a different portrait of Arafat from the ameliorative and often reasonable face he tries so hard to present to the West.

In recent months, however, his tone has softened. This is attributable to Arafat's recognition that only the United States can effectively pressure Israel to make the necessary concessions to reach some kind of settlement with the PLO. He has applauded Washington's criticism of Israel regarding human rights violations in connection with Israeli efforts to deal with the Intifada. He has even offered to assist the United States and Great Britain in bringing to justice those responsible for the bombing of Pan Am Flight 103 and to this end reportedly turned over some intelligence data to Washington.

CONCLUSION

In reality the PLO remains a revolutionary organization and not a government, and therefore, its foreign relations are conducted on two levels. The first is the PLO's public drive for international respectability and support, employing the traditional tools and methods of diplomacy, although it even has resorted to financial incentives and intimidation to win the backing of some countries. The second level involves the PLO's long-standing covert links to countries that provide it with arms and operational support, facilitating its military struggle against Israel and the West. On this level, the PLO also maintains close cooperative ties to many terrorist organizations around the globe.

5 The PLO's Financial Empire

I n the summer of 1987, close to lunchtime, the phone rang in the Jerusalem office of Adi Amorai, Israel's deputy finance minister. On the other end of the line was Shmuel Goren, who served as coordinator of activities in the territories, charged with formulating Israeli policy for the occupied West Bank and Gaza. Goren was one of Israel's top experts on Arab matters and a former intelligence officer who had risen to the number two position in the Mossad (Institute for Intelligence and Special Tasks).[1]

Goren wanted to know what to do with a Palestinian man who had been detained at the Allenby Bridge, the chief transit point between Israel and Jordan, after attempting to cross into Israeli-held territory carrying $999,000 in cash, all denominated in U.S. currency. The man offered no resistance, and there was nothing to indicate that he was engaged in any kind of illegal activity. However, Goren and his men clearly suspected that the man was a PLO courier bringing in money to support the PLO's infrastructure in the occupied territories.

Should the money be confiscated, Goren asked, and, if so, on what pretext? Or should the man be released and permitted to enter the "territories" with so much cash?

162

Amorai, who was preoccupied with Israel's stagnant economy and soaring inflation, which was running around 40 percent per annum, considered the matter for only a moment and then told Goren, "Let him go." His rationale was simple: Israel desperately needed dollars to pay for its imports, and the nation's population wanted dollars as a hedge against inflation. Amorai knew that the PLO man would rapidly have to convert the dollars into Israeli shekels in order to put them to work and that the money represented an infusion of hard currency into the ailing economy. Besides, there was little likelihood that the money would be used to support terrorist activities. It was no secret that PLO funds for the underground were shipped in far more discreetly. The money that passed across the Allenby Bridge, on the other hand, was used for ostensibly innocent purposes, such as paying the salaries of Palestinian teachers, funding schools and health care organizations, and providing survivor benefits to PLO families.

Moments later Goren called the Israeli commander at the Allenby Bridge and ordered that the man be released. The commander, in turn, walked into the sealed room at the bridge terminal where the courier was being held and handed him back the small suitcase packed with money and permitted him to leave. The courier left the terminal at a brisk pace and disappeared into the throng outside.

With the onset of the Intifada in December 1987, the Israeli government no longer permits PLO money shipments to go unimpeded. During the past year, more than twenty million dollars of PLO funds destined for the Palestinian population in the occupied territories have been confiscated by Israeli authorities.

The incident described above illustrates the strange symbiosis that existed until recently between Israel and the PLO with respect to the financial costs associated with the Israeli occupation of the West Bank and Gaza. It is also indicative of the financial power of the PLO, which has resources and assets that can be measured in the billions of dollars. Indeed, the PLO is the richest revolutionary movement in the world, with annual revenues currently exceeding the gross national products of some Third World countries. For all of its trappings as a military organization, today the PLO operates far more like a multinational corporation and must recruit accountants, public relations men, and lawyers as readily as guerrillas and covert operatives.

THE PALESTINIAN NATIONAL FUND

During its first meeting, in East Jerusalem from May 28 to June 2, 1964, the Palestinian National Council (PNC) established the Palestinian National Fund (PNF) to finance all PLO activities. The first chairman of the PNF was Abdel Majeed Shoman, son of the founder of the Arab Bank Ltd. After the death of his father in 1973, Shoman became chairman of the Arab Bank Ltd., which has come to be known over the years as the PLO bank.

The PLO at that time was headed by Saudi Arabia's former ambassador to the United Nations, Ahmed Shukeiry, and did not include Yasir Arafat's newly formed terrorist group, Fatah. However, after Arafat and his allies took over the PLO in 1969, they made a number of significant managerial and organizational changes, including several that impacted significantly on the PNF.

Arafat and Abu Iyad realized from the outset that money was the "mother's milk" of the Palestinian Revolution and that not only the PLO's independence and growth but its very survival depended on adequate funding. Initially Fatah had been a creature of the Syrian and Egyptian intelligence services, which underwrote its training, weapons, and other operational expenses. It was clear to Arafat, however, that they would support Fatah only so long as it served their national purposes and that the financial rug could be jerked out from underneath him at any time. Thus, he and his top advisers vowed to make the PLO financially sound and thereby ensure its growth and freedom of action.

In the wake of the 1967 Six-Day War and the defeat of the combined Arab armies, Fatah and the PLO were the only combat-ready Arab forces left to carry on the fight against Israel. In order to keep his forces in the field, Arafat sent

Khalil al-Wazir (Abu Jihad) and Farouk Qadoumi on an extensive tour of the oil-rich Gulf states to raise the needed funds. The Gulf sheikhdoms anted up enough to keep Fatah and the PLO going for several months, until a more permanent solution to their money needs could be found.

The Khartoum Arab summit, in late 1967, subsequently pledged sixty million dollars to fund Fatah and the PLO, as a means of continuing the struggle against Israel. During this period the PLO's chronic shortage of funds was a constant incentive to carry out terrorist operations. The PLO used such operations to justify its need for more money. By the same token, many of its benefactors regarded terrorist operations as proof that their money was being well spent. So great was the pressure on the PLO to conduct operations against Israel and its allies that it fabricated many terrorist operations in order to increase Arab largess. Such payments were routinely channeled through the PNF to the PLO, and the PNF reported back to the donors what their money was being used for.

Sometime in 1968 and 1969 the PNC imposed a 5 to 7 percent tax on the salary or income of every Palestinian worker residing in an Arab country, later expanded to include every Palestinian worker in the Islamic world. Known as the Palestinian Liberation Tax Fund (PLTF), it generated between twenty-five and thirty million dollars a year for the PLO coffers, despite a hit-and-miss tax collection system. It was by no means an ideal revenue-raising system. The various Arab governments were supposed to deduct the tax from the salary of every Palestinian wage earner; but some countries performed this obligation with more diligence than others, and there were reports that some funds were even siphoned off by corrupt officials. Governments also could delay or withhold funds as a way of putting pressure on the PLO. The levy was obviously more enforceable on salaried workers than on wealthy Palestinians and those with large investment incomes, who often escaped with token payments to the PLO.

The relatively steady flow of money produced by the levy on Palestinian incomes gave new prominence and power to the PNF. Nevertheless, the PNF was by no means the sole entity receiving funds in support of either the PLO or its constituent groups. It was simply the most visible and "respectable" entity to which funds could be transferred overtly and without complication. Not only did Arafat and his top aides create an alternative fund-raising empire known as the Chairman's Secret Fund, but every faction within the PLO had its own sources of funds, paid to it directly, often from the intelligence services of various Arab governments vying for influence within the PLO.

Since the departure of Shoman as director, the PNF has been characterized by a high degree of turnover among its top officials. Some were ousted as a result of internal struggles; others were fired, in effect, because of alleged mismanagement. At the present time, the director is a nonaligned member of the PNC, Jaweed Yaccub Ghusain (Abu Tufiq), who does not belong to a specific faction, although he enjoys close and cordial relations with Yasir Arafat. Ghusain was named to the post at the seventeenth meeting of the PNC in 1984. A wealthy contractor, Ghusain has his business headquarters in London, with branches in Kuwait and Abu Dhabi. He oversees a portfolio worth an estimated two to six billion dollars, which gives him enormous economic leverage both within the PLO and in the international banking community. There are also reports that Ghusain is responsible for the portfolios of some of the PLO's constituent groups, but such reports are impossible to verify. In his capacity as chairman of the PNF, Ghusain is, for all intents and purposes, the finance minister of the PLO. In addition, he serves on the PLO's Executive Committee, which can be likened to the PLO's Cabinet.

Arafat's top financial adviser, however, is not Ghusain but rather Nabil Shaath, president of TEAM, a Cairo-based management consulting firm. A member of the PNC, Shaath also serves as a special emissary for Arafat, especially to the United States and Western Europe. Prior to founding his own corporation, Shaath taught corporate finance at the University of Pennsylvania's Wharton School. A charming and articulate man, Shaath is one of the PLO's most effective advocates.

Prior to June 1983, the PNF's main offices were located on Baghdad Street in Damascus, Syria, although most of its portfolio activity was directed from London. When the Syrian government tried to take control of the PLO's financial empire in 1983, following the PLO's evacuation from Lebanon, the PNF moved its executive offices to Amman, Jordan. Since that time it has decentralized its operations and no longer maintains one central headquarters. Today its computers and record-keeping functions, which monitor and control its vast investments and other activities, are located in Amman, Tunis, Algiers, and Kuwait. The PNF has 110 professionals, nearly all university graduates, who manage the various portfolios and other investments.

THE PNF'S CURRENT BUDGET

The PNF has four major sources of funds: donations, taxation of Palestinians, contributions from sympathetic governments, and income from its investments. Immediately after the expulsion of the PLO from Lebanon, annual donations jumped dramatically, to more than $100 million. Today, however, donations have reportedly tapered off, and are said to be in the range of $50 million to $65 million. Most donations come from wealthy Palestinians and various Arab philanthropic organizations, such as the Geneva-based Palestinian Welfare Association. In 1987 the Palestinian Liberation Tax Fund brought in another $50 million in revenues.

Since 1979, following commitments made at the 1978 Baghdad Arab summit, seven (later six) Arab nations have annually contributed between $250 and $300 million to the PNF. This funding was a consequence of the shock and alarm felt by many Arab governments over Egyptian President Anwar el-Sadat's decision to deal directly with Israel. Since direct confrontation with Egypt or Israel was out of the question, the only alternative was to increase the PLO's ability to disrupt the Camp David accords and to put military pressure on Israel. The PLO, moreover, was viewed as the only barrier preventing the Lebanese Christians, then in ascendancy under the leadership of Bashir Gemayel, from following Sadat's lead and making a separate peace with Israel.

With the exception of Libya, which met its obligations for only two years before Qaddafi reneged on his pledge following policy differences with Arafat, all the other nations have lived up to their commitments for the past ten years, although Iraq, Algeria, Kuwait, and Qatar have, at one time or another, fallen behind on their payments. The Iran-Iraq War, for example, created severe economic problems for Iraq, and this forced Baghdad to miss a number of payments.[2] The annual payments are normally broken into three equal installments and paid to the PNF every four months. This has guaranteed the PNF an income of approximately $252.9 million a year from this one source alone, or between $2.5 and $3 billion over the past decade. While Libya suspended payments to the PLO in 1981, in 1988 Qaddafi and Arafat reconciled their differences and Libyan payments were resumed. Since 1986 Saudi Arabia has even increased its annual payment by $36 million to $121.7 million. It should be noted that Arab governments other than those on the list gave money directly to various constituent elements of the PLO or to the Chairman's Secret Fund but so far as is known did not contribute to the PNF.

The pledges undertaken by the seven countries at the Baghdad summit were as follows:

Saudi Arabia	$ 85.7 million
UAE	34.3 million
Algeria	21.4 million
Iraq	44.6 million
Qatar	19.8 million
Kuwait	47.1 million
Libya	47.1 million
TOTAL =	$ 300.0 million

In addition, the same seven Arab countries pledged $50 million in annual payments specifically for the welfare of Palestinians living under Israeli occupation:

Saudi Arabia	$15 million
UAE	6 million
Algeria	3 million
Iraq	7 million
Qatar	3 million
Kuwait	8 million
Libya	8 million
TOTAL =	$50 million

This latter fund was to be administered by the Joint Jordanian-PLO Committee for the Occupied Territories, which agreed to match the contribution of the Arab governments with another $50 million of its own. The funds were to be channeled through the PNF, and so far as is known, all the contributors, including Libya, have met their obligations.

On April 20, 1987, the PLO's Occupied Homeland Department published a report detailing the amount spent in the occupied territories from 1979 through the end of February 1987. The report had earlier been submitted to the eighteenth PNC meeting in Algiers. The $487.5 million total was broken down as follows:

Agriculture	$ 28.0 million
Industry and tourism	11.0
Water	9.7
Electricity	33.7
Transportation	101.3
Housing	61.5
Education and culture	109.4
Public health	7.7
Municipalities	47.1
Waqf (Islamic institutes)	5.5
Surveys and consulting	0.8
Emergency fund	10.9
National struggle fund	23.4
TOTAL =	$ 487.5 million[3]

THE PLO'S "OVERT" BUDGET

It is very difficult to put together a balance sheet for the PLO since it does not make any of its finances public. Most of the available data are based on estimates prepared by various intelligence services in view of the fact that even the PLO's "overt" revenues are secret. The process of developing a balance sheet is further complicated by the fact that the PNF and PLO have traditionally maintained their financial records on a fiscal-year basis (July 1 through June 30) and are presently in the process of converting over to calendar-year bookkeeping. Nevertheless, if the PLO and the PNF had publicly disclosed their "overt" revenues for 1988, a summary of their balance sheet would have looked something like this:

Donations	$ 50.0 million
Palestinian Liberation Tax Fund	46.0 million
Direct contributions by governments	216.0 million
Investment income	300.0 million
Fund for the occupied territories	62.5 million
TOTAL =	$ 674.5 million

This reflected a shortfall in projected revenues of nearly $110.5 million, although the PLO's net "overt" income of an estimated $674.5 million was hardly inconsequential. Indeed, donations were $10 million below projections, revenues from the PLTF were $4 million below projections because of the devaluation of the Jordanian dinar, contributions from governments were down by $84 million, and donations to the Palestinian population in the occupied territories declined by $12.5 million after King Hussein of Jordan withdrew his claim to sovereignty over the West Bank. Although the UAE, Kuwait, and Algeria were believed to be late in meeting their commitments to the PNF, their payments were probably received after the first of the year (1989). Late payments are a chronic problem for the PNF.

The PNF constantly pleads poverty to its government contributors, to induce them both to pay more or, at the very least, to pay on time. In December 1985 PNF Chairman Jaweed Ghusain made public what was alleged to be a summary of PNF income and expenditures, although the income figure was a line item and not broken down. According to Ghusain, the PNF's obligations were as follows: "The first $100 million goes to the Joint Palestinian-Jordanian committee to support the Palestinian people inside the occupied territories. The next $200 million goes to the PLO and its institutions such as the Red Crescent, and to the estimated 500,000 Palestinian families in Lebanon, who are in urgent need."[4] In his remarks he concentrated solely on the "humanitarian" obligations of the PNF and PLO and failed to make any mention of the PLO's military requirements. He complained that only 30 percent of all pledged monies were actually being received and that the PLO was desperately short of funds. In view of the tendency of PNF and PLO officials to exaggerate their financial situation in order to stimulate giving, it is hard to know just how serious the PLO's financial shortfall was in the wake of its evacuation from Lebanon and resettlement in Tunisia and other Arab countries. Whatever the real situation, however, by 1986–87, the PNF's situation, and therefore the PLO's, were considerably brighter. The various Arab contributors had rushed to clear up their delinquent obligations, and Palestinian contributions from throughout the world—moved by the plight of the PLO and its adherents—had flowed into the coffers of the PNF. And as noted earlier, Saudi Arabia voluntarily increased its annual payment to the PNF by more than 40 percent.

One unusual source of revenue for the PNF may be the sale of postage stamps. Apparently all the Arab countries agreed to produce individually an "Arab Liberation Stamp" and donate the revenues to the PNF. However, the present status of the effort is unknown, and there are suggestions that few of the nations that pledged to produced a stamp have done so.

CURRENT EXPENDITURES BY THE PLO

The PLO presently operates as something more than a multinational company, but less than a fully constituted government, although over the years it has taken on more and more of the trappings and obligations of statehood, including embassies, a defense force, and the funding of various social welfare programs. The present "overt" expenses of the PLO are, therefore, considerable, amounting to some $395 million in the fiscal year ending on June 30, 1988. All are paid from funds collected by the PNF.

The largest single PLO expense is the maintenance of its conventional armed militias, which is estimated at $100 million annually. Included in this category are the twelve- to fourteen-thousand-man Palestine Liberation Army (officially referred to after 1984 as the National Palestinian Liberation Army); the Lebanese National Movement (LNM), the PLO's military coalition in Lebanon; and certain other fighting militias in Lebanon that receive some PLO support. For its part, the PLA consists of three brigades, an armored corps, and a small air force, which represent no small undertaking in terms of financial resources. The average Palestinian fighter receives between $125 and $225 per month and, in addition, must be fed, clothed, and housed. The recent sharp decline in the value of the Lebanese pound has increased the financial burden on the PLO by making its activities in Lebanon far more costly. Unlike Hizballah and some of the major militias in Lebanon, however, the PNF transferred all of the organization's capital accounts out of Lebanon (and Lebanese pounds) in the late 1970's and therefore was not significantly damaged by the plummeting value of the Lebanese pound in the mid-1980's.

The PLO also pays approximately $40 million a year in expenses associated with its diplomatic activities. At the present time this involves the maintenance of nearly a hundred foreign missions (fifty-five enjoying full diplomatic status), the salaries and expenses of several hundred "diplomats," and the cost of its foreign ministry and related propaganda efforts.

The Palestinian Martyr's Fund (PMF), the PLO's equivalent of the U.S. Department of Veterans Affairs, provides stipends to the families of PLO fighters either killed in action or serving time in jail and scholarships and other benefits to their children. The PMF currently has a budget of $65 million a year.

The PNF also supports Palestinian schools and universities, newspapers, hospitals, "information" centers, the Palestinian Research Center, and the Palestinian Red Crescent, all of which costs more than $40 million per annum. In addition, funds are sent to the Palestinian populations in the West Bank and Gaza. Since the beginning of the Intifada in 1987, the PLO's expenditures in the occupied territories have doubled. Because of strikes and other disturbances that have affected worker productivity and local commerce, the large number of Palestinian breadwinners who have been jailed, and the refusal of many Palestinians to work in Israel, the

PLO has been forced to transfer $150 million to the occupied territories in the past twelve months to support the uprising and to underwrite basic services and charities. In view of these additional expenses, the 1988 Arab summit in Algiers agreed to provide the PLO with a one-time grant of $128 million, and monthly payments of $43 million, to finance the Intifada. According to Arafat, "The PLO structure is capable of absorbing everything so long as it has the resources. I assure my kinfolk in the occupied territory that we will shoulder our responsibilities."[5] Despite the pledges received at the Arab summit, Arafat indicated that as usual, he was having difficulty convincing the various Arab governments to make good on their promises.

In the final analysis, however, the PLO's $395 million annual "overt" budget is more than covered by its estimated revenues of $674.5 million, thus leaving a surplus of nearly $280 million. Some of this money may find its way into the Chairman's Secret Fund, but most of it is probably invested by the PNF, adding to its already considerable portfolio.

SAMED

In keeping with Arafat's belief that the Palestinian Revolution had to be economically independent if it were to be successful, in 1970 the PLO's Executive Committee created a new institution under the control of Fatah called Samed (pronounced "sue mud"), which in Arabic means "standing firm" or "steadfastness." Initially part of the PLO's Social Affairs Department and known as the Palestine Martyrs' Work Society, Samed was tasked with establishing various business enterprises and operating them on a profitable basis. Samed's charter contains a statement of goals:

To create the nucleus of the Palestinian revolutionary economy; to develop a self-sufficient economy for the revolution and the Palestinian masses; and to lay the foundation for the economic structure of a Palestinian state in Palestine.

To provide skills and work for the families of the martyrs of the Palestinian revolution.

To provide possible employment to every Palestinian and to develop their technical and scientific competency.

To form the material basis for Palestinian survival and provide for the continuation of the struggle inside and outside occupied Palestine.

To provide Palestinians with basic necessities at prices corresponding to their material means.

To preserve and advance Palestinian cultural traditions.

To develop economic, commercial and industrial relations with fraternal parties, democratic forces, and friendly countries.[6]

What is significant about Samed's charter is the absence of Marxist jargon and fuzzy economic theories. Samed was conceived of as a pragmatic, nonsubsidized commercial and manufacturing operation that would serve as the economic arm of the PLO's fighting forces. In addition to contributing to Palestinian economic independence, it was hoped that Samed would provide work to the families of those away fighting for an independent Palestinian state, thus enabling them to survive in the interlude. It was also a way of drawing the Palestinian rank and file into the PLO and to win public support in the Palestinian community.

The PLO's most immediate need in 1970 was for uniforms, and so Samed began—with a stake of an estimated twenty-five thousand dollars—by setting up small workshops in the Palestinian refugee camps in Lebanon and Jordan to produce them. The program was an immediate success, and since its inception Samed has grown into a multinational financial empire embracing more than a hundred different enterprises, ranging from workshops to light manufacturing plants, film studios, farms, and stores.

In the 1970's Samed's activities buttressed the PLO's goal of creating a state within a state in Lebanon and in the resettlement of the Palestinian population in areas important from a political and strategic point of view. After the PLO drove the Christian population from Damour, for example, with great brutality and loss of life, Samed moved into the void to create the economic underpinnings necessary to support a Palestinian presence in the city. By the end of 1976 Samed had set up seven workshops in the area, manufacturing cloth, woolen goods, blankets, and various metal products. In addition, the main PLO film studio was located in Damour.

In 1981 approximately 35 percent of all Samed's sales were to the PLO. The rest of its products went to Lebanon (8 percent), Arab countries (30 percent), and other world markets (27 percent).

Gross revenues were forty-five million dollars in 1982 and were expected to reach seventy million dollars in 1989. Current revenues are all the more impressive when viewed in light of the serious reverses suffered by Samed in the aftermath of the PLO's evacuation from Lebanon. According to Samed's chairman and chief executive officer, Ahmed Quary, also known as Abu A'ala, the Israeli invasion and the ensuing upheaval cost Samed seventeen million dollars. During this period the Samed enterprises—manufacturing textiles, shoes, and plastics—in the Palestinian refugee camps of Burj El-Shamali, Ein El-Hilweh, and Mijeh wa Mijeh were destroyed.

Even as late as 1986, total Samed revenues were only thirty-nine million dollars, representing a loss of six million dollars in comparison with the 1982 figure. Nevertheless, Samed was the only noncovert entity that Arafat was able to leave behind in Lebanon following the PLO's withdrawal to Tunis. During this period it provided the PLO with a presence in Lebanon and a vehicle—since 1984—that offered cover to PLO operatives infiltrating back into the country.

In the aftermath of the Lebanon catastrophe, Samed began to diversify its operations and expand into other countries. Today it has operations and investments in other Arab countries, Africa, the Communist Eastern bloc, and reportedly even Latin America. In its far-flung operations Samed employs nearly twelve thousand people, of which fifty-five hundred to seven thousand are full-time workers.

Since becoming independent of the PLO's Social Affairs Department in 1973, Samed has been organized into four main divisions: industrial, information (print and film), agricultural, and general commerce. Its activities are overseen by a board of directors and administered on a daily basis by its chairman. In 1984, following a period of sharp disagreement between Samed's board of directors and the PLO leadership over the organization's growing independence, Samed was reorganized and incorporated into the PLO's Economic Department.[7] Today it forms the nucleus of the PLO's economic "ministry" and appears to be under the full and total control of the PLO and Yasir Arafat. Abu A'ala, in addition to remaining chairman of Samed, presently serves as executive director of the PLO's Economic Department. According to A'ala, "Samed is not just an economic project striving for financial benefits. Neither is it solely a social institution for the families of martyrs. Samed is the combination of many things. It is the economic arm of our revolution and our people [nation] and is committed to the principles and policies of the revolution."[8]

SAMED TODAY

Samed has branches and operations in more than thirty countries and a pool of investment funds estimated at fifty million dollars. Samed's various industrial ventures produce clothes, wool, blankets, furniture, technical instruments, processed food products, embroidered merchandise, construction equipment, medical supplies, plastic products, shoes, and artificial limbs. It has factories in both South and North Yemen and operates joint ventures in Poland, Romania (textiles), Thailand (children's clothes), and Egypt.

Its agricultural section manages, and in most cases owns, large farms in Egypt, Zaire, Syria, the Sudan, Mali, Guinea, Guinea-Bissau, Somalia, North Yemen, and Poland (a chicken farm). A large agricultural project in Uganda was closed down last year after losing more than five million dollars.

Since 1983 Samed's film division and printing operation have been located in Jordan. Samed, however, continues to send a good deal of printing work to el-Carmel printing shop in Damascus, which is owned by the FRC, Abu Nidal's organization.

Among the general commercial investments made by Samed is the purchase of the duty-free shop at Tanzania's Dar es Salaam international airport. The PLO's representative in Zimbabwe, Ali Halimeh, described the shop as purely an "economic investment," and there were reports that Samed was negotiating for the purchase of other duty-free shops in Zimbabwe and Mozambique.[9]

Samed presently has twenty-six permanent cultural and product exhibitions in fourteen Arab and African countries and maintains thirty trade missions around the world.

What follows is a partial list of Samed's major international projects, which illustrate the diversity of its present operations:

People's Democratic Republic of Yemen (South Yemen)
    Clothing factory in Aden dedicated to the memory of Fawaz Birkdar, a Palestinian martyr. Established after the war in Lebanon, it currently employs an estimated forty people.
Yemen Arab Republic (North Yemen)
    1. Workshops for tires and electric appliances in Taiz.
    2. Agricultural project in Hodeida established in 1984, based mainly on sheep raising and the production of vegetables.
    3. Clothing factory called Arako in Sana, set up in collaboration with a North Yemeni spinning and weaving company. It manufactures military uniforms and clothing for doctors and nurses. Ninety percent of its employees are Yemenis, and production is mainly for local consumption.
Sudan
    A thirteen-hundred-hectare agricultural project about twenty kilometers from Khartoum. Samed employees grow vegetables and cereals and raise cattle, sheep, and poultry. There is also a hotel, gas station, and several swimming pools on the project.
Somalia
    An agricultural project a hundred kilometers from Mogadishu, which grows bananas, sesame, and corn.
Guinea
    An agricultural project sixty kilometers south of Conakry, which was established in 1977 and grows mangoes, pineapples, and avocados.

Guinea-Bissau
> An agricultural project and furniture factory approximately twenty kilometers from Bissau.

Poland
> 1. A poultry farm in Poznan, established in 1983.
> 2. A factory that manufactures nails.

Syria
> An agricultural project, established jointly with the East Germans, for raising cattle and poultry.

Mali
> Agricultural project about twenty-five kilometers from Bamako.

Hungary
> A shoe factory.

People's Republic of the Congo
> A factory for canned mangoes on the island of Ambamo on the Congo River, opposite Brazzaville.

In the final analysis, Samed is far from being an industrial conglomerate on a par with major Western multinationals. But it has been a PLO success story and not only has generated its own capital for further expansion but has provided work and other benefits to many Palestinian refugees. Its operations abroad have generated profits and goodwill and provided valuable experience for its Palestinian managers. Only rarely has Samed served as a front for other PLO operations.

THE ARAB BANK LTD.

The Arab Bank Ltd. is regarded throughout the world as the PLO's bank, not because of some Israeli disinformation plot, but as a result of the bank's activities and operations over many years. In other words, the Arab Bank Ltd. became known as the PLO's bank the old-fashioned way: It earned the characterization. If there was ever any doubt in anyone's mind about the bank's true identity, such concerns were put to rest in the late 1970's, when virtually every bank in Beirut—a onetime banking haven—was robbed and looted, often by PLO brigands, with the exception of the Arab Bank Ltd. Indeed, until the PLO pullout from Beirut in 1982, the Beirut branch of the Arab Bank Ltd., located in West Beirut, was guarded around the clock by elements of Force 17.[10]

Today the Arab Bank Ltd. is the world's largest Arab commercial bank, with thirteen billion dollars in assets (1987) and deposits in excess of twelve billion dollars. Ironically, the story of the Arab Bank Ltd., and how it came to be the "PLO's bank," is inextricably linked to the growth of Jewish immigration to Palestine and the emergence of the state of Israel. Indeed, it could be said that without Israel, the Arab Bank Ltd. probably would have been just another small financial institution catering to local business interests on the West Bank.

The bank was founded in May 1930 by two ambitious Palestinian Arabs, Abdel Hamid Shoman and Ahmed Hilmi. With an initial capitalization of fifteen thousand Palestinian pounds, worth approximately a hundred thousand dollars, they opened their doors at a modest location in Jerusalem. However, there was nothing modest about the name they gave their institution, the Arab Bank Ltd., which had more to do with their aspirations for the bank than actual fact. Following the example of several Jewish institutions in Palestine, the partners announced their intention of making a profit while at the same time serving the Arab population of Palestine. Ahmed Hilmi retired from the management of the bank in 1948 to serve as "Palestine's" first prime minister, leaving his partner Abdel Hamid Shoman as the sole remaining director and chief operating officer. Hilmi's selection as prime minister occurred after the Supreme Moslem Council (the most authoritative Palestinian body at that time) announced the establishment of the All-Palestine Government in Gaza, based on decisions taken by the Arab League. Hilmi remained prime minister until September 1952, when the Arab League declared that the Palestinian government had ceased to exist and that Palestine would be represented by member states of the league.

Shoman, for his part, was a member of the Palestinian al-Istiqlal party, which embraced the notion of pan-Arabism and advocated the expulsion of the British from Palestine. During World War II, the party was sympathetic to Nazi Germany both because of Nazi policies against the Jews and in the hope that a Nazi victory would mean the end of British colonialism in the Middle East. The party was supported by the grand mufti of Jerusalem, Haj Amin al-Husseini, whose violent pro-Nazi sympathies forced him to take refuge in Nazi Germany during the war.

Prior to Israel's independence, the Arab Bank Ltd. was deeply involved with projects designed to advance Palestinian self-sufficiency and political power. For example, it was the initiator of and driving force behind the Inter-Arab Economic Fair held in Palestine in 1933. The bank's resources were also used to block Jewish purchases of Palestinian land. Together with the Palestinian National Movement, the bank helped establish the Sunduq al-Umma (National Fund), which was designed to buy Palestinian land that came on the market before it was sold to Jewish or British interests.

Although the bank's growth was relatively slow prior to 1948, it managed to open small branch operations in Haifa, Jaffa, Beirut, Amman, and Cairo. After Israel's independence, Shoman moved the bank's headquarters from Jerusalem to Amman, Jordan, thereby forfeiting its branch operations in Haifa and Jaffa. In 1967, following the lightning Israeli victory in the Six-Day War, the bank was forced to shut down operations at seven branches on the West Bank (six) and Gaza Strip (one). However, far from being an economic disaster, 1967 represents a watershed year in the bank's evolution. In retrospect, it could be said that the Arab Bank Ltd. has thriven on adversity.

Deposits soared as a result of the Palestinian exodus from Israeli-held territory and the massive movement of Palestinian assets from the West Bank and Gaza to Jordan. Similarly, in 1973 the Arab Bank Ltd. was ideally positioned to take advantage of the economic boom that followed the rapid escalation in the price of crude oil. Billions of dollars flowed into the Arab Bank Ltd., which, in turn, used the money to finance development projects throughout the Arab world. The onset of the Lebanese civil war in 1975 also benefited the bank by eliminating Beirut as a rival banking and business center. Because of its relatively liberal business climate and pro-Western posture, Jordan suddenly appeared a mecca of stability in the Middle East and a convenient location for banking and other financial transactions.

To service its clients better, the bank initiated a period of rapid expansion abroad. In addition to an existing presence in London, the bank opened branches in Switzerland, France, Italy, Spain, West Germany, and the United States. The U.S. branch of the Arab Bank Ltd., located at 520 Madison Avenue in New York City, is believed to manage PLO investments in excess of one billion dollars. There is no way of knowing authoritatively the value of PLO accounts in New York because of a 1975 pledge by then Secretary of the Treasury William Simon never to reveal the magnitude, origin, or location of Arab investments in the United States.

In 1973 Abdel Hamid Shoman died and was succeeded by his son, Abdel Majeed Shoman, then chairman of the Palestinian National Fund. The younger Shoman, who was educated in the United States, has kept his father's vision of service to the Palestinian and Arab communities and, if anything, is even more committed to the goal of Palestinian self-determination. He has also been a close adviser of Jordan's King Hussein and active in Jordanian politics. In 1988 Shoman officially retired from his post as a member of the Jordanian Senate, a largely ceremonial body.[11]

In summary, despite the Arab Bank's phenomenal growth and success, it remains a highly politicized institution, which willingly provides banking and financial services to groups engaged in the Palestinian struggle, whether mainstream organizations or terrorist gangs. The Arab Bank is not the only bank committed to the Palestinian cause, but it is certainly the largest financial institution to do so.

When Arafat began pulling his funds out of Lebanon in the late 1970's, most were transferred to PLO accounts at the Cairo and Amman branches of the Arab Bank Ltd. From there some of the funds were further dispersed to Europe and the United States. Shoman has acknowledged that the Arab Bank's ties to the PLO increased in the late 1970's and that the bank began to manage a greater share of the PLO's overt investment portfolio. Indeed, Arafat's purported 1985 rejection of terrorism outside "the occupied homeland" has made it far easier for Shoman and his colleagues to support the PLO publicly.

Until July 1, 1988, the Jordanian government paid the salaries and other expenses of eighteen thousand Palestinian gov-

ernment workers (teachers, policemen, civil servants, etc.) residing in the Israeli-occupied West Bank, as a way of asserting
Jordanian sovereignty over the region. But when King Hussein terminated payment of such salaries and relinquished,
for all intents and purposes, legal and administrative claim to
the West Bank, the PLO moved into the void. In its decision
to "shoulder full responsibility toward employees and workers
in the occupied West Bank," the PLO designated the Arab
Bank in Amman as the institution where funds were on deposit to pay the salaries of Palestinian workers, at an estimated cost of between five and six million dollars a month.[12]

PALESTINIAN WELFARE ASSOCIATION (PWA)

In September 1982, after the PLO was driven from Beirut,
three of the wealthiest Palestinian businessmen in the world
met and formed the Geneva-based Palestinian Welfare Association. The three men were Hasib Sabbagh, chairman of the
Consolidated Contractors Company (CCC), headquartered in
Athens; Munib Masri, also a construction tycoon, who lives in
London; and Abdel Majeed Shoman, the chairman of the Arab
Bank Ltd. With an initial thirty million dollars in capital, the
trio set out to enlist as members and directors the hundred
richest Palestinian businessmen. In its by-laws the PWA describes its mission as to "safeguard and further the Palestinian people's aspirations, notably in the social, cultural,
humanitarian, health-care and educational fields."
   The PWA was officially registered in Geneva on October 22,
1983, and the following individuals were listed on a registration document as founding members: Abdel Majeed Shoman
(chairman), Hasib Sabbagh (vice-chairman), Issam al-Azmeh
(secretary), Munib Masri (treasurer), Abed al-Muchsein al-
Qatan (member, Kuwait), Omar al-Aggad (member, Saudi
Arabia), Basil Aqel (member, Syrian living in London), Zein
al-Abedeldin Mayasi (member, Lebanese living in Riyadh),
and George T. al-Abed Daoud (director general, living in Ge-

neva). The PWA is run by a committee with an unknown number of members.

Most of the top officials of the PWA have close ties to the PLO, and despite their public denials, few observers believe that there are no linkages between the two organizations. Hasib Sabbagh is generally considered the richest Palestinian on earth. In 1948 he launched the Consolidated Contractors Company in Beirut after fleeing his hometown of Haifa. Over the years he built CCC into the largest construction company in Saudi Arabia and the Gulf and entered into many joint ventures in the region with the California-based Bechtel Corporation. Today CCC has offices throughout the Arab world, in the Far East, and in Europe (Greece, Switzerland, and United Kingdom). It maintains an office in Washington, D.C., which is shared with Sabbagh's investment firm and another company he owns called Candia. Sabbagh speaks perfect English and is in regular contact with many major U.S. political figures, including former Presidents Jimmy Carter and Ronald Reagan.[13] It is said that he serves as a major back channel from the PLO to the governments of the United States, Jordan, Lebanon, and European nations. As one example, Sabbagh reportedly traveled to Damascus in April 1988 and met quietly with Syrian Vice-President Abdel Halim Khaddam. According to a PLO broadcast monitored by the U.S. government, Sabbagh "has paid more than one visit to the Syrian capital during the past few months in a bid to bridge the gap between the Syrians and Palestinian leadership. It is believed that during his recent visit he conveyed the Palestinian answers to demands made and conditions set by Damascus for bringing about a reconciliation between the two sides."[14]

Munib Masri's ties to the PLO are even more open and direct. He is a member of the PLO's Central Committee and a director of the Palestinian National Fund. Although not in the same league with Sabbagh, Masri's Engineering & Development Group (EDG), which has been based in London ever since leaving Beirut, has annual revenues in the range of fifty to eighty million dollars. Masri's cousin Sabih Masri is also a member of the PWA and owns and operates an agribusiness company called the Astra Farms Company, with annual revenues of approximately a hundred million dollars.

Many of the members of the PWA, like Zahi W. Khouri,

president of Gentrol, Inc., the U.S. affiliate of Saudi Arabia's largest conglomerate, the Olayan Group, contribute to the PWA as a way of supporting the Palestinian struggle without being accused of underwriting international terrorism. The fact that monies spent by the PWA free up PLO funds for the support of covert and military operations against Israel and the West is conveniently ignored.

Located at 7 Avenue Pictet-de-Rochemont in Geneva, the PWA collects and distributes money to a variety of Palestinian welfare organizations. In addition, it raises money for the general purposes of the PLO and has no clear understanding of how the money is spent. Most leading Palestinians provide annual contributions to the PWA fund, and the money is not amassed like an endowment but is spent each year. Indeed, in 1987 the PWA declared that it had only twenty-two million dollars in its fund.

The PWA also controls the Jerusalem Fund, through George T. al-Abed Daoud. The Jerusalem Fund supports a number of PLO-related newspapers and periodicals on the West Bank, including Hanna Seniora's *Al-Fajar* newspaper (in Arabic), which appears in East Jerusalem and serves as the printed voice of the PLO in the occupied territories.

THE CHAIRMAN'S SECRET FUND

Yasir Arafat is not a spellbinding orator. He is not particularly charismatic, though he possesses a certain scoundrel's charm. No Che Guevara, he is far from physically attractive; indeed, most would call him homely, even ugly. He is smart, cunning, but certainly not one of the greatest political strategists or military leaders of the twentieth century. Thus, it is often asked: What is the source of Arafat's power? Why has he been able to remain as chairman of the PLO for so long, outlasting or besting all rivals?

The answer is simple. Money is the source of Yasir Arafat's power. Without it Arafat would have been just another voice in the tumult, another salesman of broken dreams, a kind of Palestinian Willy Loman. Instead, he is a global mover and shaker, feted by kings and prime ministers, the leader of a revolution that threatens to change the map of the world. He is feared by his enemies, who know that his threats are not hollow, and loved by his followers, who know that he can be a generous patron.

The Palestinian National Fund, Samed, and the Palestinian Welfare Fund all are sources of Arafat's financial power, but even more important is the so-called Chairman's Secret Fund (CSF). In contrast with the PLO's other revenues, both the sources and the expenditures of the Chairman's Secret Fund are totally secret, hidden from view by means of multiple cutouts and banking secrecy laws. By using bearer bonds, numbered accounts, phony companies, and nominee ownership of assets, Arafat has created a financial empire that extends around the world, but that is effectively known only to him and to a lesser extent to Abu Iyad.[15] As one observer notes, "They have to keep Arafat because if he goes, no one will know where the money is."[16]

As an example of the enormous sums of money readily available to Arafat, when Brigadier Atallah Atallah (Abu Zaim), the former chief of Fatah's Intelligence and Security Apparatus (ISA), revolted against Arafat's leadership and seized, with a handful of followers, the PLO's main office in Amman in May 1986, he claims to have found two hundred million dollars in cash and other negotiable instruments. This story was also repeated by Colonel Sa'id Musa Muragha (Abu Musa) in an interview with a Beirut magazine. Atallah Atallah also described the kinds of miscellaneous expenditures that were routinely underwritten by the PLO. Among his examples were: $100,000 to Abu Mazan (Machmud Abbas), a member of the PLO's Executive Committee, for his son's wedding at a Tunisian hotel; $12 million to organize ceremonies in Aden for PLO and Fatah members expelled from Beirut in 1982; $40,000 to Abu Iyad to celebrate his twenty-fifth wedding anniversary; $15 million to Hizballah to secure the release of three kidnapped Soviet diplomats and the body of a fourth (September 1985); $480,000 to fly PNC delegates to Amman for the seventeenth PNC meeting in November 1984; and $12,000 for a translation to Arabic of the proceedings of the seventeenth

PNC meeting in Amman, despite the fact that all the delegates spoke Arabic and no translation was presumably required. Explaining his decision to break with Arafat and to declare himself commander of Fatah, Atallah Atallah accused Arafat and other top officials of the PLO of mismanagement and corruption.

There is no paper trail, and Arafat is not required to account to anyone for the expenditure of his secret funds. Details of the Chairman's Secret Fund are not reported to the Palestinian National Council or recorded with the Palestinian Central Bureau for Statistics. The combined assets of the CSF may be as much as two billion dollars, and this money is used chiefly to fund the PLO's terrorist operations and Arafat's struggles within the PLO.

But what is the source of Arafat's secret discretionary fund? Some of the funds come from Arab intelligence services eager to "hire" the covert units of the PLO to carry out specific operations, often against other Arab adversaries. Other intelligence services bankroll the PLO simply as a means of buying "protection" from such attacks. Still other services contribute to the secret fund as a way of keeping the military pressure on Israel and punishing the West for its support of the Jewish state. Some of the Arab states even have gone so far as to reward the PLO for particularly vicious or "successful" terrorist operations, such as the May 15, 1974, attack by elements of the Democratic Front for the Liberation of Palestine (DFLP) on the Israeli town of Maalot. Twenty-seven people, mostly schoolchildren, were killed in the brutal operation and another seventy were wounded, before the three terrorists were killed by Israeli troops.[17] Attacks like the one on Maalot and the March 5, 1975, Fatah operation against the Savoy Hotel in downtown Tel Aviv produced generous "contributions" from Libya, Algeria, and other Arab governments.

But for the most part, Arafat and his lieutenants operate as a multinational crime syndicate, relying on extortion, bribery, theft, narcotics trafficking, and murder to fulfill their financial needs. During the late 1960's, for example, after carrying out a string of successful hijackings and attacks against international civil aviation, the PLO realized that there was money to be made in agreeing not to target certain airlines. Accordingly, a protection racket was set up whereby airlines could reduce their vulnerability by making certain "voluntary contributions to the Palestinian cause." At least four European airlines reportedly took advantage of the PLO's "flight insurance" program. Most, it is presumed, decided that it was cheaper to pay protection money than to install comprehensive security measures. Lufthansa joined the "program" after one of its planes had been hijacked by the PFLP to Aden in February 1972. After paying the PFLP five million dollars for the release of the plane and passengers, Lufthansa annually shelled out five to ten million dollars to elements within the PLO for immunity from further attacks. The money went into the Chairman's Secret Fund and was divided up among a number of Palestinian terrorist groups, including the PFLP. This system remained in place until a Lufthansa jetliner was seized by terrorists in 1977 and ultimately diverted to Mogadishu, Somalia, where it was later stormed by West German GSG-9 commandos. Lufthansa subsequently declined to pay further "protection" money to the PLO.

A major U.S. carrier also joined the "protection program" in 1972, after one of its planes was destroyed. In 1975 the airline apparently discontinued its payments, although it is possible that it simply changed its method of payment to a more discreet channel. Indeed, some airlines found that it was not easy to stop paying protection money to the PLO. After one airline ended its three-million-dollar annual payment, its offices were bombed and its facilities were attacked. No airline is known to be paying protection money at the present time to the PLO or any other terrorist organization.

It is easy, in retrospect, to condemn the airlines for their payments. It should, however, be remembered that most airlines—especially during the early 1970's—have received little help from their national governments in protecting their planes and passengers. In some countries, including the United States, the burden of aviation-related security is placed on airports and airlines, rather than on government organizations, where it belongs. Moreover, many nations, including several in Western Europe, are characterized by weakness and vacillation in the face of terrorist threats and, indeed, continue to maintain cordial relations with the major terrorist-sponsoring states. In view of the failure of national

governments to undertake the kinds of tough actions necessary to protect the international civil aviation system, it
should come as no surprise that a few desperate airlines attempted to buy protection from Palestinian terrorists.

The PLO also received protection money from the oil indus-
try, which contributed to Fatah and related organizations as
a way of ensuring immunity from attacks against its execu-
tives and facilities. Many of the major oil companies got the
"message" after Black September attacked oil facilities in Rot-
terdam in 1972. ARAMCO (Arabian-American Oil Company)
decided to pay after fourteen of its American employees were
killed in a terrorist attack at Rome's Fiumicino (Leonardo da
Vinci) Airport. Not all the money went directly to Fatah and
the PLO; some of it was "donated" to the Center for Palestinian Studies (CPS), to the Council for the Occupied Homeland, and to the Palestinian Martyrs' Fund (PMF), but
intelligence analysts believe that most of the contributions
ended up in the Chairman's Secret Fund. "Most of these donations never reached the designated department of the PLO,"
observes a senior member of an Arab intelligence service, "but
were used according to the wishes of the chairman and Abu
Iyad for operational matters." Indeed, it is estimated that the
oil companies provided more than ten million dollars a year
to the PLO until the early 1980's. Since that time it appears
that oil company contributions are more indirect and generally go to support Palestinian organizations of a philanthropic
and scholarly nature.

OPEC (Organization of Petroleum Exporting Countries)
also anted up millions after the seizure of its headquarters in
Vienna in December 1975 by PFLP terrorists, led by the infamous Illich Ramírez Sánchez, better known as Carlos the
Jackal.[18] After a thirty-six-hour siege, the terrorists were
transported to Vienna's international airport and ultimately
to Algiers, where they ultimately surrendered and later were
released.[19] In the aftermath of the attack, Jordanian intelligence officials say that OPEC provided Wadia Haddad and his
breakaway group, the PFLP-SC, with an estimated $100 mil-
lion "to look after OPEC's interests." In addition to the money
that went directly to the PFLP-SC, it is estimated that since
1977 OPEC has paid $120 million into the Chairman's Secret

Fund. The payments, disguised as security-related expenses, continue to this day.

The rich Arab states are also contributors to the Chairman's Secret Fund. Between 1973 and 1975 alone it is believed that donations to the CSF exceeded fifty million dollars. Indeed, Saudi Arabia, Kuwait, and the Gulf states fear the PLO and have, accordingly, financed the PLO from the very beginning. The Gulf states discontinued their payments temporarily after the onset of the Lebanese civil war, but in order to secure PLO compliance with a proposed cease-fire at the Cairo summit in October 1976, they agreed to renew their "donations" and even pay back the money they'd withheld.

The seizure of the Grand Mosque at Mecca by Islamic fundamentalists on November 20, 1979, shook the Saudi government to its very core. Some observers believe that it was the single most traumatic event in that young nation's history. French GIGN (Groupement d' Intervention Gendarmerie National) counterterrorist commandos were ultimately brought in at the request of the Saudi government to assist in clearing the fundamentalists from Islam's holiest shrine. They were assisted by Jordanian commandos. The GIGN commandos arrived secretly on two aircraft, the first contingent flown to Saudi Arabia on the Concorde. They used both tear and asphyxiating gases to flush the fundamentalists from the labyrinth of tunnels beneath the Grand Mosque. When it was all over, nearly 1,000 people were dead and wounded. Of the 170 fundamentalists who surrendered to the government troops, 63 were ultimately beheaded. Contrary to published reports, the alleged Mahdi, or "final prophet," who led the operation—a religious fanatic by the name of Mohammed ibn-Abdullah Qahtani—was not killed in the last assault but rather was captured by the Saudis and brutally interrogated, despite having lost an arm. He subsequently disappeared, and it is presumed that the Saudis put him to death.

The attack on the Grand Mosque remains something of a mystery. What is known is that most of the Mahdi's followers were drawn from Bedouin tribes in southern Arabia, especially the al-Rashediya. Most of the weapons were from Libyan and Iranian military arsenals. Just before launching the attack, the rebels cried, *"Allah wa-Akbar wa-Khomeini*

Rasual Allah," instead of the traditional Islamic battle cry, *"Allah wa-Akbar wa-Muhammah Rasul Allah,"* which is indicative of Iranian Shiite involvement in the operation. Most alarming of all to the Saudi royal family was the fact that a number of members of the House of Saud were also implicated in the seizure of the Grand Mosque; at least twenty-eight high-ranking Saudis, including princes, governors, and military commanders, were quietly exiled in the aftermath of the incident.

The Saudis spent tens of millions of dollars searching for clues and information, including payments to virtually every Arab terrorist group for their cooperation or for "protection." It is estimated that the PLO, Fatah, and the PFLP all received substantial sums of money, especially since Arafat and his lieutenants were known to have some ties to the al-Rashedini-an-Iranian terrorists suspected in the attack.

But the Arab states are not the only ones that paid protection money to the PLO. Various Western European governments are suspected of having paid off the PLO, and West Germany went so far as to ask the PLO for help in dealing with the Baader-Meinhof Gang, which was terrorizing the country. Since members of the Baader-Meinhof Gang had received training in PLO camps and carried out some joint operations with the Palestinians, the West Germans apparently hoped that some kind of accommodation could be reached via the "good offices" of the PLO. As noted before, even the United States made regular payments to the PLO prior to 1982 in return for the protection of its embassies and other facilities in the Middle East, particularly in Lebanon. The PLO also agreed to provide the United States with intelligence related to the security of its operations in the Middle East and to set up an early-warning system regarding terrorist operations.

In addition to protection rackets, Arafat and Abu Iyad saw that there were enormous profits to be made in conjunction with the transportation and sale of illegal drugs. The original stimulus for becoming involved with drugs may have been the need to find an additional source of secret funds to underwrite the establishment of Black September as a covert arm of the PLO in the early 1970's. Abu Iyad, using information supplied by the PLO's intelligence unit, the Jihaz el-Razd, began hijacking drug convoys in Lebanon's Bekaa Valley. Indeed, Lebanon is a major processing area and distribution point for heroin and marijuana grown in Asia, and hashish is the principal cash crop of the Bekaa Valley, with thousands of acres devoted to its cultivation. It did not take long before Lebanon's drug lords offered the PLO a piece of the action in order to prevent the loss of further shipments. In return for Arafat's agreement not to interfere with the lucrative trade, and in some cases to provide actual protection to the drug lords and their shipments, the PLO was given 10 percent of the estimated $1.5 billion industry, netting the Chairman's Secret Fund approximately $150 million a year. The agreement that was reached meant that Arafat and the PLO would, in effect, become business partners with some of their most implacable enemies, including Jordan's Crown Prince Hassan, Hafez el-Assad's brother Rifat, and the Maronite Christian Gemayel clan.

After the collapse of the central government and the onset of chaos in Lebanon in the mid-1970's, the PLO greatly expanded its illegal operations in order to pay for the state within a state it was creating in the vacuum that had been left behind. Indeed, the Lebanese civil war provided the PLO with a golden opportunity, and Arafat and his lieutenants made the most of it. In addition to taking control of many of the major Lebanese drug routes, the PLO began levying "taxes" on ordinary businesses operating within its areas of influence and control. The PLO attached fees and levies to almost every facet of daily life. Even to drive from Beirut to the Metn Mountains required a permit, which, of course, the user had to purchase.

In northern Lebanon the PLO operated the port of Tripoli with al-Tauchid ("Islamic Unification"), the Sunni armed militia, splitting the revenues with Sheikh Sa'id Sha'aban. After the last elements of the PLO were forced out of Lebanon in 1983, Sheikh Sha'aban took over the PLO's share of the revenues, but he remains in close contact with Arafat and Abu Iyad. Despite being a Sunni Moslem, Sheikh Sha'aban appears to have a seat in the Shiite Maglis el-Shawra, or Council of Shiite Scholars, which oversees the activities of the Shiite terrorist organization Hizballah. It is not known whether he is a full member of the council or is just regularly invited to attend.[20] In addition to his being the chief point of contact between Sunni and Shiite fundamentalists, it is believed that Sha'aban serves as the PLO's chief liaison to Hizballah.

PLO gunmen also seized the ancient Phoenician ports of Tyre and Sidon and collected fees for every shipment of goods passing through either port. Higher fees were charged for contraband goods, and the PLO itself soon entered the smuggling business by selling arms, drugs, and stolen merchandise. PLO teams looted stores in Beirut, for example, and sold the goods to buyers throughout the world. All the designer clothing, for example, in a Washington, D.C., boutique operated by a Lebanese family in the early 1980's reportedly was purchased from the PLO at bargain-basement prices.

Perhaps the PLO's biggest heist was the robbery, in early 1976, of the British Bank of the Middle East, which had its worldwide headquarters in Beirut. On January 20 members of Force 17, under the command of Ali Hassan Salameh, occupied the bank by blasting through an exterior wall it shared with the Catholic Capuchin Church. Two days later a team of Corsican locksmiths and safecrackers hired by the PLO arrived in Beirut and were taken immediately to the bank, where they began work to crack the main vault. On January 24 they accomplished their mission and for the next two days looted all the money and valuables in the vault and the safe-deposit boxes. The main vault contained thousands of gold bars and millions of dollars in Lebanese and foreign currencies, as well as stock certificates and other valuables. The safe-deposit boxes were also loaded with currency, gold, jewelry, and stock certificates. So great was the volume of material carried out of the bank that it had to be hauled away in trucks. The loot was divided up, with the PLO keeping two thirds and the Corsicans receiving one third.

Once the job was completed, a chartered DC-3 landed at Beirut International Airport, and the Corsicans flew away with two hundred million dollars in gold, jewelry, and currency. Sometime in mid-March another chartered aircraft, a Bristol Britannia Series 300 four-engine turboprop, arrived in Beirut and was met by gunmen from Force 17. Under their watchful eyes, three truckloads of loot, worth close to four hundred million dollars, were loaded aboard the Britannia. In the early-morning hours, after all the loot had been loaded on board, Arafat, Abu Iyad, and Salameh arrived, and the plane departed for Geneva. The three men returned two days later on the same aircraft, after presumably depositing their loot in numbered Swiss bank accounts. Other secret accounts were maintained in Lebanon (Beirut), Cyprus (Nicosia), Greece (Athens), and West Germany (Düsseldorf).

In the following months the PLO sold many of the stocks and bonds found in the bank vault back to their original owners for twenty or thirty cents on the dollar. In many cases Arab governments and top officials were only too eager to buy back their assets since they had been illegally obtained in the first place, and disclosure of the fact that they possessed such large sums of money or owned companies doing business with their own governments would have been very embarrassing. So successful was the "fire sale" that in October 1976 a second shipment of funds and other valuables, worth an estimated $250 million, was sent to Switzerland. Once again Abu Iyad and Salameh were on board the chartered aircraft.

By contrast with some published reports, other than the British Bank of the Middle East, no major bank or financial institution in Lebanon was "cleaned out" by the PLO, Fatah, or any other organization operating under the PLO's flag. This is explained, in large measure, by the fact that virtually all the major banks had moved their cash deposits, safe-deposit boxes, and other valuables outside the country as soon as it was clear that the "troubles" afflicting Lebanon were not going to go away and, instead, were likely to escalate. Even the Bank du Liban transferred all its assets out of the country and kept on hand only those funds necessary for the transaction of ordinary business.

The erroneous reports regarding the extent of the bank robberies in Beirut during the latter half of the 1970's probably can be traced to a number of armed robberies by brigands during this period of time. Indeed, during the fourteen-year-old civil war, most large banks and virtually all their branches have been robbed, although most of the robberies were merely stickups. In addition, various armored cars, bank couriers, and wealthy citizens on their way to make substantial deposits have been robbed by criminal gangs. The haul from all these robberies, however, is estimated to be fairly modest. They were, for the most part, small operations generally conducted by rogue Palestinians or members of the various armed militias battling throughout Lebanon, like the Druze, the Sunni Murabittun, the Lebanese National Front (Maronite), and certain Shiite factions. One of the few major operations carried out, in addition to the PLO heist of the British Bank of the Middle East, was the hijacking by the Christian Forces militia of a large shipment of gold that was being shipped out of the country by a consortium of banks.

It should be noted that many major banks have shut their doors and no longer do business in Lebanon as the result of such security problems. The Bank of America closed down its operations in Beirut near the end of 1975 and referred its customers to its various branches in Western Europe. Virtually every other bank in what was once known as the banking center of the Middle East followed suit, and today only three Arab banks continue to do business in Beirut: Bank Intra, the Bank of Beirut and Riyadh, and the Commercial Bank of Lebanon.

Ironically, in 1982, when the Israelis were besieging the PLO stronghold in West Beirut, Arafat took refuge in the vault of the local branch of the Banque Nationale de Paris Internationale, which reportedly was one of the banks where he had substantial sums on deposit in Europe. In 1977, for example, Arafat had used the bank to purchase seventeen million dollars in European stock. Fearing Israeli attempts to murder him, Arafat used the vault as his operations center for five days. As the Israelis closed in on Beirut, Arafat ordered huge sums of money transferred from Lebanese banks to other banks in the Arab world and Europe, and this helped accelerate the collapse of the Lebanese pound in the mid-1980's.[21] The chairman's financial advisers were certainly more prescient than those of various Lebanese-based militias and terrorist groups that took a financial bath on the falling Lebanese pound. Once convertible at the rate of four pounds to the U.S. dollar, by late 1984 the official conversion rate was 270 to 1. The Christian Phalange saw the value of its Lebanese bank accounts, denominated in Lebanese pounds, fall from more than five hundred million to six to seven million dollars. Similarly, the Shiite Amal and Hizballah had secret Lebanese bank accounts once worth between one and two hundred million dollars, which fell in value to two to three million after the devaluation.

When the PLO pulled out of the northern port city of Tripoli, Lebanon, in 1983, under pressure from rebel Fatah forces and Syrian regulars, it is estimated that Arafat was forced to spend $300 million in a ten-day period. The money came from secret accounts controlled by Arafat ($130 million from PLO accounts and $170 million from Fatah accounts). Under pressure from the government of Tunisia, Arafat is said to have transferred as much as $200 million to Tunisian banks as a way of indicating his gratitude for that government's hospitality.[22] Brigadier Atallah Atallah (Abu Zaim) claimed that the sum was $60 million in grants and $100 million in loans. The Tunisian government, for its part, has denied that it received any kind of compensation for its hospitality to the PLO.

The PLO also paid the Tunisian government handsomely—in the form of loans and grants—for the property and services, including protection, connected with the establishment of its headquarters compound at Hammam el-Shat. In 1986 Arafat also provided Iraq with a loan of $128 million from his secret fund, as a way of compensating the Iraqis for "military facilities that were allocated to some clandestine units of the PLO."[23] Among the other loans and credits said to have been provided by the PLO to Third World countries as a way of currying political favor and support were the following: a $300 million loan to India, a $100 million loan to North Yemen to build a pipeline, a $20 million credit to the People's Republic of the Congo, a $10 million credit to Nicaragua, and an unspecified loan to Gabon.[24] In addition, Arafat is reliably reported to have provided $60 million to Lebanese President Amin Gemayel in 1985 to "facilitate" the return of the PLO to Lebanon, and another $200 million to the main Christian political party, the Katab.[25]

OTHER PLO ASSETS

In addition to the Chairman's Secret Fund, there are a variety of other cash accounts controlled directly by Arafat. Most are held in the PLO's name by the Cairo, Amman, and New York branches of the Arab Bank Ltd. These accounts are believed to total more than two billion dollars and are also used to fund

PLO covert operations, including terrorist attacks. The remaining PLO assets are salted away in other numbered accounts or invested in stocks and bonds, real estate, and even U.S. treasury bills. The PLO also has invested in corporations owned and operated by Palestinians—especially members of the PNC—living in other parts of the world, including the United States.

The PLO owns outright, or maintains a significant interest, in a wide variety of assets around the globe. Its ownership or interest is nearly always disguised and hidden from public view, and it is impossible to know whether the sums invested were from the Chairman's Secret Fund or from other secret accounts held by the PLO. In this connection, Arafat and the PLO have invested a great deal of money in media properties, including newspapers, magazines, and radio stations. Such properties allow the PLO to influence public opinion surreptitiously and are little more than propaganda organs. The PLO, for example, is the majority owner of Radio Monte Carlo,[26] which broadcasts throughout the Mediterranean and is erronously identified on a regular basis as an "independent" radio station, even by *The New York Times*. The PLO also owns radio stations in Algiers, Baghdad, and South Yemen.[27]

The PLO owns at least a dozen newspapers and magazines, including two Paris-based publications, *Fikr* (editor: Taher Abd al-Hakim) and *al-Yom al-Saba*, whose editor in chief is Bilal al-Hassan, brother of two top Arafat advisers, Hanni and Khaled al-Hassan. The main publication of the PLO is the magazine *Falestine al-Thawra*, which is edited by Ahmed al-Rahman and published in Cyprus. Three other PLO publications are also edited and printed in Cyprus: *Sawt al-Bilad* (a weekly edited by Khaled Salam), *al-Jazirah* (a weekly edited by Simon Khouri), and *Shu'un Falestinia* (a monthly edited by Sabri Jereis).

Al-Karameh, which appears in Amman, Jordan, is the monthly magazine of the Palestine Liberation Army. It is believed that the PLO owns or is the major investor in the Athens-based weekly *al-Nashra,* which was launched by Michael al-Nimri. The PLO office in Kuwait publishes a weekly newspaper, *al-Sakhra.* There is also a Palestinian news agency, known as WAFA, based in Tunis, which is operated and funded by the PLO. There are reports, not documented, that the PLO owns an interest in a variety of European and American publications that are not targeted at Arab readers, but rather are directed at mainstream audiences and designed to carry a subliminal pro-PLO message.

There are credible, although unconfirmed, reports that the PLO's real estate investments include a motel chain in the United States, a popular bar in Manhattan, and even property in California. The PLO is also believed to control various properties in Spain, France, Greece, and Great Britain. However, this cannot be documented either. Western intelligence organizations have identified a house in Larnaca (Cyprus), a villa in Nicosia (Cyprus), and a building on the island of Rhodes (Greece) as belonging to the PLO, although the deeds and registration papers are held by nominee attorneys. Most of the PLO's real estate investments are in the Middle East. An Israeli intelligence source reports that the PLO has purchased property in Jerusalem and on the West Bank. In addition to a country house in the mountains above Tripoli, Lebanon, Arafat and Abu Iyad are said personally to own a number of office buildings on the Rue Hamra in Beirut that once housed PLO offices as well as other commercial real estate in Amman and Cairo.

In 1979 the PLO once again began targeting airlines. However, this time their interest was not hijacking jetliners but buying them. After the fall of the Somoza government in Nicaragua, the PLO stepped in to assist the Sandinistas economically and militarily. The cooperation between the PLO and the Sandinistas had a long history and goes back to the late 1960's, when Sandinista guerrillas received training in Lebanon from the PFLP and other PLO units. As previously noted, in September 1970, a Sandinista skyjacker by the name of Patrick Argüello was shot to death when he and Leila Khaled attempted to hijack an El Al flight.

Shortly after the Sandinistas took power, the PLO bought a share of the national airline, Aeronica, and financed the purchase of a Boeing 727 for the company. Over the next two years the PLO's stake in Aeronica increased, and it reportedly underwrote the purchase of additional aircraft. Today Aeronica's director for operations is a former PLO operative.

The PLO is believed to be an investor in several African

airlines, and it may be the outright owner of Maldives Airways.

CONCLUSION

CIA sources estimate that the total value of all PLO accounts, investments, property holdings, and other assets is somewhere between eight and fourteen billion dollars. Whatever the precise sum, no other revolutionary organization in the world approaches the economic muscle of the PLO. Mao Zedong maintained that "Political power grows out of the barrel of a gun." For the PLO, power flows less from the barrel of a gun than from its multitudinous bank accounts. More than two decades of PLO military operations against Israel and the West have not appreciably advanced its goal of an independent Palestine. However, its massive economic resources have contributed to making the PLO a formidable political power and brought it closer to realizing its aims than ever before.

6 | Yesterday's Man: George Habash and the PFLP

G eorge Habash turned sixty-four in 1989, and the passage of time weighs heavily upon him. At an age when other men are thinking of retirement, grandchildren, and passing the afternoon sipping strong black coffee and chatting with friends, Habash is still preoccupied with the struggle for a Palestinian homeland. Though he still has dreams about the defeat of the Zionists and the destruction of Israel, in the cold light of day he admits that he and his contemporaries are unlikely to see it. "Maybe the next generation," he reflects wistfully.[1]

Although the revolutionary spirit may be willing, Habash's body isn't. The old war-horse is a sick man, and the daily struggle to overcome his physical infirmities dominates his thoughts. One side of his body is partially paralyzed, reportedly because of botched surgery he underwent in 1980 for a benign tumor in East Germany. He walks slowly, with difficulty, using two canes. He is never free from pain, both physical and mental.

He refuses to speak—even to close friends—about Bassam Abu-Sharif, whom he treated like a son and groomed as a successor. Abu-Sharif was his deputy, spokesman, and chief confidant. Even after an Israeli letter bomb exploded in Abu-

Sharif's hands in 1972, tearing away part of his face and leaving him nearly blind, Habash continued to invest his hopes for the future in the young man. That is what made Abu-Sharif's defection to Yasir Arafat's Fatah in the mid-1980's all the more painful.[2] For Habash it was the final betrayal and the one that cut deepest. After Abu-Sharif's departure, say those who know Habash, the wind went out of the old man's sails; he became brooding, detached, no longer capable of taking the initiative.

Today Habash knows that his time is rapidly passing and that younger, more energetic and aggressive men are coming to the fore to carry on the struggle: men like Feisal Husseini and Sari Nusseiba and the rest of the Shabiba, the leadership of the Intifada.

Habash passes the days in his small basement office in a highly fortified area of Damascus that serves as the headquarters of his movement, the Popular Front for the Liberation of Palestine (PFLP). On one wall is a carpet depicting the Temple Mount (Haram Ash-Sharif) and the Dome of the Rock (the Qubbat as Sakhrah), one of the holiest shrines in all Islam. There is a certain amount of irony in Habash's memento of Jerusalem since he is a Christian by birth, of Greek Orthodox extraction, though nonpracticing by all accounts. It could be said that like the nineteenth-century revolutionary theorist Mikhail Bakunin, Habash "search[ed] for God in the Revolution."[3]

Some wonder whether he still needs the intensive security that surrounds him. The Israelis reportedly long ago stopped hunting him, although it wasn't always that way. In 1973, for example, Israeli fighters intercepted a Lebanese jetliner and forced it to land in Israel, believing that Habash and his top lieutenants were on board. To the embarrassment of the Israelis, it turned out that he had changed his flight plans at the last minute.

By contrast with the ascetic Arafat, Habash has always enjoyed the "good life." Despite his infirmities, he still finds pleasure in fine food and wine and has a particular weakness for Scotch whiskey. He is the father of two daughters and sought to play more than a passing role in their lives and upbringing, though it was rarely easy. True to his medical training, he is a man of habits and precision and not an unpredictable and peripatetic "flying Dutchman," like Arafat and many of his fellow Palestinian revolutionary leaders.

THE SOFT-SPOKEN
PHYSICIAN

George Habash was born in 1925 in Palestine, in the small village of Lydia, which is now called Lod and is the site of Israel's Ben-Gurion International Airport and of one of his most spectacular terrorist operations. His father was a wheat merchant, and Habash enjoyed a comfortable childhood. Most of his formative years were spent in the Mozrara sector of Jerusalem. As a youth he dabbled in Arab nationalist politics and protested the British mandate over Palestine, to the extent that he was once jailed by British authorities. Nevertheless, he was a dutiful student and entered the American University of Beirut in 1944 to study medicine. However, the events of 1948 shattered his complacency, and he was drawn into the maelstrom of Palestinian radical politics at the university. He became a Marxist, perhaps in reaction to what he believed was Western complicity in the creation of the state of Israel. Despite his political activism, he completed his studies and was graduated in 1951.

Although he chose medicine as a career, he soon set out on a course committed to killing, rather than healing. Sometime in 1954 and 1955 he founded the Arab Nationalist Movement (ANM), which initially received support from the Egyptian government. In some respects, the grudging rivalry that still characterizes relations between Habash and Yasir Arafat may be traced back to those early days in Cairo, when ANM competed openly for influence and recruits against the General Union of Palestinian Students (GUPS), led by Arafat.

ANM, nevertheless, continued to espouse Gamal Abdel Nasser's pan-Arabist philosophy, calling for the creation of a united Arab nation that would surround and eventually destroy Israel. ANM also supported the call for Arab socialism, as articulated by Nasser. Indeed, with the birth of the Syrian and Iraqi Ba'athist parties, predicated on the ideals and ideology of Michel Aflaq, ANM served as Nasser's counterweight and continued to embrace Nasserism long after its conceptualizer had abandoned many of its tenets. The Ba'ath slogan was: "Unity, liberty, and socialism," which ANM countered with "Unity, liberty, and revenge," the revenge part referring to the destruction of Israel.

The radical politics of ANM, however, eventually brought the party into conflict with various Arab governments, and it was outlawed in Egypt. Habash and ANM were also accused of plotting to assassinate the Syrian dictator Adib Shishakli, and this incident led to Habash's arrest and incarceration for a short time in Jordan, where he was operating an ANM medical clinic. Ironically, he later was found to be part of a conspiracy to overthrow Jordan's King Hussein and forced to take refuge for some time in Syria, where he established another medical clinic. For more than a decade ANM was involved in plots and intrigues throughout the Arab world, although on the whole, the party enjoyed few real successes. Part of the problem related to its loose organization and inability to enforce party discipline on its many branches throughout the Arab world. When the local ANM branch in Aden (South Yemen) took power after the departure of the British, it immediately distanced itself from party headquarters in Amman and jettisoned its pan-Arab sentiments.

ANM cooperated with Ahmed Shukeiry's PLO and moved into open competition with Fatah for the hearts and minds of young Palestinians, at one point even accusing Fatah of being a CIA front. However, by 1966 it was clear that ANM was losing ground to Fatah, which was much more aggressive and dynamic, and Habash decided to create his own terrorist organization, the Young Avengers, despite the fact that he privately believed that any open conflict with Israel was still premature. He also established direct contact with a number of Communist countries, including Cuba, North Vietnam, and China, in an effort to enlist foreign support. Habash had been steering ANM steadily leftward ever since the breakup of the United Arab Republic in 1961, and with the formation of the Young Avengers he no longer attempted to conceal his doctrinaire Marxist orientation. Using the Young Avengers as a vehicle, Habash hoped to stake his claim as leader of the left wing of the Palestinian Revolution.

CREATION OF THE PFLP

By 1967 Habash was totally frustrated with ANM's failures, the political infighting that consumed the organization, and its relative political conservatism. With his supporters he launched the Popular Front for the Liberation of Palestine (PFLP) and adopted the political slogan "The road to Tel Aviv leads through Amman." However, in March 1968, shortly after the establishment of the PFLP, Habash was arrested in Syria, where he had gone in search of arms and munitions, and imprisoned. During his absence the PFLP began to unravel, and it became obvious that Habash's strong hand was needed if the young organization was to survive. In October 1968, for example, Ahmed Jibril broke away and started the PFLP-GC. Habash's fellow physician and PFLP member Wadia Haddad is said to have led a daring rescue mission in November to Damascus, where he and his men disguised themselves as Syrian soldiers and sprang Habash from prison. Other observers say that Habash simply cut a deal with the Syrians, agreeing to work more closely with them in the future, in exchange for his freedom, and that Haddad's mission to Damascus was staged for the benefit of the outside world.

When Habash returned to his headquarters in Amman, he found that a group of Young Turks had, for all intents and purposes, taken over the PFLP. The leaders of this group were Naif Hawatmeh and Bilal al-Hassan. The next year witnessed a series of internal clashes as Habash and his allies sought to reassert their control over the organization. When it was all over, Hawatmeh had also split ranks and left to form the Democratic Popular Front for the Liberation of Palestine (DPFLP), which later shortened its name to the Democratic Front for the Liberation of Palestine (DFLP).

In the years that followed, Habash and his operations chief, Wadia Haddad, became infamous for their bloody, but often innovative, attacks on Israel and the West. Haddad was the operational genius behind the PFLP's terrorist attacks against civil aviation. In addition to the often brilliant conceptualization and planning, it was the superb execution that contributed so much to the success of each operation. In this regard Habash and Haddad owed much to a mysterious and handsome young man by the name of Ali Shafik Ahmed Taha, who became something of a legend as Captain Kamal Rafat. Recruited in 1967 by the two physicians as a member of the PFLP, Captain Rafat was involved in virtually every PFLP operation against civil aviation until his death in 1972. He was commander in chief of the hijacking operation, from Rome to Tel Aviv, that was diverted to Algiers on July 22, 1968, the first operation designed to take the Palestinian struggle into the international arena. The hijackers were said to have believed that Israeli General Ariel Sharon, who had distinguished himself in the Sinai during the 1967 Middle East War, would be on the flight.

One of Captain Rafat's confederates was a terrorist who used the name Abu Nidal (not the same person as Sabri Khalil al-Banna) and gave directions to the pilot in the cockpit. During his debriefing later by members of the Israeli security services, the El Al pilot observed that "Abu Nidal" was very knowledgeable about aviation and might even be a pilot. Israeli authorities ultimately concluded that "Abu Nidal" had been a pilot with Gulf Air.

The Algerian government released all the non-Israeli passengers on board the El Al flight but kept the Israeli crew and passengers in custody in a barracks near the airport. The three hijackers were also detained by the Algerian government at a nearby military camp, despite efforts by George Habash, who soon arrived in Algiers, to win their freedom and to enlist the political support of the Algerian government.

In contrast with its public support for the Palestinians, the Algerian government was not happy about the hijacked aircraft's landing on its territory and suspected that it might, in reality, be an operation devised by Egyptian intelligence to embarrass Algeria. When Algeria's foreign minister, Abdel Bouteflika, met with the captive PFLP terrorists after their surrender, he accused them of serving a foreign intelligence service.

"Why did you land the plane in Algeria?" Bouteflika demanded.

"Because Algeria is a revolutionary state," came the response from one of the PFLP men.

"Algeria's revolutionary identity," Bouteflika said with a sneer, "does not need to be tested."[4]

Confronted with nearly universal international condemnation and the prospect of a boycott of Algeria by the International Federation of Air Line Pilots, Algeria capitulated six weeks later to the pressure and released the plane and the passengers and crew it was still holding. Less well known is the fact that Israel was positioning strike forces around Algeria to carry out a rescue operation. The plan called for Sayaret Matkal commandos to penetrate Algeria and make their way to the hotel where the hostages were being held after being removed from the barracks. Once they had rescued the hostages, they would rendezvous with other commandos at the airport, overwhelm the guards around the El Al plane, and use it to flee Algeria. The operation was aborted only when Algeria agreed to free the plane and the hostages. Even though the Algerian government capitulated to the Israelis and international public opinion, Captain Rafat and his colleagues had become heroes throughout the Arab world, and no effort was ever made to punish them for their deed. While still remaining a member of the PFLP, Captain Rafat subsequently became a Black September operator and coordinated PFLP input into joint operations under the auspices of Black September.

Captain Rafat resurfaced time and time again as a participant in hijackings and attacks on civil aviation, including the famous multiple hijacking in September 1970 that is described in Chapter Three. According to intelligence reports, Captain Rafat was the operational commander of the entire operation. It was this operation, part of which culminated in the Jordanian desert when three jetliners were blown up at Dawson's Field, that ultimately put into motion the Black September collision between the Palestinians and King Hussein that nearly caused the destruction of Fatah, the PFLP, and their allies.

On February 22, 1972, five of Captain Rafat's men, including Yussef al-Khatib, who had been one of his confederates during the 1968 El Al hijacking, seized a Lufthansa B-747 en route from New Delhi to Athens. The pilot landed the plane in Aden, South Yemen, where the terrorists were joined by Captain Rafat, who conducted the negotiations with Lufthansa and the West German government for the release of the plane and its passengers. On board the aircraft, but apparently unknown to the terrorists, was Joseph P. Kennedy, the nineteen-year-old son of slain Senator Robert Kennedy.[5] Although reports of the exact sum vary, Lufthansa paid a ransom of five million dollars to the terrorists and entered into an agreement providing for annual "protection" payments to the PFLP. Some intelligence officials believe that the hijacking of Lufthansa Flight 649 was a watershed in the history of the PLO and represented what amounted to a takeover of the PLO's operational apparatus by Abu Iyad. This, in turn, enabled him to coordinate closely terrorist attacks with other terrorist leaders like George Habash and Wadia Haddad.

Ten weeks later Captain Rafat carried out what was to be his final, and most brazen and dramatic, hijacking: a combined PFLP-Fatah operation hidden behind the veil of Black September. A Sabena B-707, Flight 517 from Vienna to Tel Aviv, with a stop in Athens, was seized by four heavily armed terrorists over Yugoslavia. The pilot was ordered to fly to Tel Aviv and land at Lod (Ben Gurion) International Airport. Although ostensibly acting as members of Black September, Captain Rafat's three confederates—two nurses, Rima Tannous and Therese Halaseh, and a Syrian Druze named Abdel Aziz al-Atrash—all had received training prior to the operation in a Fatah camp at Sidon, Lebanon.[6] Today it is known that operation was planned by Ali Hassan Salameh, with the full complicity and support of the PLO's leadership. After all, in addition to being Black September's chief of operations, Salameh was Abu Iyad's deputy.

On May 9, 1972, a full day after Captain Rafat and his band of terrorists took over the flight, Israel commandos from the Sayaret Matkal, under the command of Lieutenant Colonel Ehud Barak, stormed the plane.[7] Captain Rafat and al-Atrash were killed in the fire fight and the two women were captured, although Therese Halaseh was wounded. Five passengers and three soldiers were wounded in the assault, and one passenger later succumbed as a result of her wounds.

During their subsequent trial by a military court, both

women admitted to being members of Fatah. Tannous poured out a story of degradation and corruption to the court, describing how she had been an orphan raised by nuns, who ultimately guided her into nursing. Her decline into terrorism, she said, came after she had been raped by a young man and lost her self-respect, whereupon she became the mistress of a Fatah doctor. He got her hooked on drugs and forced her to sleep with numerous Fatah men, threatening to withhold the drugs or to beat her if she refused to comply. So total was his control over her life, she claimed, that she raised no complaint when he enrolled her in a terrorist unit for training.[8] Both women were handed life sentences on August 14, 1972, but were later released from jail during a major exchange of prisoners between the PLO and Israel.

Captain Rafat's influence didn't end with his death. For more than a decade and a half, young terrorists trained by him or by his pupils have continued to make war on world's civil aviation system.

HABASH THE "INTERNATIONALIST"

More than fifty Palestinian refugee camps are scattered throughout the Arab world. All are graphic testimony of the neglect demonstrated by other Arab governments to the plight of the Palestinians. Most are squalid and unhealthy places, with fetid water supplies and sewage running in the narrow streets. The only escape is television, and the roofs of the cramped huts that compose most of the camps bristle with TV antennaes and a vast cobweb of wiring that carries electricity and telephone service. In such camps young Palestinians mature to adulthood with little hope and few prospects, their bitterness and frustration fed by a steady stream of propaganda from the various Palestinian fedayeen organizations and Arab governments. Like big-city slums, the camps are breeding grounds for crime and violence and provide the PLO with most of its rank-and-file recruits.

Nahr al-Bard and Badawi are two of the many Palestinian

refugee camps. Situated along the banks of a small river in Lebanon, which is fed by the melting snows from the Jabal Lubnan mountain range, both camps are densely populated, with between fifteen to twenty thousand people packed into each.

However, it is not as a testimonial of the Palestinian plight that the two teeming camps have become world-famous. Rather it is because during the 1970's Nahr al-Bard and Badawi were synonymous with international terrorism.[9] Nahr al-Bard was a Black September stronghold that was raided by the Israelis in February 1973. As a result, the camp's name was used as the code word for the Black September execution of the U.S. ambassador and two other diplomats in Khartoum (see Chapter Eleven).

During the second week of May 1972, groups of young "tourists" began arriving at Khalde (Beirut) International Airport. From all outward appearances they were ordinary travelers and blended in with the tens of thousands of other visitors who flocked annually to the city popularly known as the Paris of the Middle East before the onset, in 1975, of the bloody violence that has torn Lebanon apart and reduced most of Beirut to rubble. Unbeknownst to Lebanese authorities, virtually all the young "tourists" traveled on forged passports.

They had been invited to Lebanon by George Habash, who wanted to create the first "terrorist summit," which he hoped would unite revolutionary elements from all over the world in a common front against Zionism and Western imperialism.[10] He had sent secret emissaries around the globe to sound out the leadership of various organizations, and most had responded favorably. Before his death at the hands of Mossad operatives on June 28, 1973, Mohammed Boudia, an actor and theatrical manager who, in reality, was a Black September operative, made contact with almost every major terrorist group in the world, especially those in Europe. He was assisted in this endeavor by Hanni al-Hassan. Many terrorist groups had other direct links to Habash. Habash also received assistance from the Soviet Union via the chief of its Middle East KGB station, who was attached to its embassy in West Beirut, with whom he maintained regular contact. Among the organizations that sent representatives were the Japanese Red Army, the Iranian Liberation Front, the Turkish Popular Liberation Army, the Irish Republican Army (Provos), and the West German Baader-Meinhof Gang (Red Army Faction).

After arriving in Lebanon, the foreign terrorists made their way to an isolated and heavily guarded two-story building on the outskirts of the Badawi camp, where they were greeted by Habash, Haddad, and three representatives of Black September: Abu Iyad, Ali Hassan Salameh, and a third individual known only as Shemali. Afterward they got down to business, and Habash described his conception of terrorist network girdling the globe that would facilitate the exchange of intelligence, weapons, safe houses, training, and other logistical support. If Black September, for example, wanted to carry out an operation in West Germany, Habash explained, wouldn't it be easier and less conspicuous for Baader-Meinhof operatives to collect the necessary intelligence and lay the groundwork for the attack? In return, the PFLP and Black September were ready to open up their training camps to recruits from the Baader-Meinhof Gang and other terrorist groups and to provide them with weapons and logistical support. Later, as a result of an agreement with Moscow, Cuban advisers were sent to the camps to assist in the training.

In addition, Habash proposed a united front against what he viewed as the globe's reactionary and imperialist regimes, thereby increasing pressure on the West and its allies in the Third World. Many of the organizations represented at the Badawi conference took Habash up on his offer, and the subsequent years saw vastly increased cooperation between international terrorists and even a number of joint operations involving terrorists from several different groups. As a result of his success, Habash became the leader of the so-called internationalist element within the PLO, which maintained that it was more important in the long run to the Arab world for reactionary regimes like Saudi Arabia and Jordan (under King Hussein's Hashemite dynasty) to be overthrown and be replaced with "progressive" regimes than to realize the establishment of a Palestinian ministate. During the 1970's Habash was also the primary moving force behind attacks directed at the United States and the West. His chief allies and fellow "internationalists" were Abu Iyad, Ali Hassan Salameh (who, despite his close relationship with Arafat, took a different doctrinal approach), Wadia Haddad, and Hanni al-Hassan, who was to become the PLO's first "ambassador" to Ayatollah Khomeini's regime in Teheran.

By contrast, the nationalist faction, which saw the establishment of a Palestinian state as its primary and in some cases exclusive goal, was led by Arafat, who was supported by Abu Jihad, Farouk Qadoumi, Naif Hawatmeh, and others. Today, despite the death of Abu Jihad, who was the power behind Arafat and served as his chief link to the rank and file, the nationalist faction appears to have won out. It is Arafat's vision, not Habash's, that is defining the PLO's present course.

Habash reportedly cannot stand Arafat personally and regards him as a "clown." He makes fun of Arafat's posturing and the way he dresses. Just as he once derided Arafat's omnipresent sunglasses, Habash now finds it amusing that Arafat, whom he speaks disparagingly of as a military commander, is rarely seen without his checked keffiyah and military uniform.

Habash is said to have once observed that if his first name hadn't been George, the fate of the Palestinian Revolution would have been far different. His remark was indicative of his long-standing rivalry with Arafat and an acknowledgment of the deep Moslem fundamentalist roots of Fatah and the PLO. Despite the fact that Habash now operates under the umbrella of the PLO and has provided crucial support to Arafat at various times, by all accounts he still doesn't fully trust the PLO chairman. Moreover, there is more than a tinge of jealousy in Habash's statement. He was, after all, a significant political-military leader of the Palestinian Revolution long before Arafat. Habash is said to believe that if he had been born a Moslem, hence named something like Mohammed, he would have been the natural leader of the armed struggle and the most likely candidate to have ascended to the chairmanship of the PLO.

In a recent interview Habash indicated that despite his misgivings over the concessions Arafat has given away to secure his present dialogue with the United States, he has no intention of breaking with the PLO. "In the past," he noted, "the Popular Front generally remained within the framework of the PNC and the PLO Central Committee whenever we disagreed with the executive leadership of the PLO on a decisive point like the Resolution 242."[11] Nevertheless, he is outspoken

in his belief that "the PLO leadership is entertaining illusions" regarding the possibility of obtaining a negotiated settlement of its grievances. He blames the problem on the fact
that the "bourgeoisie has assumed a leading and influential
position" with the Palestinian Revolution and, by implication,
the PLO.[12]

Habash vows to maintain the armed struggle and is critical
of those who believe that the Intifada is a new and more
advanced stage of the Palestinian Revolution. "We will continue struggling to change the political course and steer it in
the direction of a patriotic stance which is firm in its hostility
to the Zionist entity and imperialism. . . . The rifle has paved
the way for the stone. We can never look upon the stone as an
alternative to the rifle. In the same way the rifle has paved the
way for the stone, the stone is supposed to pave the way for
a new wave of escalated armed struggle."[13]

7 | *Ahmed Jibril and the PFLP-GC*

For Ahmed Jibril, the mistaken shootdown of an Iranian jetliner by the United States in the summer of 1988 was too good to be true. His terrorist organization, the Popular Front for the Liberation of Palestine—General Command, was nearly broke. Libya had cut off its $20 million to $25 million annual payment to the PFLP-GC, leaving only a small stipend from Syria. Operations were rapidly grinding to a halt. Jibril had four hundred to six hundred men under arms and they had to be fed, clothed, and sheltered.

Desperate for funds, Jibril had made the rounds of the radical regimes in the Middle East, pleading his case. It had been a humiliating experience. No one had offered any help, not even the Iranians.

But after the downing of the Iranian jetliner by the U.S.S. *Vincennes,* with the loss of all 290 on board, Jibril decided to take another pass at the Iranians. In view of the tragedy, they just might reconsider. After all, for a price Jibril could deliver vengeance.

Within days of the tragedy in the Persian Gulf, Jibril made contact with the Iranian Revolutionary Guards (Pasdaran) headquarters in Baalbek, the largest city in Lebanon's Bekaa

Valley and, since the expulsion of the PLO from Beirut, the terrorist capital of the world. More than a thousand heavily armed Revolutionary Guards had held the ancient city in their iron grip since the early 1980's. Countless terrorist attacks, including the 1983 bombings of the U.S. Embassy in Beirut and the marine barracks at Beirut International Airport, had either originated in Baalbek or been aided and abetted by Hizballah (Party of God) fanatics, who worked closely with the Revolutionary Guards in the Bekaa. Despite the Iranian presence, Baalbek and the surrounding region are totally under the control of the Syrian Army. Little, if anything, happens without Syrian knowledge or involvement.

Jibril's offer to the Revolutionary Guards was simple and straightforward: For a price he and the PFLP-GC would plan and execute an appropriate terrorist attack against the United States in retaliation for the Airbus shootdown. Knowing that the Iranians had an appreciation for symmetry, he indicated that a U.S. jetliner, preferably a Boeing 747, would be the target of choice.

According to intercepts of communications between Teheran and the Iranian Embassy in Beirut, Jibril also got in touch with the Iranian ambassador to Lebanon, Ahmad Dastmalchiyan, and apparently made the same offer. Aware of the fragmented nature of power in the Iranian government, Jibril apparently was afraid to leave any stone unturned, and a top PFLP-GC aide also was dispatched to make yet another pitch to Beirut-based representatives of Hizballah.

It didn't take long for the Iranians to get back to Jibril. They were interested and wanted to know more. Send someone to Teheran, they instructed, someone who can speak with authority.

THE CONSPIRACY IS LAUNCHED

For the sensitive job of cutting a deal with the Iranians, Jibril chose a trusted forty-three-year-old member of the central committee of the PFLP-GC, Hafeth el-Dalkamuni Abu Muhammad. Born in Nazareth into a poor Sunni Moslem family, Dalkamuni joined one of the predecessor organizations to the PFLP-GC in the mid-1960's.

In December 1967, Dalkamuni was part of a terrorist squad that penetrated Israel and was captured by the Israelis. He was tried and sentenced to a long jail term. But after serving more than a decade in prison, he was released as part of a POW exchange between the Israelis and the PFLP-GC in 1979. After returning to the fold, Dalkamuni had become Jibril's most trusted terrorist "operator" by 1980. Among his many responsibilities, it is known that he took part in negotiating another prisoner exchange between the Israelis and the PFLP-GC in the wake of the 1982 Israeli invasion of Lebanon. He also headed a PFLP-GC delegation to Geneva in 1984 and 1985 that negotiated an exchange of prisoners with the Israelis. Around 1987, he dropped out of sight, and Western intelligence sources speculate that he spent much of the time in Europe setting up the infrastructure for future PFLP-GC terrorist operations. This included the recruitment of Palestinian students, building up a network of safe houses, and the collection of intelligence.

In the early 1980's, he had been selected as the PFLP-GC's chief liaison with the pro-Iranian and Shiite factions in Lebanon, and therefore was Jibril's natural choice for conducting the negotiations in Teheran regarding the planned retaliation. In July 1988, Dalkamuni traveled to Teheran, where he met with his old friend Machtashimi Four, Iran's interior minister, who was responsible for the country's security services and intelligence apparatus. Four had been Iran's ambassador to Damascus in the early 1980's. He had left Syria after having lost an arm and an eye when a letter bomb exploded in his hands. The bomb had apparently been mailed to him by Israeli agents, in retaliation for his involvement with Hizballah and Revolutionary Guards operations against Israel.

Dalkamuni was observed by at least three intelligence services in Teheran: those of Israel, Iraq, and the United States. Four and Dalkamuni rapidly reached agreement in principle on the attack against the United States, and follow-on operational meetings were scheduled. It was decided that they

would be held at Iranian-Shiite strongholds in the Bekaa
Valley during the months of July and August. In payment
for the PFLP-GC's services, Four, on behalf of the Iranian
government, agreed to make up the annual PFLP-GC fiscal
shortfall. To bind the agreement, as well as underwrite the
cost of the operation against the United States, the Iranians
transferred approximately two million dollars to the PFLP-
GC. The balance was to be paid after the operation had been
successfully completed.

THE OPERATION

In September 1988, Dalkamuni surfaced in West Germany
and immediately was detected by agents of Israel's Mossad.
The Israelis tipped off West German authorities, who ultimately arrested Dalkamuni and twelve other PFLP-GC operators, after raiding PFLP-GC safe houses. Despite the fact that
the West Germans discovered two fully assembled bombs with
barometric detonators set for thirty-one thousand feet, which
were clearly designed to be used against jetliners, they failed
to mobilize quickly to head off a disaster. It was to be merely
the first of numerous West German mistakes that doomed Pan
Am Flight 103 and impeded the subsequent investigation.

Despite their discovery of a large stock of weapons and explosives, including eleven pounds of the Czech plastic explosive Semtex, in the terrorist safe houses, the West German
authorities released all PFLP-GC members but Dalkamuni
and Abdel Ghandanfar. Ghandanfar is believed to be an
Iranian, although he doesn't appear under that or any other
name in any of the major data banks of Western intelligence
agencies. The West Germans said they had insufficient evidence to hold the others.

What the West Germans did not know was that in the
Frankfurt suburbs the terrorists had yet another safe house
that had not been raided, as well as at least one other bomb
and additional weapons. All of the PFLP-GC operators who
were released immediately went underground and most

slipped out of the country, returning to either Lebanon or Syria. In addition to the two jailed members of the organization, two other members remained behind: a bomb technician and a Palestinian known in intelligence slang as a "charmer." The charmer's job was to recruit someone who could be duped into carrying the bomb aboard the target aircraft.

It is still not known authoritatively how the bomb got aboard the plane. Suspicion has centered on two young women who died in the blast, both of whom had Arab "boyfriends," and on Khalid Jaafar, a twenty-one-year-old Arab-American from Dearborn, Michigan. Investigators believe that Jaafar was a "mule," or drug courier, who frequently smuggled heroin from the Bekaa Valley into the United States, and could have been given a bomb instead of drugs. In addition, authorities are still not ruling out the possibility that one of the women might have been deceived into carrying a "Christmas present" to her family back in the States.

As soon as the bomb technician was sure that the bomb was working properly and the "package" had been delivered, the two PFLP-GC operators departed Germany, at least initially for Libya and Algeria. On December 21, four days before Christmas, Pan Am Flight 103, with 259 people on board, left London's Heathrow Airport. As it reached cruising height, thirty-one thousand feet, it exploded in midair. Investigators speculate that the blast and subsequent turbulence separated the nose and tail from the main part of the fuselage and wings. Both the nose section and tail were later found relatively intact, but the main body of the Boeing 747 landed in the village of Lockerbie, Scotland. The aircraft's fuel tanks were nearly full and the wings and fuselage, already in flames, exploded upon impact, destroying a number of homes and killing eleven people on the ground. So intense was the heat from the burning jet fuel that virtually nothing remained of the people or the main fuselage. Residents compared the fire and devastation to the effects of an atomic bomb.

Two days after Pan Am 103 went down, the Iranian Embassy in Beirut received a communication from the Interior Ministry in Teheran, which was intercepted. In this message, Teheran congratulated the ambassador on a "successful operation" and gave instructions to hand over the rest of the funds promised to the PFLP-GC.

BOMBS R US

In the 1970's Jibril had carried out several operations against Western jetliners and certainly was not a novice when it came to doing so. On February 21, 1970, Jibril's men secreted a bomb aboard a Swissair jetliner en route from Zurich to Tel Aviv, killing all forty-seven people on board. Nearly a year later, on January 9, 1971, another tragedy was narrowly averted when Israeli security personnel discovered a Peruvian girl about to board a London-to-Tel Aviv El Al flight with a valise filled with explosives. It turned out that she had been duped into carrying the valise and was an unwitting accomplice in the operation.

Finally, on August 16, 1972, a tape recorder filled with explosives exploded in the cargo bay of an El Al B-707 jetliner traveling from Rome to Tel Aviv with 148 people on board. However, because of recent reinforcement to the walls of the cargo bay, the jetliner was able to return safely to Rome with only a crack in the rear door and a hole in the skin of the aircraft. Once again it turned out that Jibril's operatives had used romance to get the bomb aboard. In this case two British women vacationing in Italy had become romantically involved with a pair of PFLP-GC operatives, Adnam Ali Hasham and Ahmed Zaid. Posing as Iranians, Hasham and Zaid prevailed on the women to fly to Israel, vowing to meet them in Jerusalem after they had picked up some money in Teheran. The men paid for the women's tickets and gave them the device—containing two hundred grams of explosive triggered by a barometric detonator—which later blew up on board the aircraft. The two terrorists were later apprehended, but in what became a pattern over the years, the Italian government could not muster sufficient courage to prosecute them. They were released from custody on the grounds that the bomb "was not adequate to destroy the airliner" and later skipped the country.[1]

Ahmed Jibril was born in 1936 in the village of Yazur, near Tel Aviv. Together with the other Arab inhabitants, he and his family fled Yazur in 1948. They took temporary refuge in Beirut and later moved to Damascus. Jibril became a Syrian citizen and served in the Syrian Army, as an officer in the engineer corps. During the period of unification between Syria and Egypt as the United Arab Republic (1958–61), he was tapped as a potential candidate for the new combined intelligence service. However, the Egyptians rejected him as a "Communist" and forced him to resign from the Syrian military. He remained in Damascus, and there are reports that he did some work during this period for the Deuxième Bureau, the Syrian intelligence service.

THE PLF: JIBRIL JOINS THE STRUGGLE

As the euphoria accompanying the independence of Algeria swept through the Arab world in 1962, young Palestinian militants formed a plethora of new revolutionary organizations dedicated to the "liberation" of Palestine. Each claimed to have the formula for translating the Algerian experience into a successful struggle against the hated Zionists. Among the organizations that appeared in Beirut were the Arab Front for the Liberation of Palestine, the Palestinian Revolutionary Movement, and the Palestinian Association Command. The Palestinian refugee camps saw the rise of the Organization of Palestine's Army, the Palestinian-Arab Fedayeen, the Red Palm, and the Black Hand. In Damascus, in the fall of 1962, the Front of Palestine's Rebels and the Palestinian Liberation Front were born.

Most of the organizations were longer on rhetoric than action, and after a few meetings, the printing of brochures, and a public rally or two, they disappeared. The Palestinian Liberation Front (PLF), however, was the exception. Founded by former Captain Ahmed Jibril and two of his friends, Ali Bushnak (a relative of Jibril's who died of a heart attack during the Black September crisis of 1970) and Fadel Sharuru (who is the PFLP-GC's spokesman today), the PLF steadily gathered momentum as its numbers swelled. Jibril recruited members from the Palestinian refugee camps around Damascus as well as from those in Jordan and Kuwait. With the cooperation and support of Syria's intelligence services and its ruling Ba'ath party, Jibril and his colleagues were permitted to set up training facilities for their recruits, the largest at the Yarmuk refugee camp near Damascus.

Despite their outward support for the Palestinian militants, however, within the Syrian government and the Ba'ath party there was real concern over the issue of Palestinian terrorism. Some circles feared that Palestinian terrorist strikes against Israel would precipitate Israeli retaliation against Syria, which would lead inevitably to war, a war that Syria could not win. Nevertheless, the PLF and other Palestinian fedayeen organizations enjoyed the support of Michel Aflaq, the Syrian Christian writer who was the chief ideologue of the Ba'ath movement.

After the collapse of unification efforts between Syria and Egypt, mutual suspicion and bitterness replaced the goodwill that previously existed between the two nations. At the behest of their Syrian intelligence masters, Jibril and some of his men infiltrated into Egypt and joined the underground that was actively working against the Nasser regime. In 1963 Jibril was captured by the Egyptian Muchabarat (intelligence service) and served some time in prison before finally being deported to Beirut. From Beirut he returned to Damascus, where he devoted his full energies to building up the PLF and conducting operations against Israel.

In order to control and channel Palestinian revolutionary fervor, the Syrian government sought influence within the various fedayeen organizations, in some cases by means of money and support but in other instances by murdering or subverting an organization's leadership and substituting its own agents and proxies. Such efforts were not always successful. The Deuxième Bureau, for example, assigned one of its agents, Captain Yussef Ur'aabi, to gain influence in and ultimate control over Fatah. When Ur'aabi moved prematurely and declared himself the new chief of Fatah in February 1966, he was hunted down and killed inside a Palestinian refugee camp near Damascus by agents of Yasir Arafat. Indeed, during this period the Syrians used the PLF as a counterweight to siphon off men and matériel from the PLO, which was still led by the ineffectual Ahmed Shukeiry, and to advance their

own agenda, such as terrorist operations against the Hashemite kingdom of Jordan. So effective were these operations
that King Hussein was frightened into seeking an accommodation with Haj Amin al-Husseini, the former grand mufti of
Jerusalem and the man behind the assassination of his grandfather, King Abdullah (Abdullah Ibn Hussein al-Hashemi). In
addition, the Syrians did everything in their power to see that
the PLF's claims as the legitimate military arm of the Palestinian revolution would appear more valid than those of Fatah
and other Palestinian organizations.

The PLF, therefore, continued to prosper because of its close
relationship to the Syrian government and its willingness to
take orders from Damascus. From 1966 to 1969 Jibril was
"operated" by Syria's intelligence chief, Colonel Abed al-
Karim Jundi. So as to minimize potentially dangerous clashes
with the Israeli Army, Jibril and the PLF were restricted to
operating from a base in Syria near the Jordanian, not Israeli,
border. Each operation against Israel was coordinated in advance with the Syrian regional military commander, Syrian
field security elements, and Syria's military intelligence apparatus. The Syrian government also provided the PLF with
arms and training, and though it numbered no more than 150
men at this time, the PLF rapidly evolved as one of the most
technically proficient Palestinian terrorist groups, adept at
hitting Israeli infrastructure targets (water, electricity, transportation, etc.). In October 1966 the PLF carried out two operations against Israel—the sabotage of a water pumping
station in the upper Galilee and a bomb blast that severed the
rail link between Jerusalem and Tel Aviv, although credit for
the attacks was claimed by the "Abed al-Kader al-Husseini"
organization.[2]

BIRTH OF THE PFLP-GC

In the aftermath of the 1967 Six-Day War the PLF merged
with the forces of Dr. George Habash to form the Popular
Front for the Liberation of Palestine (PFLP). For Jibril it was
a difficult decision, and for some time he considered joining

Fatah; but in the end Habash seemed to present a better alternative. Not only were both men Marxists, but their individual weaknesses were balanced by each other's strengths. Unlike Habash, who had no real military experience, Jibril was a professional military man who had run operations inside Israel. He had a small but well-trained and equipped force of terrorists/commandos. Habash, on the other hand, was a capable political leader with substantial financial resources, who was backed by a political party (the Arab Nationalist Movement, or ANM) and supported by a number of Arab governments.

Egypt's Gamal Abdel Nasser became the principal military and financial backer of the newly formed PFLP as a way of checking the growing power and influence of Fatah. However, Jibril could not adjust to the anti-Syrian line promoted by the ANM and the Egyptians, and within months of the merger considerable friction had developed between Habash and Jibril. When Habash was jailed by the Syrians in 1968, Jibril demanded that the PFLP adopt a more conciliatory posture toward Syria as a way of solving the dispute. His views were rejected. In October he was summarily dismissed as military commander of the PFLP. He responded by breaking completely with the PFLP and, with those still loyal to him, setting up a new organization, known as the Popular Front for the Liberation of Palestine—General Command (PFLP-GC). Although he looked to Damascus rather than Cairo for support, his political and military philosophy remained almost identical to Habash's. They both viewed the armed struggle for Palestine as producing the vanguard for a broader revolution throughout the Arab world, which would topple the conservative and traditionalist regimes allied with the West. Only when the so-called nonprogressive Arab governments had been swept away, they maintained, was there any real hope for Arab unity. Thus, unlike many other Palestinian leaders, both Jibril and Habash believed that non-Palestinians should actively be recruited as members of their organizations.

Both the PFLP and the PFLP-GC initially vied with Fatah for control of the PLO but failed—over time—to make any headway. At the meeting of the Palestinian National Council in 1969, out of 105 total seats, Jibril's PFLP-GC was awarded

4 seats, Habash's PFLP got 8 seats, and Fatah received 33 seats. The ratio between the three organizations remained roughly the same even after the PNC had quadrupled in size.

Jibril's personal animus toward Yasir Arafat may be traced to this period. He hates Arafat with a passion, both personally and ideologically. He views Arafat as an accommodationist, interested only in realizing the goal of a Palestinian state, not as a real revolutionary committed to Arab unity and the destruction of nonprogressive regimes. Arafat, he believes, is a toady for the conservative oil-rich states that provide so much funding to the PLO. On several occasions Jibril has tried to have Arafat assassinated, but every attempt has failed.

Arafat has responded in kind to Jibril's threats and opposition. When the PLO held sway in Lebanon prior to 1982, Fatah gunmen often raided Jibril's camps, disarmed his men, and confiscated their weapons. In 1982, just prior to the Israeli invasion of Lebanon, when Arafat learned that Jibril was going to try to disrupt the cease-fire agreement negotiated by U.S. envoy Philip Habib (with considerable Saudi assistance) by carrying out a major attack against targets in northern Israel, Fatah's Intelligence and Security Apparatus (ISA) moved against all of Jibril's camps and bases in Lebanon. The PFLP-GC's plans were disrupted, its weapons caches were confiscated, and Jibril was warned to stay on the sidelines and adhere to Arafat's leadership.

During the Israeli siege of West Beirut, both Arafat and Jibril were trapped in the shattered city. Jibril used this period to undermine Arafat's leadership and to foment the rebellion that broke out in 1983 within the PLO. While Fatah and other large Palestinian organizations were forced by the Israelis to withdraw from Beirut, Jibril ordered his men to go underground, and most remained in the city, even though he himself was forced to leave. In the bitter fighting around Tripoli the following year, Jibril's men stood shoulder to shoulder with the Syrian regulars besieging Arafat's remaining forces in Lebanon. During the struggle Jibril boasted to his men that he would kill Arafat with his bare hands. The open conflict between the PLO/Fatah and the PFLP-GC continued inside the Palestinian refugee camps in Lebanon until around 1988. At that time Abu Musa and his pro-Syrian elements took over control of all of the camps.

The PFLP-GC fragmented over the Syrian invasion of Lebanon in 1976, with the Abbas-Yaqub faction breaking away to form the Palestinian Liberation Front, resurrecting the name of Jibril's old organization. Yet another split in the PFLP-GC occurred in 1983, when Abu Jaber, the chief of "Central Security," and approximately 100 to 150 supporters, broke away and joined Colonel Hawari's Special Operations Group, which is part of Fatah.

TIES TO SYRIA AND LIBYA

The PFLP-GC has traditionally been supported by both Syria and Libya. It is headquartered in the Rehan sector of Damascus and uses Syrian military facilities, especially the 17 September camp at Ein Saheb, for training and launching operations against Israel and the West. In preparation for a hang glider attack on Israel in November 1987, Jibril was permitted to use a deserted Syrian Army base on the road between Homs and Damascus to train his terrorists. The Syrians also gave him the East German hang gliders used in the operation as well as made arrangements for East German flying instructors to teach Jibril's men how to operate them.

Syria, moreover, provides the PFLP-GC with weapons, logistical support, intelligence, and false documents. The PFLP-GC's forces are divided into an artillery unit, a company-size unit outfitted with rocket launchers, a small naval force, and a semiregular army regiment. The PFLP-GC also maintains a number of bases in Lebanon. The bases are located in Tripoli, Sidon, inside the Sabra and Shatilla refugee camps in West Beirut, near Beirut International Airport, and at al-Na'imah, near Damour. The al-Na'imah base, which is employed as a staging area for raids on Israel, was the target of an Israeli military operation on December 9, 1988, which left at least twenty PFLP-GC men dead. Three PFLP-GC commanders were wounded in the raid. Jibril claimed that Israel, the United States, Yasir Arafat, and Egyptian President Hosni Mubarak were behind the raid.

Libya provided the PFLP-GC with money for operations,

salaries, and arms not available from the Syrians. In addition, Qaddafi has made available to Jibril both training and R&R facilities in the Benghazi area. In an interview with a Lebanese newspaper Jibril described the support he and other Palestinian groups received from the Libyans: "I would like to stress again the support of our Libyan brothers, who supply us with weapons and equipment. They give not only to the General Command but to all the groups of the Palestinian resistance including Fatah and the Liberation Movement. The quantities are such that we are not dependent on any other Arab support. I estimate the value of this supply, without exaggeration, by hundreds of millions of dollars and this on top of grants and other help."[3] Jibril went on to say that Libya was also sending volunteers to fight with the PFLP-GC ("hundreds of them are with us right now") and that some of them had already been killed in action in southern Lebanon.[4] Jibril, in turn, repaid Qaddafi in 1987 by sending a small militia battalion of PFLP-GC men (two to three hundred) to Libya to assist Qaddafi in his war in Chad. Although they trained with Libyan units and participated in exercises, the PFLP-GC contingent never saw action in the Sahara against French and Chadian forces.

Interestingly, in September 1988 Muammar Qaddafi, who finally reached an uneasy peace with Arafat, attempted to facilitate a reconciliation between Arafat and two of his leading adversaries, Ahmed Jibril and the commander in chief of the Fatah Provisional Command (FPC), Abu Musa, which presumably would have resulted in both organizations returning to the PLO and accepting Arafat's nominal leadership. The reconciliation never got off the ground as both leaders refused to meet with Arafat, despite the fact that all three men were in Tripoli. Indeed, in early 1988 Qaddafi cut off the PFLP-GC's annual $20 million to $25 million stipend.

Every PFLP-GC operation against Israel is coordinated by Jibril with Syria's intelligence chiefs. He meets regularly, for example, with Brigadier Kanaan, head of Syria's intelligence services in Lebanon. Jibril's primary handler, however, is General Ali Duba, Syria's chief of intelligence and special operations.

As a result of contacts established through Brigadier Ghazi Kanaan, the PFLP-GC has also developed close ties to the

This innocent-looking doll's head, which was found in a PLO bunker in Lebanon in 1982, was actually made of plastic explosive. *From the authors' personal collection*

Weapons captured from Palestinian terrorists by the Israelis in July 1988 *From the authors' personal collection*

Naif Hawatmeh, chief of the Democratic Front for the Liberation of Palestine (DFLP), a pro-Soviet group with close ties to Syria. The DFLP is a member of the PLO. *From the authors' personal collection*

PLO sticker showing Arafat and Abu Jihad before the Dome of the Rock in Jerusalem. *From the authors' personal collection*

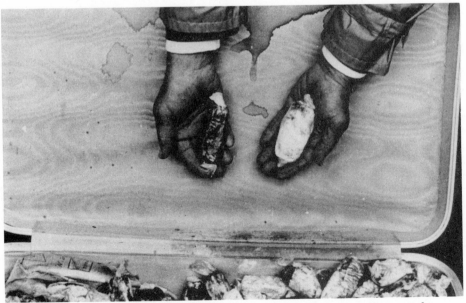

Shipment of PLO plastic explosive, disguised to look like marzipan candy, confiscated by authorities at an airport in Cyprus. The telltale "sweating" of the explosive (see stains on bag) tipped off authorities. *From the authors' personal collection*

Abdul Aziz Shaheen, one of the leaders of the Fatah's Western Section. The forty-nine-year-old Shaheen, who currently resides in Baghdad, has been involved in the planning and execution of many terrorist attacks on Israel. *From the authors' personal collection*

Ahmed Jibril, head of the Popular Front for the Liberation of Palestine-General Command (PFLP-GC), and mastermind of the plot to destroy Pan Am 103. Jibril's organization, which presently is not part of the PLO, has carried out dozens of bloody terrorist attacks during the past two decades. *From the authors' personal collection*

Rare photo of Abu Hul, the fifty-year-old Fatah intelligence chief. A highly regarded intelligence professional, Abu Hul has—for the most part—stayed out of the internal quarrels within the PLO. *From the authors' personal collection*

George Habash, the physician-turned-terrorist leader of the Popular Front for the Liberation of Palestine (PFLP), a member organization of the PLO. Although in ill health, Habash remains one of the most radical PLO leaders. *From the authors' personal collection*

Abu Abbas (Mohammed Zaiden Abbas), leader of one of the three organizations that call themselves the Palestine Liberation Front (PLF). Abbas planned the seajacking of the *Achille Lauro* cruise ship. He was aboard the EgyptAir jetliner forced to land by U.S. warplanes at a NATO airbase in Sicily, but was permitted to escape by the Italian government. *From the authors' personal collection*

Abu Jihad (Khalil Ibrahim Machmud al-Wazir), the former military chieftan of the PLO. Abu Jihad was generally considered the second most powerful man in the organization until his death at the hands of Israeli commandos in April 1988. *From the authors' personal collection*

Abu Daoud (Mohammed Daoud Machmud Auda), who was the overall operational commander of Black September's attack at the Munich Olympics. Captured by the Jordanians, during his interrogation he described the Black September's covert links to Fatah and Arafat. After being shot and seriously wounded in Warsaw in the late 1970s, he has disappeared back into the shadows. He has been spotted in recent years in Egypt and Jordan. *From the authors' personal collection*

The only published picture of Hafez Machmed Kassem al-Dalkamuni, a leader of the PFLP-GC, who played a key role in the bombing of Pan Am 103. Dalkamuni is currently being held in a West German prison. *From the authors' personal collection*

Above, Arafat leaving Beirut in August 1982, being shielded by his bodyguards. This photo was taken secretly by an Israeli intelligence operative.
An Israeli defense ministry official gave a copy of this photo to U.S. special
envoy Philip Habib to demonstrate that Israeli commandos had Arafat in
their gunsights and did not "take him out." *From the authors' personal
collection*

Left, rare photo of Abu Zaim (Brigadier Atallah Atallah), which was obtained by an intelligence service. It
may have been a passport photo. Abu
Zaim is the former chief of ISA and
led a revolt against Arafat. *From the
author's personal collection*

Iranian Pasdaran (Revolutionary Guards) and to certain Iranian elements in Lebanon. Recent intelligence reports suggest that the Iranians have conducted joint training sessions with the PFLP-GC in Libya.

On March 5, 1989, Jibril attempted to ingratiate himself to the Iranian government by vowing to kill Salman Rushdie, author of the book *The Satanic Verses,* after the ayatollah Khomeini called for his execution. The Iranian government has labeled the book "blasphemous."

"STILL A FIRE IN HIS BELLY"[5]

Over the years Jibril has put on a good deal of weight, a testimonial to his love of food. He's not a gourmet, say intelligence reports, just a hearty eater. His hair is thin and wispy and has turned white, in contrast with his bushy mustache, which is still dark. He often wears a leather coat over his Syrian commando tunic. He is not known to have any serious vices and has been married to his wife, Samira (Um-Firas, the "mother of a hero"), for many years. They have three sons, the eldest named Firas.

According to those who know him, Jibril is a bitter and cynical man who is fed up with Palestinian politics and the demands of his Syrian masters, whose orders he has obeyed for so many years. He is, they say, dedicated solely to violence. A recent Israeli intelligence assessment describes Jibril as "no less dangerous than Abu Nidal."

Jibril realizes that his goal of destroying the hated Zionist state is more distant today than when he began the struggle. He remains, however, the most unreconstructed of the Palestinian guerrilla leaders, opposed to any accommodation with Israel. Unlike Habash, he has not mellowed with time but continues to believe that "fighting and armed struggle is [*sic*] the only road to Palestine."[6] He has been outspoken in his criticism of Arafat for his dialogue with the United States and for moving toward a negotiated settlement with Israel. "The return to Palestine will be only on the ruins of Israel," he told a pro-Libyan magazine in 1983. "Only the armed struggle will lead us there and there is no place for short cuts, neither through the United States nor through Europe."[7] As long ago as 1976 he vowed to block any political solution to the Palestinian question with acts of terrorism, which he hoped would poison the atmosphere in which any negotiations might take place.

8 | *Abu Nidal*

abri Khalil al-Banna, better known as Abu Nidal, was born in 1940 (or 1937, according to other sources) in Jaffa, then Palestine. He was one of eleven children. His father was a devout Moslem and prosperous businessman, who owned more than six thousand acres of orchards, including orange groves in Ashkelon, Yavne, and Kfar Sava. The al-Banna family lived in a twenty-room house (later converted into an Israeli police station) in the Ajami section of Jaffa. Ironically, until his death Sabri's father, Haj Khalil al-Banna, was a close friend of Israel's first president, Chaim Weizmann, as well as the founder of the Haganah (the Jewish underground army), Avraham Shapira. Mohammed al-Banna, one of Sabri's brothers, was one of the largest fruit and vegetable merchants on the occupied West Bank and was known to enjoy cordial relations with the Israeli government. According to Mohammed, he remembers "as a boy twice visiting the Weizmann house in Rehovot."

As a young man Sabri al-Banna led a privileged existence. He was brought to and from school in a chauffeur-driven car, virtually unheard of in those days. But following the bitter struggle that accompanied the establishment of the state of Israel in 1948, all of the al-Banna family orchards and property in Israel were declared "properties of absentees" and taken over by the Israeli government.

Suddenly Sabri al-Banna was just one more stateless Palestinian refugee. His father had died in 1945, and the task of supporting the family fell to his older brothers. The family moved first to Nablus and later to Beirut (in the mid-1950's). Despite the loss of their lands in Israel, the family had been able to save much of its wealth, including houses in Beirut, Damascus, Nablus, Marseilles, and Istanbul. Since their wealth was intact, Sabri never had to live in a refugee camp but went to school in East Jerusalem, where he studied, among other things, English and French.

There are unconfirmed reports that Sabri attended the American University of Beirut. What is known is that in 1955 he matriculated at Cairo University for two years, studying to become a mechanical engineer. Without completing his degree, he returned to Nablus and taught at a local school. But he soon yearned for excitement and the challenges of a broader world. In 1960 he journeyed to Saudi Arabia and was hired as an electrician's assistant by a construction company. He married a young woman, also from Nablus, and had three children: two daughters and a son named Nidal ("Struggle"). It did not take him long to become involved in radical Palestinian politics, and shortly after Fatah launched its first operation in 1965, as part of the Palestinian reawakening, he joined up and adopted the nom de guerre Abu Nidal, or "father of the struggle."

It was not until after the disastrous Arab defeat in the Six-Day War in 1967, however, that he began to devote his whole life to the Palestinian cause. By 1970, a rising star, he had become a member of the PLO Executive Committee and shortly thereafter was sent to the Sudan as the PLO's "ambassador." It was during his time in Khartoum that he first began secretly to recruit young Palestinians to his own covert fighting force.

In 1971 he left his post in Khartoum and went to Baghdad, to become the PLO's chief representative in a country that was one of the most outspoken proponents of the Palestinian cause. Once in Baghdad, he continued to develop his own organization and openly advocated a more aggressive PLO strategy, calling for stepped-up violence against Israel and its allies.

In September 1973 he began to put his philosophy into action. With the help of the Iraqi government, a group of armed Palestinian fighters from one of Abu Nidal's training camps near Baghdad traveled to Paris and seized the Saudi Arabian Embassy. Within months Abu Nidal reportedly broke with Arafat, whom he accused of being too conservative and of undermining Palestinian aspirations. He formed the Fatah Revolutionary Council (FRC) and declared his intention to kill Arafat. Arafat, in turn, allegedly had Abu Nidal condemned to death in absentia. In the years that followed, Abu Nidal's organization became more popularly known as Black June, although at one time or another it has also operated under names—some borrowed from other groups—such as Black September, the Arab Revolutionary Brigades, and the Revolutionary Organization of Socialist Moslems.

He has purportedly given occasional interviews to the media, such as the one in the West German periodical *Der Spiegel,* in which he described himself as "the evil spirit of the secret services. I am the evil spirit which moves around only at night causing them nightmares." He openly acknowledges that he has served as a surrogate, at different times, of the Iraqis, Syrians, and Libyans.

Intelligence files on Abu Nidal are revealing. One file describes him as "highly ambitious, with a magnetic personality and extraordinary will power. He always strives to make a powerful impression upon others. He demands blind obedience." In another, he is characterized as "an opportunist with an unlimited lust for power."

There are reports that sometime in 1987 Abu Nidal traveled to East Berlin for treatment of a cancer condition and that he recuperated in East Germany and Bulgaria. He also reached a secret understanding with Abu Iyad whereby Arafat and the PLO gave him a free hand to operate in Southern Lebanon, since the FRC militia had become a force to reckon with. In return, it is believed that Abu Nidal agreed to carry out some operations in Europe on behalf of the PLO.

MASTER OF MAYHEM

A recent U.S. Defense Department report has described the Abu Nidal organization as "the most dangerous terrorist organization in existence, and its area of operations is one of the most extensive."[1] During the past decade Abu Nidal's name has been linked to scores of terrorist attacks, including the shooting of Israel's ambassador to the United Kingdom, Shlomo Argov, which became the pretext for Israel's 1982 invasion of Lebanon, and the hijacking of an EgyptAir jetliner to Malta in 1984. Sixty people lost their lives when Egyptian commandos botched an attempt to rescue the plane.

U.S. and Israeli intelligence sources indicate that since its inception Abu Nidal's organization has carried out more than 250 terrorist attacks. For the two-year period from 1983 to 1985 alone, more than 100 terrorist attacks can be linked to Abu Nidal. Of these, 69 were directed at Arab targets, 16 against Israeli targets, and 15 at European and American targets. Among his 1985 operations were the assassination of West Bank Mayor Fahd Qawasma; an attempt to blow up a Jordanian plane en route to Kuwait; an attack on the offices of the Jordanian national airline, Alia, in Rome; the assassination of a Jordanian diplomat in Ankara; the bombing of a coffee shop in Kuwait; the assassination of a British diplomat in India; an attack on the U.S. Embassy in Cairo; and attacks on a Jewish-owned store in Paris and the El Al office in Amsterdam. His bloodiest operations occurred two days after Christmas, when Palestinian gunmen killed 14 people and injured 115 in coordinated attacks at the airports in Rome and Vienna.

On September 5, 1986, more than a hundred people were killed and injured after a Pan Am jumbo jet was hijacked by Abu Nidal terrorists in Karachi, Pakistan. Before the terrorists panicked and opened fire on the passengers, they had asked stewardesses to identify those aboard with American passports. The following day, September 6, two gunmen employed by Abu Nidal murdered twenty-two Jewish worshipers in an Istanbul synagogue. The attackers slipped into the synagogue and bolted the door with an iron bar to prevent anyone from escaping. Then they opened fire on the those inside with Czech-made submachine guns and grenades. In retrospect, it appears that the attack on the synagogue was designed to derail a planned meeting between Israeli Prime Minister Shimon Peres and Egypt's President Hosni Mubarak.

INTERNATIONAL TIES

Following his alleged break with Arafat, Abu Nidal located his headquarters in Baghdad and for at least a decade enjoyed the support, protection, and funding of the Iraqi government and its strong man, Saddam Hussein. After the Iraqi government became embroiled in its protracted war with Iran, it began seeking closer ties with the West. In 1983, under strong U.S. pressure, the Iraqi government told Abu Nidal to pack his bags and leave. He subsequently moved to Damascus, and it was from Syria that he launched most of his bloodiest operations in the mid-1980's. In fact, his headquarters was not far from the U.S. Embassy. The FRC also established a small publishing arm that continues to produce a periodical, which is printed by el-Carmel printing shop.

Evidence of Abu Nidal's close ties to the Syrian government abounds. The Rome and Vienna airport attacks provide indisputable evidence of this relationship. On December 27, 1985, FRC terrorists launched an attack with grenades and assault rifles on passengers near El Al's check-in counter at Rome's Fiumicino (Leonardo da Vinci) Airport in which twelve people were killed and seventy-four wounded. Five of the dead were Americans, including the eleven-year-old daughter of an Associated Press editor. A simultaneous attack was carried out at Vienna's international airport, leaving another two dead and forty wounded. In Rome, three of the terrorists were killed, and the fourth, Mohammed Sarham, was wounded and taken into custody.[2] He admitted to Italian investigators that he was a member of Abu Nidal's Fatah Revolutionary Council (FRC), and he described his training at a Syrian military facility in the Bekaa Valley. He also stated that Syrian intelligence officers had authorized the attacks in Rome and Vienna and given Sarham and his confederates a final briefing before their departure from Syria for Europe. Sarham and his three confederates flew from Damascus to Belgrade, Yugoslavia, and then took a train to Rome. The three terrorists who carried out the Vienna operation, by contrast, flew from Damascus to Budapest, Hungary, where they caught a flight for Vienna.[3]

The passports and other documents carried by the terrorists were provided to them in Damascus. Some of the terrorists carried genuine Moroccan passports, which had been obtained in their blank or unissued state by Syrian intelligence. The passports were then filled out, using the false names and other data adopted by the terrorists, along with actual photos. As a result, it was impossible to discern the passports from the real thing. A few of the terrorists utilized Tunisian passports obtained from the Libyans, who confiscated them during the forced expulsion of Tunisian laborers from Libya.[4] Libya also provided the weapons and grenades used in the Fiumicino attack, which had been shipped to Rome in November in the Libyan diplomatic pouch (DIP). They were stored in the Libyan People's Bureau, which serves as the Libyan Embassy, until being turned over to the terrorists immediately prior to the operation. This is why, on December 31, 1985, former Italian Prime Minister Bettino Craxi publicly accused the Libyan government of complicity in the attack. Two days earlier the Libyan news agency had described the attacks as "heroic." Sarham is also reported to have told Italian authorities where to find additional arms caches secreted in Europe and elsewhere by Abu Nidal's organization.

By early 1986 Abu Nidal had become too hot even for the Syrians to handle, at least publicly. Because of their increasing isolation from the rest of the international community, the Syrians were under a great deal of pressure, especially from the United States, to take some public steps to indicate that they were reducing their support of international terrorism. Syrian President Hafez al-Assad personally told Abu Nidal that he and his headquarters would have to leave. Nevertheless, the Syrians indicated their interest in maintaining a direct link to his organization and even provided him with official entrée to the Khomeini regime in Iran.

Some observers believe that the FRC's estrangement from

Syria was an elaborate charade designed to take foreign pressure off Assad; others maintain that it was, at best, a short-term cooling of relations. Whatever the explanation, it was clear by 1987 that Syria had reestablished its close ties with the FRC and that all of the organization's former offices in Damascus were again functioning. There are reports that the FRC's rapprochement with Syria followed meetings between Abu Nidal and Abu Iyad that occurred in conjunction with the 1987 Palestinian National Council gathering in Algiers, during which Abu Nidal was present in Algeria. The FRC's primary office in Damascus is located in the Meisset Building. Abu Nidal also maintains a personal office near the Nakura Restaurant on Masra'a Street. And just behind the Litani Hospital there is a third FRC office facility.

According to intelligence sources, the FRC's main training base in Syria is the Duma camp near Damascus. Another base near Chibbin, specializes in training terrorists for suicide operations. The FRC's chief representative in Syria, Ibrahim al-Raheb, known as Abu Khaled, and his top deputy, Mohammed Khalil Shahin, during 1988 regularly coordinated their activities with two Syrian intelligence officers, Air Force Colonels Haitham al-Sa'id and Khaled al-Hassan.[5]

The Syrians actually set up a committee within its intelligence establishment to coordinate activities with Abu Nidal. Members of the committee are Ali Duba, chief of Syrian intelligence; Brigadier General Mohammed al-Huli, former head of Syria's air force intelligence; Colonel Saleiman al-Khuli, the former deputy chief of Syria's air force; and Abu Nidal's permanent representative in Damascus, Abu Khaled.[6] Both al-Huli and al-Khuli were "reprimanded" for their roles in the April 17, 1986, attempt to bomb an El Al plane en route from New York to Tel Aviv, via London. Mustafa Murad, the FRC's spokesman, serves as liaison with the Syrian intelligence chiefs. Abu Nidal occasionally meets with Syrian intelligence officials himself. On October 3, 1986, for example, he met with the Syrian intelligence chief in Lebanon, Brigadier General Ghazi Kanaan, at Anjar, in the Bekaa Valley near the Syrian border, to coordinate a forthcoming operation in Europe. As a direct result of the meeting, four members of a fanatic Islamic fundamentalist organization, apparently retained by either the Syrians or Abu Nidal, departed from Beirut on

October 12 for Bulgaria. A follow-up meeting between Abu Nidal and other Syrian intelligence officials—all presumed to be staff officers reporting to General Kanaan—took place a week later, on October 10, also at Anjar. The operation that was the purpose of the meetings apparently was preempted by Western intelligence services and has never been revealed.

In 1983 the FRC took an active role in the fighting around Tripoli, Lebanon, and at the Badawi refuge camp, as Arafat and the PLO made their last stand on Lebanese soil. Initially the FRC forces fought under Syrian command against their own Palestinian brothers. However, when the FRC's relationship with the Syrians began to sour, Abu Nidal switched sides and threw his support to Arafat in battles against the Syrian-backed Amal militia.

Today, with the reestablishment of close links to the Syrian government, the FRC has been permitted to maintain a number of operational bases in the Syrian-controlled sector of eastern Lebanon. One terrorist training camp is located northwest of Yanta in the Bekaa Valley, almost on the Syrian-Lebanese border. Another training camp has been identified near the village of Hamara, also on the Syrian-Lebanese border, and a third camp is located inside the Nabi Zahour Syrian military base. The FRC even has a small naval base in northern Lebanon at the port of Behnin.

The FRC has established the Abu Nidal Militia in the Palestinian refugee camps near Beirut and in southern Lebanon. This armed militia took part in the most recent battles between rival Palestinian factions in and around Beirut. Promising young recruits are sent either to Libya or to one of the bases in the Bekaa Valley for advanced training, including instruction on how to conduct terrorist operations.

In addition, the FRC has opened a local headquarters in Sidon, in southern Lebanon, which processes and trains new recruits and represents Abu Nidal's interests in the area. There are recent reports that Abu Nidal is trying to establish a shadow network in the occupied West Bank and Gaza and that the Israelis have exposed at least four of his cells.

Today the FRC maintains ties to a variety of other terrorist organizations, including the Japanese Red Army (Arab Section), the Irish Republican Army (IRA), the Red Army Faction of West Germany, and what is left of the Cells Combatante

Communiste (CCC) of Belgium and France's Direct Action. The FRC's closest relationship, however, is with the Marxist Armenian Secret Army for the Liberation of Armenia (ASALA). It is too early to tell what impact the 1988 death of its leader, Hagop Hagopian, will have on the relationship. The link to ASALA is maintained via Syrian Air Force intelligence.

Contrary to most other terrorist groups, Abu Nidal buys his weapons and lethal supplies on the open market in the arms bazaars of the world. Sometimes the weapons are shipped to operatives in Libyan or Syrian diplomatic pouches.

Today Abu Nidal's annual budget is estimated to be in the neighborhood of twenty million dollars. Libya provides fourteen to fifteen million dollars of the budget, with the balance coming from other Arab governments and from a network of companies that Abu Nidal and his organization own surreptitiously. Iraq's last known cash payment to the FRC was in 1983, and Syria's in 1985.

Abu Nidal also maintains close ties to Eastern bloc intelligence and regularly travels in and out of Eastern Europe. Indeed, CIA sources report that he actually maintains offices in Poland and East Germany. In this connection the FRC owns a number of trading companies based in Poland and East Germany. One of the Polish-based companies is SAS-CII, which has an office in the Intraco II building on Stawski Street in Warsaw. According to former Director of Central Intelligence William Casey, "The Soviets don't run him or control him, but they use him and his group for their own purposes."

ABU NIDAL'S PLO CONNECTION

Although the PLO allegedly sentenced Abu Nidal to death and put a price on his head after his purported break with Arafat in the early 1970's, there is no evidence that it ever really tried to get him, even when it knew where he was. This may be the strongest evidence to indicate that Abu Nidal's relations with

Arafat, Abu Iyad, and the PLO are not as strained as some observers might suggest or as the PLO wants everyone to believe.

Over the years Abu Nidal and his organization have served the interests of the Iraqis, the Libyans, and the Syrians as "guns for hire," and there is no reason to believe that he has any particular aversion to conducting operations on behalf of the PLO. Indeed, there are indications that Abu Nidal has carried out contract operations for the PLO since the mid-1970's. In a number of cases when the PLO found itself with a particularly discreet or dirty operation that had to be done but that—for political or other considerations—had to be totally deniable, it appears that Arafat turned to Abu Nidal. According to former Romanian intelligence official Ion Pacepa, Hanni al-Hassan of the PLO confirmed this in a conversation. According to Pacepa, al-Hassan told him that "we've taken over control of his 'Black June' through the agents I had there. All the top jobs under Nidal are held by my men. We're the ones who are really running 'Black June' now, not Nidal. We, not Nidal, now have the last word in setting its terrorist priorities."[7]

While we do not doubt the substance of the conversation between Pacepa and al-Hassan, it appears that the PLO man misrepresented the amount of control the PLO has over Abu Nidal. The PLO may believe that he is its proxy, but the known facts just don't support this conclusion. Nevertheless, intelligence sources suggest that Abu Nidal has carried out a number of killings at Arafat's behest. These include the murders (in Spain) of Issam Sertawi, who was engaged in negotiations with Israel's left-wing political parties; (in Jordan) of Fahd Qawasma, the former mayor of Hebron and once a member of the PLO's Executive Committee; and Sa'id Hamami, the PLO representative in London. In all three instances, the victims were targeted because of political differences with Arafat.

Western intelligence services are divided on the question of whether or not Abu Nidal serves in any appreciable sense as a covert instrument of the PLO. Sources in the U.S. intelligence establishment say that the evidence is inconclusive. The Israelis, for their part, are engaged in an internal disagreement on this question. A high-ranking official of AMAN, Israel's military intelligence organization, says, "All we have indicates the opposite: that Abu Nidal is not linked in a hidden form to the PLO." On the other hand, a Mossad official indicates, "There are many indications to prove this thesis [that Abu Nidal is closely tied to the PLO]."

Whatever the real truth, there is little question that the PLO has closer ties to Abu Nidal's FRC than either organization publicly acknowledges. Interestingly, one of Abu Nidal's relatives, a Palestinian woman named Janine al-Banna, works for the PLO in Tunis and maintains close ties to both Arafat and Abu Iyad. She became acquainted with the two men when she lived in Beirut and worked for WAFA, the PLO news agency. However, her real role with the PLO has never been established. It is known that she has a French passport, possibly forged, in the name of Janine el-Bina and that she was observed frequently in the company of Rita Yorinio, a young Italian woman who served as a Red Brigades courier. In addition, both women were often seen with Bassam Abu-Sharif. Prior to 1983, Janine al-Banna used to travel often to Syria and Iraq, although the purpose of her visits is not known.[8]

THE HUNT FOR ABU NIDAL

Abu Nidal remains the most elusive and mysterious terrorist leader in the world. According to a former antiterrorism adviser to the Israeli prime minister, "Abu Nidal does not use his own travel documents, even when going from one safe country to another. He does not attend major gatherings and only rarely talks to his own people. He is always on the move or behind the Iron Curtain. He hands his orders, in written form, to three operators who are very close to him. He has only one aide." In addition, it is believed that he never speaks by telephone, which he regards as unsafe, nor has he ever been heard on a radio broadcast. No one even knows for certain what he looks like. The photo most often reproduced of him, allegedly taken in North Korea, may not be genuine. At the very least, it is fifteen years old.

Yet the search for Abu Nidal goes on.

On September 9, 1986, CIA chief William Casey was in a jubilant mood. He was seated behind his broad desk in his imposing office on the third floor of the Old Executive Office Building, adjoining the White House. As the first director of central intelligence with Cabinet rank, Casey also was the first to have an office in the White House complex.

"We have located Abu Nidal's main headquarters," he told a visitor. By contrast with previous intelligence, continued Casey, Abu Nidal was living on a secret base in Lebanon's Bekaa Valley. Casey hinted that the United States and Israel were considering a joint strike against Abu Nidal, either to destroy his base of operations or to snatch him and bring him back to the United States to stand trial for his role in the Rome and Vienna airport attacks. However, locating a terrorist leader and actually having the time to pull together an operation against him are not easy. One high official in the Reagan administration compared it with "trying to paint a moving train."

Nevertheless, Ronald Reagan wanted Abu Nidal. According to a senior U.S. policy maker, Reagan was profoundly affected by the death of the eleven-year-old American girl, Natasha Simpson, in the Rome airport attack, and he ordered National Security Council planners to hit Libya, which had given aid and assistance to Abu Nidal, at the next opportunity. This, not the terrorist bombing of a West Berlin disco in early April, was the real genesis of the April 1986 U.S. bombing raid on Libya. Even after the raid, however, Reagan was not satisfied, and he ordered stepped-up U.S. efforts to find Abu Nidal. Although former National Security Council staff member Oliver North had said that the United States was ready to go to "the ends of the earth" in order to bring Abu Nidal to justice for his role in the Rome and Vienna airport attacks, the operation envisioned by Casey never materialized. It was overtaken by both events and the Iran-contra scandal. By the time that Israeli intelligence could get a fix on the secret base, Abu Nidal had slipped away. Subsequent efforts to track him down were sidetracked by the firing of Oliver North and Casey's incapacitation in December 1986.

The Israelis, on the other hand, have not slackened their efforts to capture or kill Abu Nidal. When he attacked the Istanbul synagogue, he signed his death warrant, if he had not done so already. Former Israeli Prime Minister Menachem Begin never believed that Abu Nidal had actually split with Yasir Arafat. The Abu Nidal terrorist group, according to Begin, was simply a successor to Black September and other deniable units of the PLO. "He [Abu Nidal] is the secret arm of those who want to disguise their real intentions," a top-ranking Arab intelligence official suggests, buttressing Begin's contention.

Today intelligence organizations from the United States, Israel, several conservative Arab regimes, and a few European nations monitor Abu Nidal's activities on a continuous basis. Only the Israelis are known to be actively hunting him. However, even this effort has taken a back seat to the more immediate problem of the Intifada. Nevertheless, Abu Nidal's name is likely to remain at the top of the Israeli "most wanted" list. Since the mid-1980's the Israelis have labeled Abu Nidal and his group "enemy number one" of the state of Israel and its people.

The prevailing belief within the Israeli intelligence community is that once it eliminates Abu Nidal, his organization will lose its momentum and dynamism, if not cease to exist altogether. In order to target him, the Israelis have established an interagency group composed of top-ranking officials from the Mossad, AMAN, and the Shin-Bet, together with representatives from the prime minister's office (the antiterrorism adviser's office) and the Foreign Ministry.

The needs and requirements of the interagency group are given priority with respect to the tasking and allocation of intelligence assets. To the extent possible, the group monitors every move the terrorist leader makes, every meeting with his couriers, every contact with a foreign government. Its goal, of course, is to assemble all the operational intelligence that will be required to carry out a successful "hit."

At least twice in 1988, the interagency group thought that it had reliable intelligence indicating that Abu Nidal was in a "reachable" location. On both occasions Mossad intelligence-gathering teams were sent to the suspected locations to assemble operational data. One of the locations was Libya. However, it appears that Abu Nidal left the country before a commando operation against him could be mounted successfully. In the other location, which was far more distant from Israel, the

Mossad team was unable to confirm his whereabouts. It should be noted that Abu Nidal uses many different real and forged passports, in a variety of names, when he travels. During the past two years, he has traveled exclusively on a Norwegian passport.

In 1988 Abu Nidal spent a great deal of time behind the Iron Curtain, mostly in Bulgaria, where in the past his host, Bulgarian intelligence, provided him with an official security detail and other state courtesies. With the winds of change sweeping through the Soviet Union and its satellites, and the onset of the dialogue between the United States and the PLO, Abu Nidal's world is shrinking; there are fewer countries where he is welcome and which will permit their territory to be used to launch terrorist attacks. Yet he remains an extremely dangerous and wily foe. Like a cornered animal, however, he may be even more dangerous and unpredictable as the world closes in on him.

9
Abu Abbas, the PLF,
and the Hijacking of
the Achille Lauro

Mohammed Zaidan Abbas (Abu Abbas) was born in 1941 in the area of Sefad in the Galilee but fled with his family to Syria in 1948. In the late 1960's Abbas joined George Habash's Popular Front for the Liberation of Palestine, but he soon found the organization—despite its Marxist orientation—too conservative for his tastes. According to a Lebanese intelligence report, he was a Black September operator in the early 1970's, allegedly working in Europe under the command of Ali Hassan Salameh.[1] He joined Ahmed Jibril's pro-Syrian PFLP-GC in 1973, after Black September for all practical purposes was disbanded, and quickly rose through the ranks, becoming a top aide to Jibril and the PFLP-GC's spokesman. The role of spokesman is particularly important in most terrorist organizations since publicity is the chief aim of the majority of all terrorist operations. The spokesman, therefore, is generally involved in all the planning and operational discussions.

It wasn't long, however, before Abbas began to grow disenchanted with Syrian control over the PFLP-GC. In 1976, when the Syrians invaded Lebanon to save the Christians and the Lebanese Forces from extinction, Abbas turned to the Iraqis, who opposed the Syrian role in Lebanon, and cultivated close relations with Baghdad. In contrast with a majority of the members of the PFLP-GC, Abbas favored all-out resistance to the Syrian invaders and lined up with Tal'at Yaqub and other anti-Syrian elements to oppose Jibril.

After the anti-Syrian faction within the PFLP-GC failed to oust Jibril in what amounted to an attempted coup d'état, the internal struggle within the PFLP-GC erupted into open warfare. There were military clashes between the two factions, and key members of each group were assassinated. Only the decision by Yaqub, Abbas, and approximately four hundred followers to break away from the PFLP-GC and form their own organization, the Palestine Liberation Front, resurrecting the name of Jibril's old organization, brought the violence to an end.

Like its predecessor organizations, the newly created PLF was also riven by dissension and, after the 1982 Israeli invasion of Lebanon, broke into three factions. One faction led by Abed al-Fatah Ghanem, declared itself pro-Syrian and set up its headquarters and a base inside Syria, while a second faction followed Yaqub. The third faction, headed by Mohammed Abbas, evacuated Beirut with the rest of the PLO and went to Tunis, where it established its headquarters and declared itself loyal to Yasir Arafat.

As a reward for his loyalty, in November 1984, during a meeting in Amman, Jordan, Abbas was named to the PLO Executive Committee under Arafat's sponsorship. The PLO also helped Abbas establish a headquarters at Hammam el-Shat and provided him with a budget of a hundred thousand dollars a month. Indeed, the PLF/Abbas faction's decision to join the PLO represented a victory for Arafat, who has always preached unity among rival Palestinian groups. Coming on the heels of the PLO's expulsion from Beirut, at a time when Fatah and the PLO were torn by strife, Abbas's action was particularly welcome. The Syrians had managed to split Fatah by encouraging and supporting Abu Musa's rebellion, so Arafat lavished praise and rewards on Abbas in order to demonstrate the handsome benefits flowing to those who pledged their allegiance to the chairman.

Under Arafat's patronage, overnight Abbas became a force within the Palestinian movement. The PLF cemented its close ties with the Ba'ath regime in Iraq and continued to oppose

Syrian ambitions in Lebanon. The Iraqis supplemented the aid provided by Arafat to the PLF, giving the organization additional money, training, arms, and, when required, safe haven. Abbas maintained an Iraqi diplomatic passport and set up a liaison office in Baghdad and also served as a second channel of communication between Yasir Arafat and the PLO to Saddam Hussein and the Ba'ath party in Iraq.

In September 1985 the PLF Congress observed its annual meeting in Baghdad. Arafat was the guest of honor, sharing the podium with Abbas and delivering the keynote address on September 5. Both men praised Saddam Hussein and the Iraqi government for their support and condemned Syria's Hafez al-Assad and Libya's Muammar Qaddafi as enemies of the Palestinian Revolution.[2]

Shortly thereafter, however, the PLF's relationship with the Iraqi government began to decline, reportedly owing more to repeated PLF operational failures than to pressure from the United States and other Western countries.

As an architect of terrorism Abbas lacks the brilliant planning and organizational skills of an Abu Nidal or the audacity of an Immad Mugniyeh, operational chief of Hizballah. Abbas and the PLF are, in many respects, the "gang that couldn't shoot straight," and apart from a few cold-blooded murders against unarmed targets, the PLF has not distinguished itself as a terrorist organization. In 1978 PLF guerrillas were driven back when they attempted to attack the Israeli settlement of Kiryat Shemoneh. The following year four PLF infiltrators landed in Israel in a rubber dinghy and killed four Israelis: a policeman, a father and his daughter, and another young girl. Although their intent was deadly serious, the PLF's next three operations recalled Wile E. Coyote of Roadrunner fame. In July 1980 a PLF terrorist sought to slip into Israel undetected in a hot-air balloon, but the balloon exploded shortly after takeoff, killing the terrorist. On March 7, 1981, two PLF terrorists penetrated Israel on hang gliders, intending to drop explosive charges on a refinery in the Haifa area. One of the bombs on the first hang glider slipped away prematurely and the terrorist/pilot jettisoned the second bomb before reaching the target. He ran out of fuel a short time later and landed near the Kibbutz Afek, where he was later apprehended. The second hang glider crash-landed in southern Lebanon, where the terrorist/pilot was captured by the South Lebanon Army (SLA), a pro-Israeli Christian militia, and turned over to the Israel Defense Forces (IDF).

Five weeks later, on April 16, two more PLF terrorists attempted to cross into Israel from Lebanon in a hot-air balloon but were shot down by IDF antiaircraft fire. They crashed in Lebanon, and after a short pursuit both were killed by Israeli soldiers. Finally, on June 5, 1984, the PLF launched an attack from Syria on the Israeli kibbutz of Ein-Gev, located on the eastern shore of the Sea of Galilee. All four members of the raiding party were captured.

Aware of his slipping support within the PLO and from Saddam Hussein, Abbas decided to launch a "bold" terrorist operation that would restore his credibility and gain respect and fear for the PLF. His target would be the Italian cruise ship *Achille Lauro.*

THE *ACHILLE LAURO* AFFAIR

On October 5, 1985, Abbas commiserated with Arafat in Tunis regarding the Israeli air raid on Hammam el-Shat, which had destroyed Force 17's headquarters. What else they discussed is unknown, but just two days later four PLF terrorists seized the *Achille Lauro* en route from Alexandria, Egypt, to Port Said. Most of the passengers had left the ship in Alexandria in order to take an excursion to the Sphinx, the Pyramids, and the various Egyptian museums and were scheduled to rejoin the ship at Port Said.

The decision to seize the 624-foot vessel was probably motivated by tightened security at European airports following the hijacking of TWA Flight 847. Like other cruise ships plying the Mediterranean, the *Achille Lauro* had no security on board, nor was any effort made to screen passengers or inspect their luggage. Apparently the original plan devised by Abbas and his henchmen called for the seizure of the ship once it had anchored at the Israeli port of Ashdod and to threaten the Israelis with its destruction unless their demands were met. It is also believed, in some circles, that the PLF team had been instructed to sail to Syrian waters and then execute the Jewish and American passengers. The operation, says one source, was first conceived in late 1984 or early 1985, though the precise target was probably not agreed upon until much later. While the PLF later claimed that the seizure of the *Achille Lauro* had been undertaken in response to the Israeli bombing on Hammam el-Shat, it is inconceivable that such a complicated operation could have been launched less than a week after the raid, especially by a group like the PLF, which was not known for its success or expertise in carrying out complicated operations. Indeed, the seizure had required a good deal of intelligence, the stockpiling of weapons in Genoa, and the selection and positioning of the terrorists.

In one version of events, the terrorists were forced to advance their timetable after being discovered with their weapons by one of the ship's stewards. According to Israeli intelligence reports and information made public—in part—by Italian Defense Minister Giovanni Spadolini, immediately before the seizure of the ship on October 7, 1985, the terrorists were in contact, via the ship's radio telephone, with a PLF coordinator in Genoa. He, in turn, got in touch with the PLO headquarters in Tunis for final instructions.

Minutes later, at approximately 8:45 A.M., the terrorists burst into the vessel's dining room with guns blazing, injuring two people with their wild gunfire. They quickly took control of the vessel and ordered the captain to steam toward Tartus, Syria, and demanded the release of some fifty Palestinians incarcerated in Israel. Following a call to Syrian President Hafez al-Assad from U.S. Ambassador to the United Nations Vernon Walters, the Syrians refused to permit the vessel to enter the port of Tartus. A short time later the terrorists murdered a wheelchair-bound sixty-nine-year-old American named Leon Klinghoffer. The terrorists allegedly shuffled the passports of the American hostages to see who would be killed first, and Klinghoffer's ended up on top of the stack. The terrorists then ordered several of the other passengers to throw Klinghoffer's lifeless body over the side. "We threw the first body into the water after shooting him in the head," they boasted over the ship's radio. "Minutes from now we will follow up with the second one. Do not worry, Tartus, we have a lot of them here."

At this point it was clear to Arafat and his advisers that something had gone terribly wrong with the *Achille Lauro* operation and that it was going to be a public relations disaster for the PLO. After weighing the options, they decided to move quickly to cut their losses.

On October 8, the second day of the crisis, Mohammed Abbas arrived in Port Said, purporting to be a disinterested good Samaritan and saying that he had been "dispatched by Arafat to resolve the hijacking."[3] Intelligence sources now believe that Abbas had flown to Port Said in order to take charge of the operation. Such a conclusion is supported by conversations that Abbas conducted with the hijackers using a ship-to-shore (STS) telephone link. From tape recordings of the intercepted communications, released by the Israeli government on October 16, 1985, it is clear that Abbas knew the terrorists by name and was attempting to extricate them from their dilemma before the situation aboard the vessel deteriorated any further or the United States mounted a rescue attempt. He identified himself by another nom de guerre, Abu Khalid, and then uttered a code word, according to the Israelis, to confirm his identity. The following is a transcript of the conversation on October 9:

PORT SAID [Abbas]: Here is Abu Khalid, here is Abu Khalid, how do you hear me?
SHIP: Go ahead.
PORT SAID: This is Abu Khalid. Who is talking? Is it Magid?
SHIP: Correct.
PORT SAID: How are you feeling, Magid?
SHIP: Good. Thank God."
PORT SAID: Listen to me carefully. First, you have to treat the passengers very well. You have to apologize to them and to the ship's crew and tell them it was not our goal to take control of the ship. Tell them your main goal and who—
SHIP: Right. We spoke to them and told them that our goal was not to seize the ship.[4]

In Washington the same day a U.S. Justice Department official stated that "the evidence we have right now is that he [Mohammed Abbas] participated in all of this, guiding them [the hijackers] throughout."[5] Similarly, Attorney General

Edwin Meese III announced that the United States had "hard evidence" that Abbas was "a principal in the hijacking."[6]

U.S. military action to rescue the ship was imminent, and Abbas desperately wanted to bring the hijacking to a close before Washington's patience ran out. He was well aware that most Western countries operate on an unspoken rule of thumb that once terrorists start killing their hostages, it is time to act to resolve the situation, if appropriate to the circumstances, by force.

U.S. RESPONSE

Approximately two hours after the takeover of the *Achille Lauro* on October 7, the White House situation room was made aware of the incident. Initially, its main source of information was radio communications between the cruise ship's captain and his home office in Genoa, Italy.

Soon afterward three U.S. military C-141 transport planes were airborne. Two planes, which departed from Charleston Air Force Base, carried members of SEAL Team Six and their equipment, while elements of the U.S. Army's Delta Force, from Fort Bragg, North Carolina, were aboard the third aircraft. The destination of all three planes was the Royal Air Force air base at Akrotiri, Cyprus, which would serve as a staging area in the event that a rescue operation was mounted. Immediately upon arrival at Akrotiri, Brigadier General Carl W. Stiner began making plans to retake the ship.

Meanwhile, back in Washington officials were attempting to pull together all relevant intelligence and line up support among America's allies for any eventualities that might arise. Two major pieces of intelligence were missing: the number of terrorists on board the ship and its exact location. Despite the fact that the vessel's captain had indicated, in one of his transmissions, that only a few terrorists were on board, crisis managers at the U.S. Joint Special Operations Command (JSOC) were reluctant to accept such information at face value since it was assumed that the terrorists might be forcing the captain to transmit misleading or erroneous data.

If at all possible, Stiner and his men wanted to hit the ship in international waters, in order to avoid sovereignty questions and so that the United States would not have to request permission of a foreign government to rescue the ship, especially since such a request might be rejected or be leaked to the media, thereby compromising the mission's security.

After the *Achille Lauro* was turned away from Syria, the U.S. Navy lost track of the ship twice during the next day and a half. Although U.S. Secretary of Defense Caspar Weinberger ordered the Joint Chiefs of Staff (JSC) and JSOC not to seek assistance from the Israelis in locating the vessel, Israeli military intelligence (AMAN), responding to a request from Lieutenant Colonel Oliver North of the National Security Council, provided the *Achille Lauro*'s location directly to the NSC.

The rescue operation was subsequently set for Wednesday, October 9, at about 8:15 P.M. local time (2:15 P.M. in Washington), about an hour and a half after sunset. The combined force of SEAL and Delta operators was divided into three groups. Team One would be dropped into the ship's wake from helicopters and was to approach the *Achille Lauro* from the stern in high-speed Zodiac rafts and board the ship's fantail. The choppers would then circle until Team One had reached its objective, at which time they would hover overhead while Team Two fast roped down onto the bridge and main deck and secured the radio room as their first priority. Team Three would remain aboard the choppers in reserve and would provide fire support to the men on the *Achille Lauro*. The choppers were equipped with FLIR (forward-looking infrared radar), permitting them to operate at night. All the SEAL and Delta operators wore night-vision goggles over the black hoods that masked their faces and were dressed in tight black overalls. They carried an assortment of silenced Uzis, pistols, and other custom weapons. All were outfitted with small radio sets that enabled them to communicate with each other and with the operational commander, who was directing the operation from a nearby helicopter gunship.

The goal of the commandos was to regain control of the ship and bring it into a safe harbor. Any terrorist who resisted was to be killed.

Before the operation could take place, however, the *Achille Lauro* returned to Port Said, where, later on October 9, after "negotiations" with Mohammed Abbas, the hijackers surrendered to Egyptian authorities. The Egyptians, at the urging of Abbas, allegedly promised the terrorists "safe conduct" out of Egypt. The following day an EgyptAir jetliner left Egypt for Tunis with Abbas and the four hijackers on board. However, it was intercepted by F-14 jets and forced to land at Sigonella Air Base in Sicily, where U.S. commandos from SEAL Team Six surrounded the plane.[7] After a tense standoff with Italian carabinieri, the United States turned over Abbas and the hijackers to the Italians.[8]

BETRAYAL

In an act of extraordinary cowardice and betrayal, the Italian government of Prime Minister Bettino Craxi put Abbas and another PLO official on a Yugoslav Airline flight bound for Belgrade, rather than antagonize the PLO and the Arab world by handing them over to the United States. According to then Director of the FBI William Webster, once he reached Yugoslavia, Abbas stayed at "the PLO embassy in Belgrade."[9]

The Italian government later offered a number of lame excuses justifying its action, including the suggestion that "the United States had offered only unprovable, circumstantial evidence of his [Abbas's] involvement in the hijacking."[10] Antonio Badini, foreign policy adviser to Prime Minister Craxi, later testified, "We knew at the time only that Abbas had offered his good offices [to end the hijacking] as a sort of intermediary." Badinni also alleged that Abbas had been on an official Egyptian mission and enjoyed diplomatic immunity.

Italy also refused to extradite the four hijackers to the United States. However, the West German government later extradicted to Italy another Palestinian suspected of providing the false passports used by the hijackers. The Italians subsequently tried the five men, along with ten others in absentia, including Abbas, whom Italian prosecutors later identified as the mastermind of the *Achille Lauro* operation. According to the report by the Genoa magistrates, Abbas "created the action, chose the perpetrators, trained them for their particular task, gave the orders to the 'commando'."[11] Italian investigators also concluded that Abdel Rahim Khaled a top PLF operative, was the operational commander of the mission and that he had been on board the vessel until it reached Egypt. After giving last-minute instructions to the four terrorists who seized the ship, he disembarked at Alexandria.

The five terrorists in Italian custody all were convicted of various crimes. Yussef Magid Molqi, who confessed to killing Klinghoffer but later recanted his confession, received the stiffest sentence, thirty years. Nevertheless, it was decidedly less severe than the life sentence demanded by the Italian prosecutor. Molqi was so relieved by the light sentence that he began chanting in the courtroom, "Long live Italian justice, long live Palestine." Molqi's deputy, Ibrahim Abdelatif Fataier, was handed a twenty-four-year-and-two-month sentence, and Marouf Assadi was given fifteen years and two months. The fourth hijacker, Bassam al-Ashker, had been declared a minor at the time of the hijacking and had been handed over to a juvenile court pending trial.

Two other defendants in Italian custody also received sentences as accessories to the hijacking. Mohammed Issa Abbas, a distant cousin of Mohammed Zaidan Abbas, was handed a six-month jail term for using a false passport and giving a false name. Mowefaq Gandura, a PLF colonel, was convicted of aiding and abetting the crime and making false statements; he was given an eight-month sentence but was released from jail because he had already served more than eight months awaiting trial. In a hollow gesture, the Italians convicted Abbas and a number of henchmen in absentia, giving life sentences to Abbas; his chief of staff, Ozuddin Badratkan; and the PLF treasurer, Omar al-Ziad. Many U.S. officials and the Klinghoffer family were outraged by the relatively short sentences meted out to those actually in Italian custody.

In the aftermath of the hijacking, the United States indicted Abbas and offered "a reward of up to $250,000 for information leading to the apprehension and effective prosecution and punishment of Abu el Abbas as well as any others not yet in custody responsible for the terrorist action which resulted in the seizure of the Achille Lauro on October 7, 1985, the taking of hostages including 14 Americans, and the killing of one American, Leon Klinghoffer."[12] However, in January 1988 the

Justice Department withdrew the arrest warrant on the flimsy grounds that Abbas had already been convicted in Italy and it served no real public purpose that he also be tried and convicted in the United States. The government's decision was decried by the Klinghoffer family. According to a family member, "This was forfeiting our right for our father's murderer to be held accountable in an American court of law. We see no purpose served by abandoning the warrant and we appeal to the president to have the Department of Justice retract the decision."[13]

ABBAS AND THE PLO

At the outset of the *Achille Lauro* hostage drama, the PLO leadership moved quickly to deny any connection to the hijackers. On the first day Abu Iyad claimed that the gunmen who hijacked the ship were part of a new small Palestinian faction with no affiliation to the PLO.[14] The following day the PLO issued an official statement maintaining that the hijackers did not belong to any group loyal to Yasir Arafat, another outright untruth.[15] As negative world public opinion mounted, on October 9 Arafat himself met with the international media to deny any PLO involvement in the hijacking.[16] Attempts to disassociate the PLO from the *Achille Lauro* affair became more and more desperate, and on October 10, following a meeting of the United Nations Security Council in New York, the PLO's foreign secretary, Farouk Qadoumi, told assembled members of the media that reports an elderly American had been slain on board the *Achille Lauro* amounted to a "big lie fabricated by the intelligence services of the United States."[17]

It soon became clear, however, that no amount of obfuscation and denial could change the fact that the PLF/Abbas faction was an integral part of the PLO, ostensibly loyal to Yasir Arafat. Indeed, ten days after the seizure of the *Achille Lauro,* Arafat and Abu Iyad were interviewed on Radio Monte Carlo, which, as noted earlier, is owned—in part—by the PLO. Abu Iyad stated, in no uncertain terms, that the PLO "will not abandon Abu Abbas." In late November Arafat finally admitted publicly that Abbas was one of his loyal followers. "The PLF is made up of four groups," Arafat told the Budapest Television Service, "[and] Abu Abbas is the [*sic*] leader with us in Tunis."[18] In an interview Abbas later described how he reported the details of the *Achille Lauro* seizure to Arafat in their first meeting after the incident. He told an Arab newspaper, "It has been my duty to inform brother Abu Amar [Arafat] of the details [of the *Achille Lauro*] during our first meeting."[19]

Just as it was impossible to hide the PLF's ties to the PLO, so there was no way to avoid the unsavory image of armed Palestinian terrorists murdering an elderly Jew in a wheelchair and dumping his body over the side of the *Achille Lauro*. Although Abbas came under a great deal of internal criticism within the PLO for the clumsily executed terrorist attack, he remained defiant. At a PLO Executive Committee meeting in Baghdad he reportedly jumped to his feet and shouted at his critics, "Maybe it was wrong. But who else here has carried out any successful operations at the heart of Palestine?"[20]

In an interview in May 1986, broadcast on *NBC Evening News*, Abbas called Ronald Reagan "enemy number one" and vowed further attacks on American citizens. While acknowledging that his men had carried out the *Achille Lauro* operation, he denied, using extremely indelicate language, that his gunmen had killed Klinghoffer. "What is the use of killing an old man anyway?" he told the NBC correspondent. "Why? After all, he is old and would soon be dead anyway without killing. I do not believe our comrades on the boat carried out any killing."[21]

Efforts by Abbas and the PLO to disassociate themselves from the Klinghoffer murder became even more outrageous. In December 1985 Farouk Qadoumi told an Arab League luncheon, which was attended by UN Secretary-General Javier Pérez de Cuellar, that "perhaps it might be his wife pushed him [Klinghoffer] over into the sea to have the insurance. Nobody even had the evidence that he was killed."[22] And at the Algiers meeting of the Palestinian National Council in late 1988, Abbas went so far as to joke that maybe the sixty-nine-year-old Klinghoffer had died "trying to swim for it."[23] He went on to complain, "I wish that the names of our victims and martyrs were as well-known as the name of Kling-hoffer."[24]

In a moment of rare candor, however, Abbas admitted to the French magazine *Journal Dimanche* that the *Achille Lauro* seajacking had been an "operational failure" and that the murder of Leon Klinghoffer "was the act of a young PLO fighter, without experience and not stable."[25] Despite his disparaging comments about Molqi, Klinghoffer's murderer, Abbas conspired to secure his freedom and that of the other PLF men incarcerated in Italy. Like so many of his operations, this one also went sour. On November 27, 1985, Italian authorities arrested Omar Sadat Abdel Fatch, at the house of his cousin, an Italian citizen named Folavia Bonni, in Verona. In the basement of the house they discovered twenty kilograms of explosives, two Czech-made machine pistols, two pistols, radio equipment, and a great deal of ammunition. The thirty-three-year-old Fatch, who was using a Jordanian passport, had just returned from Yugoslavia after meeting with Abbas. He gave police the details of a terrorist operation that Abbas had instructed him to mount as a way of winning the freedom of the *Achille Lauro* hijackers. During his interrogation Fatch described himself as a PLO officer who "receives direct orders from Arafat."

Mohammed Abbas is, by no means, one of the stars of the Palestinian terrorist network. Nevertheless, he remains a dangerous, if often incompetent, fanatic, obsessed by overcoming past failures and demonstrating that he is someone to be reckoned with. Although held in relatively low esteem by other senior PLO officials, he commands a loyal following and has a reputation for hands-on involvement in every facet of his organization's operations. According to a secret document submitted by the IDF to the U.S. State Department, "Abu al-Abbas is behind the planning of his organization's attacks and is personally involved in all stages of the operations carried out by it. He is also personally involved in the recruitment of foreign volunteers and in the procurement of means for the perpetration of attacks."

10 | *The PLO and Hizballah*

E arly on August 21, 1982, as dawn was breaking over Beirut, U.S. Marines landed at the port of Beirut and relieved the Israeli troops controlling the area. Fifteen minutes later, at 5:45 A.M., French paratroopers, including a contingent from the Foreign Legion, took up positions along the so-called green, or demarcation, line dividing West and East Beirut. Italian troops, white plumes in their helmets, were the next to arrive, taking control of the checkpoints that permitted access to the warring halves of the city. Small French and Italian units also joined the Marines at the port of Beirut in order to emphasize the multinational nature of the Western presence.

By midmorning all was in readiness for the evacuation from Beirut of the embattled PLO. At 10:20 A.M. PLO fighters began evacuating their strongholds in the Fakhani section of West Beirut and boarding six U.S.-made trucks for what was to be their last ride through the shattered city, now encircled by Israeli armor. They tried to salvage a little pride by donning crisp new uniforms. Each man carried his personal AK-47 assault rifle and little else. It was an emotional scene, as their families and friends pressed close around the vehicles to bid them farewell. Thousands of other Palestinians, many from the refugee camps on the outskirts of the city, jammed the streets leading to the harbor, where a ferry, the *Sol Gregouri-ous,* painted white and flying both Cypriot and United Nations flags, lay at anchor, waiting to take them into exile and an uncertain future.

As the trucks started rolling toward the harbor, their comrades began firing in the air as a final salute to those about to depart. Slowly the sound began to build until it seemed that every rifle and antiaircraft gun in the city had erupted. At 11:45 A.M. the trucks arrived at the waterfront, which was secured by the multinational force, and the PLO men climbed off the trucks and scrambled up the gangplank leading to the *Sol Gregourious.* One of the last to board was a red-bereted PLA colonel, who told one of the authors, "We are withdrawing now, but we shall return to Beirut, as we shall return to Palestine." Then, with no further fanfare, at 12:09 P.M. the ferry pushed away from the pier and slipped out of the port, under the watchful gaze of Western warships.

Within ten days the PLO was gone, allowed to withdraw peacefully from the city which it had dominated for a decade. It had escaped total destruction at the hands of the Israelis only by the most slender of margins. The evacuation was the result of an agreement, forged at the last minute, among the governments of the United States, Lebanon, Syria, and Israel. The Lebanese government, which had reached an understanding with Arafat, negotiated on behalf of the PLO.

By August 30, 14,398 Palestinian and Syrian fighters and assorted terrorists, their faces masked to conceal their identities, had been pulled out of Beirut, along with 664 women and children. Of these, 8,144, nearly all Palestinians, had left by sea, together with the women and children. The Syrian Eighty-fifth Brigade and a contingent of Syrian commandos, both stationed in Beirut since 1976, and the remnants of the Palestine Liberation Army (PLA) evacuated Beirut by land, using the Damascus highway.

Unbeknownst to the various terrorists who slipped out of the besieged city with their identities concealed, silent Israeli drones, mounted with cameras, took their pictures from high overhead, as they crowded the decks of the evacuation vessels.

The pictures from the drones were transmitted to an air-conditioned command and control center on the twelfth floor of the Lebanese Electric Company building in Christian East Beirut, near the green line. There, on a large screen, the evacuation was closely monitored by senior Israeli and Lebanese Forces intelligence and military officials.

Arafat departed Beirut on August 26, aboard a Greek-registered yacht named the *Atlantis,* which was also painted white and bore the United Nations flag along with the colors of Greece. In order to ensure his safe passage, he had been accompanied from the Fakhani district to the waterfront by Red Cross officials, United Nations representatives, and the Greek and French ambassadors. They had formed a kind of human barrier around him, to shield him from harm. A spy camera mounted to a drone, however, monitored Arafat's every move and relayed it back to the screen in the Lebanese Electric Company Building. Arafat and his protectors were also unaware of the Sayaret Matkal snipers, hidden in buildings and on rooftops, who followed him in their gunsights every inch of the way to the *Atlantis.*

Arafat received a tumultuous sendoff, the largely Palestinian crowd beside itself with despair. There was wailing, shrieking, men beating their breasts and firing their weapons in the air, and the high-pitched undulating trills of the Palestinian women. As the *Atlantis* pulled out of the harbor, Arafat slumped in a deck chair at the stern of the vessel and watched the Beirut skyline recede into the distance, observed, even then, by a drone soaring overhead. He remained motionless, absorbed in thought, his aides giving him wide berth.

It was the end of an era.

"HOTHOUSE" OF INTERNATIONAL TERRORISM

For more than two decades Lebanon has been the hothouse of international terrorism. The political strife that started in the late 1950's and engulfed the eastern Mediterranean nation in the mid-1970's has spawned dozens of terrorist groups and factions. Not only did various terrorist groups mirror the violent passions and hatreds of the region, but the collapse of Lebanon's central government produced a state of anarchy that resulted in the country's becoming the chief terrorist safe haven in the world.

No terrorist, including Abu Nidal, has had more impact on the United States during the last decade than Immad al-Haj Mugniyeh, leader of the Musawi clan and chief of security of Hizballah ("The Party of God").[1] As operational head of Hizballah, Mugniyeh was the architect of the terrorist attacks that, in effect, drove the United States and its Western allies from Lebanon in the mid-1980's. His first major target was the U.S. Embassy.[2] On April 18, 1983, a pickup truck filled with explosives (two thousand pounds of TNT) detonated at the entrance of the U.S. Embassy in Beirut, shearing off the front of the building, killing at least sixty-three people and injuring many others. Forty-seven of the dead, including seventeen Americans, were employees of the embassy.

Of the seventeen American casualties, many were members of the CIA station in Lebanon. Nearly the whole station was lost, including the agency's top Middle East expert, Robert C. Ames, who was visiting that day. Indeed, a working lunch was being held for Ames, and the embassy's kitchen had been alerted to prepare something special. It was a Lebanese employee of the kitchen who passed the information along to Hizballah and precipitated Mugniyeh's decision to carry out the attack on the eighteenth at 1:05 P.M.

U.S. and Lebanese authorities assembled a good deal of reliable intelligence information affixing blame for the attack on Mugniyeh. One of the most persuasive pieces of evidence was the statement of the commander of a Christian Lebanese Forces checkpoint near the embassy, who was an intelligence operative with Elias Hobeika's Lebanese Forces intelligence (LFI) unit. He later admitted, while being tortured by representatives of the LFI and in the presence of U.S. intelligence officials, that he had been bribed by Hizballah to permit the bomb-laden pickup to pass through the checkpoint without scrutinizing it. The man ultimately died in the interrogation chair.[3] Interestingly, in late 1985 Hobeika defected to the Syrians and is presently in the Bekaa Valley near Baalbek, mounting terrorist operations on behalf of Syria's intelligence chief in Lebanon, Brigadier General Ghazi Kanaan.

The following October 23, at 6:20 A.M., the four-story U.S. Marine battalion landing team (BLT) headquarters at the Beirut airport was turned to a pile of smoldering rubble by another vehicle bomb. The gas-enhanced bomb, composed of approximately twelve thousand pounds of explosives, was one of the largest conventional explosive devices on record. In the blast 241 Americans, nearly all marines, were killed.

In the aftermath of the April bombing of the U.S. Embassy, members of the French contingent of the multinational force in Lebanon had rapidly come to the aid of the stricken Americans, throwing up a security cordon around the shattered embassy and helping dig the victims out from underneath the collapsed masonry. However, on October 23, the French were too preoccupied with their own problems to help. Two miles from the Beirut airport, they, too, were frantically digging for survivors after a vehicle bomber hit a building housing French paratroopers. Fifty-nine legionnaires were dead.

Once again the perpetrator of the attacks was Immad Mugniyeh, although both Syria and Iran played significant roles in the slaughter.[4] Sheikh Mohammed Hussein Fadlallah, the supreme leader of Hizballah in Lebanon and Mugniyeh's superior, denied any role in the bombings.[5] In an interview published in the Washington *Post* less than a week after the attacks, Fadlallah "said he was a peaceful man, harbored no grudges against either the U.S. Marines or the French and has always preached against violence."[6] Interestingly, Mugniyeh's name fails to surface in any of the media reports regarding the Beirut incidents.

Nearly a year later Mugniyeh's men carried out their third major attack against an American target in seventeen months, this time hitting the U.S. Embassy annex in East Beirut and leaving nearly fifty people dead and wounded. Mugniyeh later masterminded the 1985 hijacking of TWA Flight 847. One American, a U.S. Navy diver, was murdered in cold blood during the seventeen-day ordeal. Mugniyeh was also responsible for the kidnapping of four Soviet diplomats in Beirut on September 30, 1985. One of the hostages, a consular secretary named Arkady Katkov, was executed by the terrorists and his body dumped near the Beirut sports stadium. The three surviving diplomats were later released unharmed. In 1988 terrorists under Mugniyeh's control were responsible for the hijacking of a Kuwaiti jetliner.

Not only did Mugniyeh play a major role in bombing the United States, France, and Italy out of Beirut in 1983 and 1984, but he is behind the seizure of nearly all of the Western hostages in Beirut over the past five years. In short, Mugniyeh is the modern equivalent of the "old man of the mountain," the master terrorist and leader of the Islamic sect once known as the assassins.[7]

But just who is Immad Mugniyeh and where is he from? What motivates him?

THE MASTER TERRORIST

Little is actually known about Immad Mugniyeh. Reportedly between thirty-two and thirty-five years old, he is regarded as extremely close to Sheikh Mohammed Fadlallah, the founder and supreme leader of Hizballah (not just the "spiritual" leader of the organization, which is how he is frequently identified). Fadlallah is the revolutionary government of Iran's chief link inside Lebanon. It was Fadlallah who established close working ties with the Pasdaran, Iran's powerful Revolutionary Guards, who subsequently have provided Hizballah with men, military training (in both Lebanon and Iran), and weaponry.

Mugniyeh reportedly was born in southern Lebanon and grew up in the Chai e-Salum or Bir al-Abed section of Beirut, among the poorest Shiite neighborhoods in the city. Mugniyeh and many other impoverished Shiite youths, all under the age of twenty, were recruited during the latter part of 1975 by Fatah, the largest single component of the PLO. The young Shiites joined Fatah at a time when the endemic sectarian violence in Lebanon was escalating into an all-out civil war, pitting the various factions—Christians, Druzes, Palestinians, Moslems (both Sunnis and Shiites), and Syrians—against each other. Most of the Shiite youths were unemployed, with few prospects and little hope for the future. Fatah offered them good salaries, military training, and the opportunity to play a role in the battle for Lebanon's future.

After receiving basic training in the Palestinian refugee camps around Beirut, some of the more promising Shiite recruits, familiar with Beirut and its environs—by then the chief battleground of the conflict—were selected to join Force 17, one of the most elite elements of Fatah. As noted previously, Force 17 is responsible for the security of Chairman Yasir Arafat and other top PLO officials and also serves as the PLO's counterintelligence apparatus, charged with eliminating traitors and enemy agents from the PLO's ranks. Initially the Shiite recruits performed relatively menial security tasks, but in time some of the young men gradually evolved into skilled special operators.

Mugniyeh remained with Force 17 from early 1976 until sometime in 1982, although few facts about his actual service have been reported. According to intelligence sources, during this period Force 17 was generally not involved in external terrorist operations but confined its activities, for the most part, to settling disputes among rival Palestinian factions and dealing with Arafat's enemies.

DISCIPLE OF ALI HASSAN SALAMEH

The original leader of Force 17 was Ali Hassan Salameh, the legendary former chief of operations for Black September. Black September, which was for all intents and purposes an artifice to put distance between the PLO and various terrorist operations, had been "disbanded" after the Israeli government declared war on the group and initiated a systematic effort to hunt down and kill its leadership.

In 1979 Salameh was killed by the Israelis, who had hunted him ever since the massacre at the Munich Olympics in 1972. Their operations against him had failed on a number of occasions, the most notable being the attack in Lillehammer, Norway, in 1973, when Israeli agents murdered a Moroccan waiter, Ahmed Bouchiki, they had misidentified as Salameh. The gunmen, believing they had finally cornered Israel's most wanted terrorist, pumped twenty-two rounds into the unfortunate man, who bore a remarkable resemblance to Salameh, and then fled the scene of the crime. Six members of the hit team were later arrested by Norwegian authorities and tried, and five of them were convicted and sentenced to jail terms.

On January 22, 1979, the "long arm" of the Mossad finally caught up to Salameh, in the heart of West Beirut, as he traveled through the city's narrow streets to visit his mother. Sometime during the previous November an Israeli agent of English origin who used the name Erika Mary Chambers, and was known to her neighbors as Penelope, took up residence in the West Beirut neighborhood transited by Salameh on his daily comings and goings to and from Fatah headquarters. Accompanied by heavily armed bodyguards, he normally traveled in a tan station wagon, followed by a Land-Rover. Chambers meticulously gathered intelligence about his movements, and in January she was joined by four other Mossad agents, who entered Lebanon on British passports and rented cars from a local agency.

The night before the operation one hundred pounds of plastic explosive were delivered to a deserted beach near Beirut by members of Israel's naval commando unit, Flotilla 13. The commandos came ashore in rubber dinghies from an Israeli missile boat and transferred the explosive to the Mossad agents. The explosive was packed into a rented Volkswagen parked on the Rue Madame Curie. At approximately 4:00 P.M. Salameh's tan station wagon turned onto the Rue Madame Curie, followed by the Land-Rover. As the station wagon pulled abreast of the Volkswagen, Chambers triggered the explosive device by remote control.

The blast destroyed the Volkswagen and turned the station wagon and Land-Rover into torches, killing Salameh and his eight bodyguards. The surrounding buildings sustained considerable damage as well, and several pedestrians died in the attack. Within days of Salameh's emotional funeral, his deputy, Abu Tayeb, had become commander of Force 17.[8]

In 1982 the Israelis drove deep into Lebanon and laid siege to Beirut. It was the first time Palestinians troops had engaged in large-scale direct combat with Israel, and within a days it became clear that they were no match for the Israeli war machine. Their dream of defeating Israel on the battlefield quickly dissolved; the very best they could hope for was to delay the Israeli advance and salvage a modicum of pride by fighting an effective rearguard action. In eastern Lebanon, Syrian regulars inflicted heavy casualties on the Israelis and covered the Palestinian withdrawal.

Within a week the PLO was surrounded in Beirut. For its part, Lebanon's large Shiite community tried to remain on the sidelines. Al-Amal, (the Hope) the main Shiite militia under the control of Nabih Berri, steered a neutral course and avoided confronting either the Israelis or the Palestinians. However, not all Shiites agreed with Berri's approach. The most radical elements in the Shiite community coalesced into a new political and fighting body known as Hizballah, or the Party of God. Under the leadership of Sheikh Mohammed Hussein Fadlallah, Hizballah advocated armed struggle against all foreign forces in Lebanon, although this did not include fraternal forces from the Islamic regime of Ayatollah Khomeini, which had sent a detachment of Revolutionary Guards (the Pasdaran) to Baalbek, in the Bekaa Valley. A Libyan military force was also dispatched by Colonel Qaddafi to Baalbek in late 1982, and it remained there until 1988, providing logistical support to the pro-Syrian Palestinian organizations based in the Bekaa, such as Abu Musa's Fatah Provisional Command, the PFLP-GC, and Habash's PFLP.

THE PLO-HIZBALLAH AXIS

During the summer of 1982, as the Israeli noose closed around Beirut, the Shiite fighters from Force 17—including Mugniyeh—defected with their arms to Hizballah, apparently with Arafat's blessing. Sheikh Fadlallah, who made his headquarters in Bir al-Abed, the Shiite section of Beirut, knew Mugniyeh personally. Because of Mugniyeh's experience with Force 17, Fadlallah tapped him as Hizballah's chief of security in Beirut, in effect making him the operational chief of the organization. In August the PLO agreed to evacuate Beirut, and its exodus, as noted earlier, was overseen by a twenty-one-hundred-man multinational force (MNF) composed of U.S., French, and Italian troops. Unbeknownst to the Israelis or the intelligence services of the MNF nations, a small unit of Force 17 remained secretly behind.[9]

With the PLO infrastructure gone, the unit turned to its former comrades in Hizballah for arms, intelligence, and protection. Immad Mugniyeh offered the Force 17 unit any support it required, and a regular channel of communication was established between the unit and Hizballah. "It was a clandestine-operational line of communication which helped both sides," observes one intelligence official, who notes that the link has, in recent years, been institutionalized and upgraded and today involves regular contact between Mugniyeh and Abu Tayeb.[10]

To express Force 17's gratitude for the assistance rendered to it during the difficult period following the PLO's evacuation from Beirut, the PLO, specifically Fatah, transferred a large sum of money to Hizballah. Ever since then the PLO has continued to provide regular funding, as well as arms, to Hizballah. The payments are made directly from Abu Tayeb to Mugniyeh, and every transaction is personally approved by Yasir Arafat. In return for the financial support, Hizballah has assisted Force 17 and the fighting elements of Fatah in reestablishing their presence in Lebanon, especially around Beirut. According to one intelligence source, "Mugniyeh's people met the Fatah people at various points of entry and arranged safe transportation for them into West Beirut."[11] Hizballah operatives provide regular logistical support to the PLO, especially in and around Beirut, and there is even some sharing of intelligence. This did not prevent the PLO and Fatah from engaging in bitter fighting with the Shiite Amal militia both in Beirut and in southern Lebanon.

In the aftermath of the bombing of the U.S. Embassy in Beirut and the U.S. Marine barracks at the airport, Western intelligence questioned to what extent, if at all, Hizballah received direct outside assistance in carrying out the bloody attacks, especially from the PLO.

The ties between PLO elements and Hizballah have remained intact despite the shifting political tides in Lebanon and occasional political differences. They are not predicated on either politics or ideology and are strictly operational and based on mutual expediency.

In 1986 Arafat initiated an effort to secure the freedom of the foreign hostages in Lebanon as a way of currying international support and demonstrating the PLO's "moderation." At the time most of the foreign hostages were prisoners of Hizballah. An undetermined number were being held captive in a building on the outskirts of West Beirut, not far from the Beirut International Airport. The building, which had two stories above ground and two below, served as a Hizballah outpost and dormitory. A number of Shiite families were housed on the two upper floors, and there was a carpenter shop in the front, on the ground level, that did business with the public. A garage led to the two floors beneath the ground, and the hostages were kept in isolated cells on the lowest level.[12]

Arafat and his senior advisers believed that Hizballah was ready to negotiate the release of the hostages, sensing that they had become a burden to the terrorist organization, tying up its men and resources and making it difficult to operate as a result of the intense effort by the United States and other Western nations to recover their hostages. The United States was spreading millions of dollars around Beirut and in the eastern Mediterranean in an effort to gather intelligence regarding the hostages and had even repositioned and reprogrammed—at an enormous cost—a spy satellite over Lebanon to provide high-resolution photos of every inch of Beirut and its environs. Every form of technological eavesdropping was being used to intercept Hizballah's signals and other communications.

Lebanon was becoming claustrophobic for Hizballah, and Arafat knew it. He also knew that Mugniyeh and some of his senior operatives were growing increasingly apprehensive about the Reagan administration's willingness to use military force against terrorism, as had been demonstrated with the dramatic midair interception of the EgyptAir jetliner carrying the *Achille Lauro* pirates in 1985 and the air raid on Libya in April 1986. Direct intervention by the United States to retrieve the passengers on board TWA Flight 847 had also been narrowly avoided in 1985. Indeed, there were many rumors concerning impending joint military operations in Lebanon by the Americans and the Israelis and by the Americans and the French. The United States, moreover, had already indicated its willingness to play hardball with a series of covert operations, carried out by its agents and proxies from the Lebanese central government, against Hizballah and other terrorists in Lebanon. In one operation, defective bomb detonators were sold to a Hizballah unit. As the terrorists loaded a bomb into a vehicle, the ultrasensitive detonator triggered the device, dropping an apartment building on their heads.

What Arafat did not know, of course, was that the United States was already secretly negotiating directly with Iran for the return of the hostages. Arafat, accordingly, instructed Abu Tayeb to make contact with Immad Mugniyeh to see if some kind of "deal" could be brokered, with the PLO serving as the middleman. Fadlallah, however, who presumably knew something of the secret dealings between the National Security Council and emissaries of Speaker of the Iranian Parliament Hashemi Rafsanjani, instructed Mugniyeh to reject the PLO overture. That was not the end of it, though. Periodically the PLO has tried to get its hands on the hostages in order to use them as collateral in its dealings with the West, but Fadlallah has stood firmly by his original decision. Summarizing the PLO's efforts, one intelligence source observed that "relations between Fatah and Hizballah are close and good. But they exist solely on the operational level. No exchange exists on the political level. And the transfer of hostages is a political decision that Hussein Fadlallah has not taken."[13]

In late 1988 news reports surfaced that elements of the PLO actually had control of some of the hostages, but they were discounted by Western intelligence sources. Similarly, a report in the *Wall Street Journal* that American hostage Lieutenant Colonel William Higgins was being held in a Fatah jail was also dismissed as highly improbable.

In retrospect, there is no evidence that the PLO, or any of its constituent elements, assisted Hizballah in mounting its attacks in Lebanon on the United States. On the other hand, there is every indication that both Syria and Iran provided direct assistance to Hizballah in terms of intelligence, explosives, training, and money. The PLO's contribution was Mugniyeh's seven-year apprenticeship with Force 17, where he learned to plan and execute terrorist operations with a great deal of efficiency and sophistication. The only real question remaining is whether Abu Tayeb or any elements within Force 17 or Fatah had any indication, in advance, regarding the Hizballah plots against the U.S. Embassy in Beirut or the Marine barracks. "It is conceivable, yet the probabilities are low," concludes a senior Israeli intelligence official who has closely monitored PLO/Fatah activities since 1974.[14]

Prior to both major attacks it was widely rumored around Beirut that Hizballah was planning something "big" against the Americans; but the rumors were unspecific, and Beirut was awash in rumors of this kind. The PLO was surely aware of the rumors, but it is doubtful that Mugniyeh or any of his senior operatives shared with the PLO any specific knowledge of the impending attacks against either the embassy or the barracks. There was no reason to do so, and the larger the circle of people who knew about a forthcoming operation, the more risk there was of its being exposed in advance. Thus, the PLO's principal contribution to the attacks seems to have been the comprehensive terrorist training provided to Mugniyeh when he was a member of Force 17.

Mugniyeh has interesting ties to at least two other terrorist organizations. Indeed, it could be said that terrorism runs in the family. His brother-in-law, Mustafa Yussef, is one of the operational leaders of al-Dawa ("The Call"), an Iranian-backed terrorist organization seeking to overthrow the Iraqi regime of Saddam Hussein. It was Yussef who planned and organized the attack against the U.S. Embassy in Kuwait on December 12, 1983, leaving four dead and twenty wounded. The U.S. Embassy was only one of six targets hit that day in Kuwait. Yussef and sixteen others, including a cousin of Mugniyeh's, were captured a short time later by the Kuwaitis and sentenced to death. The various hijackings and kidnappings subsequently carried out by Hizballah have been, in large measure, designed to force the Kuwaiti government to release the seventeen.

Another cousin of Mugniyeh's, by marriage, is Palestinian and a senior member of the Abu Nidal terrorist organization. The cousin, who travels on a Moroccan passport, is one of only two aides who meet regularly with Abu Nidal and carry his orders to the organization's field operatives.

On August 1, 1986, a Fatah unit composed of six experienced terrorists (four Palestinians, one Syrian, and one Lebanese) arrived in West Beirut, with orders to set up a base on New Fakhani Street and to make contact with Hizballah, after which it would operate under Hizballah's command. The leader of the unit, a Palestinian by the name of Mohammed Sa'id Salem (Abu Ghazi), and his men reported at Hizballah headquarters on August 6, 1986, after establishing themselves on the second floor of the Hashisho Building, near Hammoud Hospital in Saida. The Fatah unit has subsequently been engaged in Hizballah operations in and around Beirut, but no specifics are known.

11 | *Operation Cold River (Nahr al-Bard)*

Khartoum is the capital of Africa's largest nation, the Sudan. Situated at the confluence of the White Nile and the Blue Nile, the city was an Egyptian army camp 160 years ago. Today a traveler from the nineteenth century would still feel more at home in Khartoum than someone from the contemporary world. Indeed, it's as if the twentieth century had taken a detour around Khartoum. Arriving at the city's ramshackle airport, the first-time visitor senses that he has stepped back in time, into a place at once both exotic and wretched, full of the sights, sounds, filth, and tumult of a bygone age.

Minarets, not high rises, dominate the skyline. A few high-rise buildings loom over the city center, housing the burgeoning foreign aid community, perhaps the only sector of the economy that is growing. Most of the city's buildings, like everything else in the country, are in disrepair, the only exceptions being the presidential palace, a cluster of government ministries and army installations, the foreign embassies and the residences of the diplomatic corps, and a brief ribbon of attractive villas clinging to the banks of the Blue Nile.

City services are almost nonexistent. Most of Khartoum's half million or more inhabitants do without plumbing

276

or running water. There are few sidewalks; only the main roads are paved, and they are full of potholes. Telephone service is sporadic, as is electricity.

A layer of dust covers everything and makes the city almost indistinguishable from the desert around it. The few scraggly palms that dot the cityscape and provide some shade and relief from the the searing heat also are covered in dust. Indeed, it is the dust that the visitor finds the city's most pervasive feature. It sets the teeth on edge and parches the throat. Even the water tastes of dust.

Khartoum wasn't much different on the night of March 1, 1973, when eight Palestinian terrorists, all members of Black September, burst into the Embassy of Saudi Arabia during an all-male farewell party being thrown by the Saudi ambassador, Sheikh Abdullah al-Malhouk, in honor of the departing U.S. chargé d'affaires George Curtis Moore. Some guests escaped during the takeover, and others were released a short time later, including all the diplomats from the Eastern bloc and "sympathetic" Arab and Third World countries. Moore, recently arrived U.S. Ambassador Cleo A. Noel, the Belgian chargé d'affaires, Guy Eid, the Saudi ambassador, and Jordanian Chargé d'Affaires Adli al-Nassr were among those taken hostage. Both Noel and Eid sustained leg wounds in the takeover. The West German ambassador also had been a prime target, but he had left the party before the terrorists arrived.

In exchange for their hostages the terrorists demanded the release of a grab bag of international outlaws, including Black September leader Abu Daoud, then imprisoned in Jordan; Sirhan Sirhan, the murderer of Senator Robert Kennedy; and several members of the notorious Baader-Meinhof Gang, serving long prison sentences in West Germany.

The terrorists had been provided with all the critical intelligence needed to storm the Saudi Embassy—such as the guest list, security arrangements, and a diagram of the building—by the Palestine Liberation Organization's representative in the Sudan, Fawaz Yassin Abdel Rahman (Abu Marwan).[1] Prior to becoming the PLO's top man in the Sudan, Abu Marwan was in charge of the Voice of al-Asifa (The Storm). The Voice of al-Asifa was Fatah's main propaganda broadcast and was transmitted by Cairo Radio and later rebroadcast by Baghdad

Radio. The program had aired every evening for one hour since May 1968, when it first appeared. Abu Marwan oversaw the content of the program, which included a mix of interviews, segments devoted to instructing listeners on the principles of the Revolution, and military announcements, punctuated with Palestinian poems and songs. Among the more famous musical offerings was the "Kalashnikov Song," a paean to the Communist-manufactured assault rifle pronounced "Klashin" in Arabic:

> Klashin makes the blood run out in torrents,
> Haifa and Jaffa are calling us.
> Commando, go ahead and do not worry.
> Open fire and break the silence of the night.

Abu Marwan, who enjoyed full diplomatic immunity, apparently got cold feet and departed the Sudan for Libya on the eve of the attack, leaving behind incriminating documents that left no doubt about his role and that of the PLO high command in the plot. His deputy, Salim Rizak (Abu Ghassan), the PLO's number two man in the Sudan, who also had full diplomatic immunity, assumed command of the operation and actually led the attack. He was joined by six PLO gunmen, Abdel Latif Abu Hijlah (Abu Tariq) and five others known only by their first names or code names (Khalid, Salah, Gamal, Mahir, and Farouk). They had just arrived from Beirut the previous day. The final member of the operation was the third-ranking PLO operative in the Sudan, known today only as Karam, who was in charge of Palestinian student scholarships. It was Karam who actually drove the terrorists through the gate of the Saudi Embassy in the PLO delegation's Land-Rover, bearing its official diplomatic plates. The weapons and explosives used in the attack were shipped to Khartoum by Libya in a diplomatic pouch.

As a sandstorm swept toward Khartoum, negotiations for the release of the hostage diplomats got under way, reflecting the gloom hanging over the city. The United States, Jordan, and West Germany all indicated that the terrorist demands were out of the question. In a public statement President Richard Nixon declared that the United States would not pay blackmail. "We cannot do so and we will not do so," Nixon affirmed.

"REMEMBER NAHR AL-BARD"

All the terrorists were members of Black September, and throughout the entire hostage standoff in Khartoum, they remained in close and constant contact with Fatah headquarters in Beirut, using both a telephone and a shortwave radio (single side band, or SSB, high-frequency transmitter). When it became clear that the United States and the other nations holding the terrorists demanded by the Black Septembrists in exchange for their hostages were not going to capitulate, the terrorists looked to their headquarters for instructions.

Shortly after 8:00 P.M. on Friday, March 2, 1973, twenty-five hours after the Black Septembrists had stormed the embassy, Abu Iyad instructed Abu Ghassan, the commander of the terrorist operation in Khartoum, "Remember Nahr al-Bard. The people's blood in the Nahr al-Bard cries out for vengeance. These are our final orders. We and the rest of the world are watching you."[2] Nahr al-Bard ("Cold River") was a refugee camp and terrorist training facility near Tripoli, Lebanon, and one of two (the other being Badawi) that had been raided by Israeli paratroopers and naval commandos on the night of February 20–21, 1973, ten days before the Khartoum operation was launched. The training camp, which was located within the refugee camp, was run jointly by Fatah, via Black September, and the Popular Front for the Liberation of Palestine (PFLP), and served as the chief instructional center for international terrorists from all over the world.[3]

"Nahr al-Bard" was also the code phrase instructing the terrorists in Khartoum to kill the Western diplomats. Abu Iyad repeated the key phrase twice to underscore his order. At Fatah headquarters in Beirut there was still concern over whether the proper message had been received and understood. To eliminate any possible confusion, according to intelligence sources, Ali Hassan Salameh contacted the Embassy of Sudan in Beirut and requested that the same message ("Remember Nahr al-Bard") be transmitted to the terrorists at the Saudi Embassy in Khartoum. Sudanese officials were assured by Salameh that the message would bring the hostage crisis to a speedy conclusion. Accordingly, they transmitted it to the Sudanese Foreign Ministry in Khartoum, and it was delivered by courier to Abu Ghassan. The second message, however, was unnecessary. Noel, Moore, and Eid had already been executed in the basement of the embassy.

The execution had been a particularly brutal affair. Informed that he was about to die, Ambassador Noel, with great dignity, thanked the Saudi ambassador for his hospitality and assured him that he should not feel any guilt over what was about to happen. At 9:06 P.M. the three men were lined up against the wall and forty rounds were pumped into their bodies. At the command of Abu Tariq (Hijlah), who led the assassination squad, the terrorists fired from the floor upward, to prolong the agony of their victims by striking them first in the feet and legs, before administering the coup de grâce. When they were finished, Abu Ghassan telephoned the U.S. Embassy in Khartoum and informed it that the two Americans and the Belgian diplomat were dead.

A few minutes later Fatah headquarters once again established contact with its men in Khartoum. But this time it was the "old man," as Yasir Arafat was commonly known, calling. Arafat asked Abu Ghassan if the Nahr al-Bard code word had been understood. Abu Ghassan responded in the affirmative and told Arafat that the order had already been carried out. Arafat then expressed concern over the fate of the two Arab hostages, the Saudi ambassador and the Jordanian chargé d'affaires. He was assured that they were all right. Employing another set of code words, Arafat instructed Abu Ghassan to demand safe passage to Libya or Egypt. If the Sudanese government would accede to this demand, he continued, Abu Ghassan and his seven team members were to free the two remaining hostages and surrender to the government of Sudan.[4] In addition, Arafat personally contacted a top Sudanese official by telephone to urge that no precipitous action be taken, such as an effort to storm the embassy. He asked the Sudanese to "be patient" until a senior PLO official arrived on the scene. According to Beirut newspaper reports described in a confidential U.S. State Department cable, the PLO emissary was carrying an order from the PLO Executive Committee informing the terrorists that their "mission" was over and instructing them to surrender to the Sudanese authorities.[5]

The State Department later speculated that "Arafat's last minute move to help avert assassination of Saudi and Jordanian ambassadors may have been designed [to] maintain some slight credit with Arab moderates and those within Fedayeen movement who believe that extremists like Salah Khalaf [Abu Iyad] are leading movement to destruction."[6] Even if we concede such an interpretation to Arafat's actions, it is clear that he and Abu Iyad were in charge of the operation.

Further evidence of their guilt is provided by the U.S. Embassy in West Beirut, some two miles north of Fatah's headquarters in the Fakhani section of the city, which subsequently intercepted another radio transmission from Arafat to his men inside the Saudi Embassy in Khartoum. "Your mission has ended," he told them. "Release Saudi and Jordanian diplomats. Submit in courage to Sudanese authorities to explain your just cause to [the] great Sudanese Arab masses and international opinion. We are with you on the same road. Glory and immortality to [the] martyrs of the Nahr al-Bard and Libyan aircraft."[7] This is the first time that Libya is referred to, and it suggests that the operation may have been carried out, in part, in retaliation for the Israeli downing of a Libyan passenger jet on February 21, 1973. Former Deputy Chief of Mossad Shlomo Cohen Abarbanel was convinced that the Libyans were intimately involved in the operation. According to Cohen Abarbanel, they "were all over the operation. They offered their assistance once they were approached by Fatah and apparently paid for the operation after it was carried out."[8]

Although the Sudanese government failed to promise the terrorists safe passage out of the country, at the end of a sixty-hour siege they surrendered without harming their Saudi or Jordanian hostages. After their surrender, speaking from Beirut, Black September issued the following statement: "Now that our youth have given themselves up as instructed, we wish to make following position: (A) Their operation was aimed at liberating Abu Daoud and his companions and Sirhan Beshara Sirhan who are being jailed in violation of all human ethics."[9] The rest of the statement, in fractured English, accused Ambassador Noel of conducting spying operations against Palestinians in the region and claimed that Moore was a CIA operative who assisted the Jordanian government in its "massacre" of civilians in September 1970. No evidence was presented to substantiate either charge.

The Black September terrorists were brought before a Sudanese court of inquiry, but two of them were, unbelievably, released for "lack of evidence." The other six were subsequently tried and on June 24, 1973, found guilty of murdering the three diplomats. During the trial Abu Ghassan, the terrorist commander, told the court, "We carried out this operation on the orders of the Palestine Liberation Organization and should only be questioned by that organization."[10] Additional evidence of the PLO's full complicity in the savage operation had earlier been supplied by Sudanese Vice-President Mohammed Bakir, who said one of the terrorists had made a full confession and described in detail Fatah's play-by-play direction of the operation from its Beirut headquarters. According to Bakir, "At the outset, the terrorists received instructions as to the method of storming the Saudi Embassy in Khartoum and whom to seize as hostages. They relied on radio messages from Beirut Fatah headquarters, both for the order to kill the three diplomats and for their own surrender Sunday morning."

The Black Septembrists were sentenced to life imprisonment, but later the same day their sentences were reduced to seven years by Sudanese President Gaafur Nimeiry. Twenty-four hours later they were spirited out of the Sudan and handed over to the PLO.

AFTERMATH

Prior to the Khartoum murders terrorism had been viewed by U.S. officials chiefly as an Israeli and European problem, not as a direct threat to the United States. But the incident in Khartoum changed all that. It was clear that the PLO was prepared to wage war against the United States and its citizens, not only because the United States was Israel's leading protector and patron but also because the PLO was fundamentally at odds with America from an ideological point of view. The PLO had lined up with the Soviet bloc and America's Third World enemies, who were committed to a violent restructuring of the global order and the destruction of the political, economic, and moral values embraced by the West.

The United States, however, hesitated to directly retaliate against Black September and the PLO. Instead, Secretary of State Henry Kissinger dispatched Lieutenant General Vernon Walters to a still-secret meeting with two top PLO figures, Khaled al-Hassan and Majid Abu Sharar, in Rabat, Morocco.[11] According to a published interview, Walters said his meeting was with "a very senior PLO guy, but not Arafat directly." As for what he told the PLO officials, Walters will only say: "Stop killing Americans or there would be serious consequences."[12]

U.S. officials had ample evidence of Arafat's and the PLO's direct involvement in the Khartoum murders but chose—for reasons never made clear—to suppress the evidence, including the intercepts of the radiotelephone conversations between Abu Ghassan and Fatah headquarters in Beirut. The National Security Agency (NSA) had monitoring stations throughout the region and obviously would have paid particular attention to communications between Khartoum and Beirut during the period in question. Among these stations were the huge Kagnew "listening post" in Asmara, Ethiopia, and signals intelligence facilities in Turkey, Italy, Saudi Arabia, and Cyprus. The communications may also have been monitored by U.S. naval vessels belonging to the Sixth Fleet and by U.S. RC-135's based in Greece.

In addition, the U.S. Embassy in Khartoum was equipped with a Fairchild Band Hopper, an electronic device able to scan the entire range of radio transmission frequencies searching for signals.[13] Once it locks in on a signal, it can record the transmission. It is hard to imagine, therefore, that the embassy failed to intercept the critical communications (including the coded message to kill the Western diplomats) between Fatah headquarters in Beirut and the Saudi Embassy in Khartoum. Indeed, a March 7, 1973, cable from the U.S. Embassy in Khartoum to the secretary of state actually re-

ferred to what are, presumably, taped intercepts. "Embassy
. . . has obtained . . . recitation of communications (based on
tapes) between Al Fatah Radio in Beirut to terrorists at Saudi
Embassy in Khartoum," reads the heavily censored cable.
"Notable that the terrorists were apparently under external
control from Beirut and did not murder Ambassador Noel and
Moore nor surrender to GOS [government of Sudan] until
receiving specific codeword instructions."[14]

A confidential source has confimed that the CIA station at
the U.S. Embassy in Khartoum did monitor the communications between the terrorists and their headquarters in Beirut.
According to this source, when the crucial "Cold River" command was intercepted, the CIA operatives at the station did
not immediately understand its significance. This was due to
the fact that the term "Nahr al-Bard" was translated literally,
and no connection was made with the Israeli raid in Lebanon
ten days earlier. Thus, it was only in retrospect that the station realized that the Nahr al-Bard message was the command
to execute the Western hostages.

At the time of the Khartoum incident, in addition to the
elaborate U.S. signals collection net, Israel monitored all communications from Fatah headquarters to its far-flung stations
and operatives.[15] The Israelis have never released the actual
taped intercepts, but transcripts exist of the communications
between the terrorists in Khartoum and their Beirut headquarters.

Although General Walters, who served as U.S. ambassador
to the United Nations during the Reagan administration, has
been quoted as saying that the existence of the critical tape,
wherein Abu Iyad and, subsequently, Arafat gave the order to
kill the Western diplomats, was "common knowledge," the
tape has never surfaced. Crucial State Department cables
from the U.S. Embassy in Khartoum also reportedly were
destroyed.[16]

The only answer for the Nixon administration's reluctance
to make public all that was known about the Khartoum incident in 1973 is that top American policy makers feared that
to do so would force the government's hand. The public and
the Congress would surely have cried out for some kind of
retaliation against Arafat and the PLO if their direct involvement in the murders of Noel and Moore was proved. There

may also have been concern that the situation could easily escalate out of control, placing many other Americans in jeopardy, as the United States and the PLO flailed away at each other.

In addition, it should be remembered that in the spring of 1973 the Nixon administration was distracted by the protracted war in Vietnam and the growing Watergate scandal. Another crisis was the last thing anyone desired. As the recently named secretary of state, Henry Kissinger also had to be mindful of the negative impact in the Arab world of any direct U.S. military operation against the PLO, especially on his efforts to forge some kind of lasting peace agreement between Israel and its Arab neighbors. Kissinger may have suspected, but had no way of knowing, that within months the Middle East would once again be enveloped by war when Egypt and Syria launched a surprise attack against Israel on Yom Kippur.

WHERE ARE THEY NOW?

It has been more than sixteen years since the incident in Khartoum, and the United States is presently conducting a dialogue with the PLO that U.S. policy makers hope will lead to some kind of resolution of the Palestinian question. Nevertheless, it should be asked: What became of the perpetrators of the Khartoum incident and those who murdered the three diplomats in the basement of the Saudi Embassy?

On November 13, 1974, Yasir Arafat addressed the United Nations General Assembly in New York. Prior to Arafat's appearance, three members of the Black September team who were intimately involved in the planning and execution of the Khartoum operation were spotted by Western intelligence agents at Heathrow Airport en route to New York. The three terrorists—Fawaz Yassin Abdel Rahman (Abu Marwan), Abdel Latif Abu Hijlah (Abu Tariq), and Farouk el-Husseini— all were members of Arafat's entourage, using diplomatic passports and traveling under false names.

El-Husseini, who was described as a "counterterrorism expert," was with Arafat's security detail in New York, and even liaised with U.S. authorities responsible for the PLO chairman's protection. Rahman, by contrast, was part of the PLO's diplomatic delegation, assigned to work with various Arab delegations at the UN. Until recently Rahman was the PLO's ambassador to the Arab League.

By 1974, Hijlah (Abu Tariq) was a senior official in the Foreign Affairs Department of the PLO and was in New York as one of the principal members of Arafat's delegation. All three men had been granted visas for the duration of Arafat's visit, and no attempt was made to arrest them or otherwise retaliate against them while they were within the grasp of U.S. law enforcement and intelligence agencies.

Arafat was also accompanied to the United Nations by the new commander of Force 17, Ali Hassan Salameh, the mastermind of the Khartoum incident and former operations chief of Black September. After Arafat's speech, which he delivered wearing a sidearm on his hip, the PLO leader was mobbed by reporters and television cameras as he departed the United Nations building. Right behind Arafat, Salameh, dressed in his traditional black garb, was clearly visible.

Since Rahman had left the Sudan immediately prior to the storming of the Saudi Embassy, his second-in-command, Abu Salim Rizak (Abu Ghassan), actually headed the operation and was the terrorist commander on the scene. It was Rizak who received the instructions, from Fatah headquarters in the Fakhani section of Beirut, to kill the three diplomats. Rizak's present whereabouts are unknown.

Perhaps the most disturbing reappearance of one of the Khartoum terrorists occurred in December 1988, after the United States opened a direct dialogue with the PLO in Tunis. According to an Agence France-Presse dispatch transmitted to Paris on December 16, 1988, at 4:11 P.M. (GMT):

Tunis, Dec. 16 (AFP)—The first official meeting between U.S. and PLO representatives for more than 13 years opened near here on Friday at 4:30 P.M. (1520 GMT).

U.S. Ambassador to Tunisia Robert Pelletreau and a four-man Palestinian delegation held a brief session for photographers before entering talks in closed session.

The Palestine Liberation Organization delegates were Executive Committee members Yassir 'Abd Rabbuh and Abdallah Hurani, Foreign Affairs Director 'Abd al-Latif Abu Hijlah, and the PLO representative in Tunisia, Hakim Bal'awi. A single session of talks was envisioned.[17]

Before the session started, U.S. Ambassador to Tunisia Robert H. Pelletreau, Jr., a former CIA official named the American representative to the talks, shook hands with Hijlah (Abu Tariq), the man who fifteen years earlier had emptied the magazine of his Russian-made assault rifle into Ambassador Cleo Noel, George C. Moore, and Belgian Chargé d'Affaires Guy Eid. There is no direct evidence that Pelletreau knew of Hijlah's unsavory past, but it is difficult to believe that U.S. intelligence agencies had not provided the ambassador with full profiles of the four PLO officials he was scheduled to meet with.

Arafat and the PLO could have chosen anyone to represent them at the first official talks with the U.S. government. Instead, for a variety of reasons, Hijlah was deliberately selected as one of the PLO's representatives. The chief purpose was to send Washington and the incoming Bush administration a blunt message, not in English but in Arabic. The message was that the past should be forgotten, that no matter what direction the U.S.-PLO dialogue would take, the talks should be predicated on current realities and mutual hopes for the future, not on past animosities. Sending Hijlah to meet with Ambassador Pelletreau was a particularly Arab/Bedouin gesture, which finds its origins in the Sulach, or reconciliation ceremony, which permits a murderer to sit down with the family of the murdered and to put the past behind them.

Hijlah's presence at the meeting was also a way for Arafat and his lieutenants to test the depth of the U.S. commitment to the dialogue. There was little question that U.S. intelligence would quickly identify him and ascertain his involvement in the Khartoum murders. If the United States reaction was harsh and public, Arafat would have to back off, replace Hijlah, and approach the talks with far more sensitivity. If the U.S. failed to react, Arafat knew that he would have much more latitude in conducting the talks.

Finally, the choice of Hijlah was a gesture to the radical forces within the PLO that opposed the dialogue with the

United States and the formal renunciation of terrorism. It also represented a none too subtle message to the United States and the rest of the world, signaling that the PLO could always return to terrorism to achieve its goals in the event that diplomacy failed to meet the PLO's expectations.

12

The Future of
the PLO

O
n May 2, 1989, during an official visit to Paris
that included a meeting with French President François Mitterrand, Yasir Arafat said
of the 1964 Palestinian National Covenant, which calls for the
destruction of Israel, that it is "null and void" or "lapsed"
(c'est caduque). Arafat's description of the covenant caught
many observers, including some top PLO officials, by surprise
since the Palestinian National Council, which originally
adopted the covenant, has never formally renounced it. Arafat
went on to say that he favored a referendum by all Palestinians on the efficacy of the covenant in its present form. PFLP
chieftain George Habash lashed out at Arafat, saying that if
Arafat believed the covenant was obsolete, he should resign as
leader of the PLO.

The confusion over the covenant is indicative of the contradictions and inconsistencies that exist within the PLO. The
question is: Who really speaks for the PLO and can he be
trusted? Is the PLO's leadership ready to make a decisive
break with the past and shed its commitment to violence and
terrorism? Can the PLO be demilitarized and its various ter-
rorist/commando organizations dismantled, their energies
channeled into nation building instead of destructive pur-

suits? Will the PLO relinquish its commitment to armed
struggle and adopt a truly realistic strategy for achieving
peace with Israel and the creation of a Palestinian ministate,
and in the event that such a ministate is realized, will the PLO
and its adherents be satisfied with it? Considering the PLO's
past hostility toward the United States and frequent collaboration with its enemies, is it in America's interest to help the
Palestinians achieve an independent homeland? Does the
world really need another wild card—that is to say, another
erratic and unpredictable nation?

It is impossible to predict with certainty the future or to
know how the PLO will govern in the event that it achieves
its goal of an independent state composed, most likely, of the
West Bank and Gaza Strip, without any portion of Jerusalem,
which Israel vows will never again be a divided city. The only
way to gauge the PLO's fitness to rule and assess its real
intentions is to look at its past, at its history, and thereby
attempt to draw some conclusions which may serve as a guide
to the future.

In this regard there is little in the PLO's past that is very
reassuring from a U.S. or Israeli perspective. Moreover, recent
statements by the leadership of the PLO raise doubts about its
willingness to settle for a truncated ministate with few resources, little infrastructure, indefensible borders, and a large
and vocal population. On December 18, 1988, for example, Abu
Iyad told a Kuwaiti newspaper that the PLO seeks "at first a
small state, and with Allah's help, it will be made large and
expand to the east, west, north, and south. . . . I am interested
in the liberation of Palestine step-by-step."[1] Such statements
suggest that Abu Iyad's long-held strategy of a "phased" program to redeem the Palestinian nation has not changed and
that he clearly views the attainment of a Palestinian state on
the West Bank and Gaza merely as the first stage in his ultimate quest to recover all the land now occupied by Israel.
Thus, the eventual destruction of the state of Israel appears
still to be his, and the PLO's, ultimate goal.

It is also hard to imagine that either the leadership or the
rank and file of the PLO, which has been at war with Israel
and much of the rest of the world for a generation, will
abruptly shed its revolutionary character, relocate to a West
Bank/Gaza Palestinian state, and settle down to ordinary jobs

and the task of raising families. Many observers within the Palestinian community have expressed their own doubts on whether "Arafat will be inclined to spend his time taking care of such things as garbage collection on the West Bank." In the past Arafat and his confederates have given little indication that they were really interested in ruling a Palestinian state. The PLO has been talking since 1968 about establishing a provisional government-in-exile and could not come to terms with the idea until late 1988, when, under pressure from the Intifada, Arafat and the old guard were forced to take action in order to assert their leadership over the developments in the occupied territories.

Indeed, there has been speculation that the PLO might remain intact as a revolutionary organization even after the establishment of a Palestinian state, something that would certainly not be welcomed by Israel or the United States or frankly by the rest of the Arab world. This would be consistent with Habash's notion of the PFLP and other Palestinian commando/terrorist organizations as a revolutionary vanguard that would "cleanse and purify" the entire Arab world with the destruction of conservative and pro-Western regimes. It could well be that Arafat, Habash, and their generation of Palestinians have been involved in the struggle for so long that the Revolution is even more sacred than Palestine itself, which for many of them represents the modern equivalent of the green light at the end of Daisy's dock in *The Great Gatsby*, the unattainable ideal that is richer and more fulfilling in the abstract than in the reality.

The question of whether or not Arafat would actually become the leader of a new Palestinian state is also intriguing. Over the years he has demonstrated little aptitude for management chores, most often delegating them to others, preferring instead the role of spokesman, roving ambassador, and chief energizer of the Palestinian movement. It has been suggested that Farouk Qadoumi (Abu Lutf), head of the PLO's Political Department, might be the most likely choice as prime minister if Arafat were not in the running. Faisal al-Husseini, son of the legendary Abed al-Kader al-Husseini and probably the most universally respected Palestinian, is a good bet for foreign minister. Although loyal to the PLO and a relative of Arafat's, Husseini spends most of his time on the

West Bank and is not actively involved in the day-to-day operations of the PLO. The real power in a future Palestinian state, however, is likely to be Abu Iyad, who would no doubt emerge as interior minister.

Despite such speculation, ultimately the most important question may be whether the Palestinian population of the West Bank and Gaza would—in the event that an independent Palestinian state comes into being—accept the leadership of the PLO being imposed on it. After all, almost no one in the PLO's leadership and few in the rank and file come from the West Bank. Virtually all the top officials of the PLO and most of its members are from places that are now part of Israel proper. Not only have few of them, for obvious reasons, visited the West Bank in the past twenty years, but recent years have seen the emergence of a West Bank identity that is separate and apart from the pre-Israel Palestinian identity and even the pre-1967 Six-Day War identity. As a consequence, says Yitzhak Rabin, "There is the chance, the potential, that local Palestinians [on the West Bank and in Gaza] will determine their own leadership, and this is a direct threat to the PLO."[2] This should come as no surprise considering that more than half the Palestinians of the West Bank and Gaza were born after the 1967 war and the onset of Israeli occupation. They have no firsthand memory of the PLO's leadership or of a Palestine not under Israeli occupation. For most West Bank and Gaza residents, Arafat and the other leaders of the PLO are remote and idealized figures, familiar largely through books and newspapers, unlike their own youthful leaders, who were born and raised on the West Bank and in Gaza and possess flesh and substance.

In the final analysis, the Intifada may have simultaneously breathed new life into the PLO and accelerated its decline by catapulting a new generation of Palestinians—with different aspirations, experiences, and values—into the forefront of the struggle for Palestinian respect and self-determination. Thus, it would be dangerous for Israel, the United States, or any other country to read too much into the PLO's present posture of accommodation and compromise. It could turn out to be extremely ephemeral. Moreover, a careful analysis of recent events raises serious doubts that the PLO will be able to deliver on its promises and commitments, even if it wants to. A far more sinister interpretation holds that the PLO has no intention of adhering permanently to its promises and commitments, that it has always had a secret agenda, and that this agenda remains as real as ever.

With respect to the PLO's "secret agenda," it is instructive to recall a little-noted or long-remembered 1977 press conference held in Damascus that spoke volumes about the true nature of the Middle East conflict.

THE PLO'S "SECRET AGENDA"

Just prior to his historic visit to Jerusalem, Egyptian President Anwar Sadat traveled to Syria to meet with Syria's Hafez al-Assad in a desperate attempt to generate some kind of support for his peace initiative with Israel. Sadat met with Assad for seven hours, and at the conclusion of their talks the Egyptian president held a press conference at the Tishrin Palace in Damascus. Although extremely significant, the press conference went almost unnoticed in the general climate of euphoria and excitement that overtook the world's media during this tumultuous week.

The two men clearly disagreed over the wisdom and advisability of Sadat's initiative. However, what is notable about the press conference is that Sadat took great pains to reassure Assad that their differences were merely a matter of tactics rather than goals. "We have often disagreed on tactics," explained Sadat, "but not on strategy [with respect to Israel]. We will never disagree on strategy."[3] In other words, Sadat had not suddenly fallen in love with Israel and decided to spurn his own culture, religion, and place in the Arab world. Like Assad, he would have preferred that Israel disappear from the face of the earth, but—by contrast with his Syrian counterpart—he recognized that Israel was, for at least the time being, a reality and that the nearly continuous state of belligerency that had existed for three decades was serving only to make Israel stronger and the Arabs weaker.

Three days after his meeting with Assad, Sadat's plane landed at Israel's David Ben-Gurion Airport. The world hailed the Egyptian president for his boldness and courage, and he was lionized in the international media as a peacemaker. While he certainly deserved credit and approbation for his historic initiative, whatever his motivations, lost in the frenzy of the moment was the meaning of the Damascus press conference and Sadat's underlying rationale for entering into the peace accord—the first between Israel and an Arab state—formalized on the south lawn of the White House sixteen months later.

By the same token, it must be recognized that the PLO's dramatic about-face, involving the recognition of the state of Israel and a formal renunciation of terrorism, does not necessarily mean that the PLO is abruptly putting aside all past differences with Israel and is ready to forge a lasting peace with the Jewish state. It is hard to believe that the PLO is reconciled to accepting Israel as a permanent reality in the Middle East, any more than Sadat was. Although many divisions presently exist within the Palestinian community, as former Israeli Prime Minister Yitzhak Rabin has observed, "The Palestinian community has its more extreme elements and less extreme elements, and argue among themselves over almost every issue. But there is no argument over the final goal."[4]

Afterword

At the time of this writing, Yasir Arafat has announced that he will come to the United States in late November 1989 to address the United Nations General Assembly. Arafat's action comes less than a year after he was denied a visa by the Reagan administration for precisely the same purpose. How President Bush and his State Department respond to Arafat's overture will say a great deal about the Bush administration's commitment to combating terrorism and its willingness to put aside the past, which witnessed frequent PLO attacks on American citizens and interests.

Although the facts surrounding the bombing of Pan Am 103 in December 1988 are well known, and involve a conspiracy by the Iranian government and the Popular Front for the Liberation of Palestine—General Command to bomb the plane in retaliation for the downing of an Iranian jetliner by a U.S. warship in the Persian Gulf, the Bush administration has so far failed to take any action to punish the perpetrators. It has even been reluctant to acknowledge the facts or to make public the results of its investigation. At the present time, the victims of Pan Am 103 are stark reminders of American timidity and vacillation in the face of egregious provocation by terrorists. Such weakness serves only to undermine the forces of moderation in the Middle East, both Arab and Israeli, by demonstrating that violence succeeds.

295

The Palestinian uprising, or Intifada, is in its third year and shows few signs of abating. Indeed, it may herald a permanant state of insurrection in the Israeli-occupied territories of Gaza and the West Bank. However, Palestinian supporters of the Intifada have little to show for three years of strife and bloody confrontation with Israeli authorities. The bad press that greeted heavy-handed Israeli efforts to deal with the violence has subsided, since the Israelis have become far more sophisticated in their techniques for handling the disturbances. If the Intifada has demonstrated, in the words of its graffiti, that "we exist" and that "we are here to stay," it has done little else. Strikes and work stoppages have combined with the endemic violence to paralyze the occupied territories and to sap their economic vitality. Many schools and colleges serving the Palestinian community remain closed. And, perhaps most tragic of all, the rift between Israelis and Palestinians has become a chasm. In Israel, the Intifada has served to bolster the political fortunes of hard-liners and those preaching no accommodation ever with the PLO or the Palestinian population in the occupied territories.

The Intifada took an even uglier turn in 1989, as Palestinian supporters of the uprising turned their anger on their own community, using strong-arm tactics and even murder to maintain revolutionary discipline and to prevent Palestinians from cooperating on any level with the Israelis. More than one fifth of the total casualties of the Intifada are Palestinians killed by other Palestinians. The PLO maintains that those who died at the hands of their own compatriots were collaborators with ties to Israel's internal security service, the Shin-Bet. This may have been true of a small number, but many were victims of grudges and personal vendettas or casualties of brutal efforts by the leadership of the Intifada to enforce their will on the populace.

In recent weeks there have been reports that the Intifada may evolve into an armed struggle, with radical elements in the Palestinian community, including some within the PLO, calling for arming the Palestinian population of the West Bank and Gaza. Israeli officials believe that there are already enough weapons in Palestinian hands to equip a force of over two thousand fighters, and that the number of weapons being smuggled in each week is on the increase. The authors believe that any resort to armed insurrection would be a catastrophe for Palestinian aspirations in the occupied territories, and would produce a swift and brutal reaction on the part of the Israeli government. Both sides would be losers in such a conflict. The only winners would be Israeli extremists like Rabbi Meir Kahane in Israel and, on the Palestinian side, the Jibrils,

Mugniyehs, Abu Nidals, and other members of the so-called rejectionist front, which opposes any accommodation with Israel.

On the other hand, if the forces of moderation within the Palestinian community can prevail, Palestinians in the occupied territories could find themselves masters of their own destiny within a few years. Acceptance of the Israeli government proposal for elections and limited self-rule will not, in the short term, give Palestinians everything they desire. Initially they will have a homeland, but not a nation. Nationhood, in any real sense, will take time to achieve. It will be a gradual and evolutionary process, and depend on the degree of cooperation and coexistence that can be forged with Israel. In addition, it will be affected by events in Jordan, where an aging, and some reports suggest ill, King Hussein and his Bedouin followers rule over an increasingly restless Palestinian majority.

For its part, the PLO has shown a remarkable ability to control its many factions and splinter groups. Since Arafat's address before the special session of the UN General Assembly in Geneva in late 1988, terrorist actions by organizations affiliated with the PLO have declined by more than 50 percent, and almost all those that have occurred were conducted against Israel rather than against Western targets. Nevertheless, the PLO is riven with internal disputes and factionalism. The debate over which path to take—violence or accommodation—is far from settled, although Arafat and the "moderates" still appear to have the upper hand at the present time. The PLO remains an organization uncertain of its future and uncomfortable with its past.

Appendix One

LIST OF ALL MEETINGS OF THE PALESTINIAN NATIONAL COUNCIL (PNC), AS OF JANUARY 1989

1. May 28–June 2, 1964, at the Hotel Ambassador in East Jerusalem. It ratified the Palestinian Covenant (al-Qomi Ahed al-Falestinia).

2. May 31–June 4, 1965, in Cairo.

3. May 20, 1966, in the town of Gaza, inside the Gaza Strip.

4. July 10–17, 1968, in Cairo. Ahmed Shukeiry resigned as chairman of the Executive Committee, and Yechye Hamuda was elected to replace him. Fatah became the dominant organization within the PLO at this meeting, paving the way for Arafat to become chairman the following year. The Palestinian Covenant was edited, and four chapters were added. The Palestinian Covenant was renamed the Palestinian National Covenant.

5. February 1–4, 1969, in Cairo. Yasir Arafat and the fedayeen* movement took over the PLO and the PNC. Arafat was elected chairman of the Executive Committee.

6. September 1–6, 1969, in Cairo. The Palestinian Red Crescent organization was absorbed as an integral part of the PLO.

7. June 4–5, 1970, in Cairo.

8. February 28–March 5, 1971, in Cairo.

9. July 7–13, 1971, in Cairo.

10. April 6–12, 1972, in Cairo (emergency meeting).

11. January 6–12, 1973, in Cairo. During this meeting the Palestinian Central Council (PCC) was established.

12. June 1–9, 1974, in Cairo. The doctrine of phased stages was adopted during this meeting.

13. March 12–22, 1977, in Cairo.

14. January 15–22, 1979, in Damascus. The site of the PNC meeting was shifted from Cairo to the Syrian capital in the wake of Anwar Sadat's historic trip to Jerusalem.

15. April 11–19, 1981, in Damascus.

16. February 1983, in Algiers. This meeting took place after the expulsion from Lebanon and the loss of the PLO's safe haven and main base of operations. This meeting saw the reorganization and renaming of the PLA, henceforth to be called the National Palestinian Liberation Army (NPLA). Overshadowing the meeting were the rift between the PLO and Syria and the rebellion in the Fatah ranks that led to the creation of the Fatah Provisional Command, headed by Abu Musa.

17. November 22–29, 1984, in Amman. A reconciliation with Jordan was ratified, and the PLO accepted the idea of a Palestinian-Jordanian confederation.

18. March 1987, in Algiers. This was the so-called unification PNC, during which the PFLP (Habash) and the DFLP (Hawatmeh) returned to the fold and rejoined the PNC and PLO. Negotiations along the same lines were held by Abu Iyad with Abu Nidal, the leader of the FRC, who was in Algiers but did not attend the confer-

---

*"Fedayeen" refers to Palestinian fighters willing to sacrifice themselves for the cause.

ence. However, they were inconclusive. The notion of a Palestinian-Jordanian confederation was rejected, and the PNC came out unequivocally for the creation of an independent Palestinian state.

19. November 1988, in Algiers. This is the historic meeting during which a Palestinian declaration of independence was approved, and UN Security Council Resolutions 242 and 338 were accepted.

Appendix Two

MEMBERS OF THE PLO'S EXECUTIVE COMMITTEE AS OF JANUARY 1989

YASIR ARAFAT (Abu Amar), Fatah, chairman of the Executive Committee, head of the Military Department, "Commander in Chief of Revolutionary Forces," and chairman of Fatah's Central Committee.

FAROUK QADOUMI (Abu Lutf), Fatah, head of the Political Department and member of Fatah's Central Committee.

MACHMUD ABBAS (Abu Mazan), Fatah, head of the National Department and member of Fatah's Central Committee.

MUSTAFA EL-ZABARI (Abu Ali Mustafa), Popular Front for the Liberation of Palestine (PFLP), head of the Palestinian Refugee (Camps) Department and deputy secretary-general of the PFLP.

YASIR ABED RABA (Abu Bashir), Democratic Front for the Liberation of Palestine (DFLP), head of the Propaganda and Information Department, and deputy secretary-general of the DFLP.

ABED EL-RAHIM AHMED, Arab Liberation Front (ALF), head of the Popular Organization Department and secretary-general of the ALF.

MOHAMMED ZAIDAN ABBAS (Abu Abbas), Palestine Liberation Front (PLF), without portfolio and head of one of the two PLF factions loyal to Arafat.

SULEIMAN NAJAB, Revolutionary Palestinian Communist party (RPCP), head of the Social Affairs Department and secretary-general of the RPCP.

JAMEL SURANI (Abu Amar), independent, secretary-general of the Executive Committee and head of the Organizations Department.

ILIA HURI (Abu Mahar), independent, without portfolio, considered the Christian representative on the Executive Committee.

MOHAMMED HASSAN MILHAM (Abu A'ala), independent, head of the Occupied Homeland Department and the Higher Education Department.

ABED AL-RAZAK YAHIA (Abu Anas), independent, head of the Economic Department and the senior PLO representative in Jordan.

JAWEED YACCUB GHUSAIN (Abu Tufiq), independent, chairman of the Board of Directors of the Palestinian National Fund (PNF).

ABDULLAH HURANI, independent, head of the Cultural Affairs Department.

MACHMUD DARWISH, independent, chairman of the Supreme Council for Education, Propaganda, and Heritage. A well-known Palestinian poet.

Notes

INTRODUCTION

1. In Arabic *hammam* means "bath," *el* is "the," and *shat* is "sea." Thus, the phrase means "the sea bath" or, more elegantly put "the bathing shore."
2. See Washington *Post,* State Department statement on the rejection of PLO leader Yasir Arafat's application for a visa to visit the United States, November 27, 1988, p. A34.
3. Yasir Arafat, address to the United Nations General Assembly in Geneva on December 13, 1988. See *The New York Times,* December 15, 1988.
4. Yasir Arafat, statement in Geneva, December 14, 1988. See *The New York Times,* December 15, 1988.

CHAPTER ONE: THE DEATH OF ABU JIHAD

1. Interview with former Israeli intelligence officer, Tel Aviv, December 1988.

2. Interview with former Israeli chief of naval operations, February 1989.

3. News agency reports originating in Beirut, April 22, 1985.

4. Yossef Argaman, "To Beirut and Back," *Bamachaneh,* IDF official weekly publication (April 13, 1988), p. 35. See also David B. Tinnin, with Dag Christensen, *Hit Team* (New York: Little, Brown & Co., 1976).

5. He even named his eldest son Jihad.

6. "Abu Jihad Khalil al Wazir," Israeli intelligence report, December 1988.

7. Amnon Kapelyuk, "Abu Jihad Told Me: 'When the War Ends, I'll Learn Hebrew,' " *Yediot Achronot* (Israeli daily), April 22, 1988.

8. Interview with senior signals intelligence (sigint) officer, April 1988.

9. Most authoritative sources in the West, including the chief newspapers of record, spell the unit's name as "Sayaret Matkal." This, however, is an imperfect transliteration from Hebrew to English, and in the authors' opinion the unit's name should appear as Sayeret Matkal. Nevertheless, now that we are on record, in the interest of consistency with other sources we will continue to spell the unit's name with an *a* rather than an *e.*

10. The mutually recognized understanding not to target each other's top leaders is not locked in concrete. Rather, it amounts to a realization that the deliberate assassination of an opposing leader could set off a chain reaction of violence and counterviolence that might be impossible to bring to an end. Nevertheless, top leaders on both sides occasionally have been targeted for perceived transgressions or violations of prevailing norms. The Israelis have, for example, attempted to kill Arafat on a number of occasions, including a number of times during the 1982 siege of Beirut. The PLO, by contrast, tried to assassinate former Israeli Defense Minister Moshe Dayan and several other senior Israeli officials. The acceptability of revenge is very much a part of the Middle Eastern mentality, and both Israelis and Arabs subscribe to the notion of "an eye for an eye."

11. U.S. Government, *Foreign Broadcast Information Service,* interview with Abu Iyad, April 26, 1988.

CHAPTER TWO: THE RISE OF THE PLO

1. Larry Collins and Dominique Lapierre describe the coercive tactics employed by Israel Amir of the Haganah: "His first tactics

were psychological. His men would sneak into the areas at night and plaster the walls and doors of Arab houses with threatening posters. Handbills telling their owners to 'leave for your own safety' were stuck to the windshields of Arab cars. Anonymous threatening calls were made to Arab leaders in each [Jewish] neighborhood." See Collins and Lapierre, *O Jerusalem!* (New York: Simon & Schuster, 1988), p. 112.

2. The full name of the Irgun was National Military Organization, or Etzel, its abbreviation in Hebrew. Although popularly known as the Stern Group, or Gang by its detractors, which were many, its real name was Israel's Freedom Fighters, abbreviated in Hebrew as Lechi.

3. Abu Iyad, with Eric Rouleau, *My Home, My Land* (New York: Times Books, 1981), p. 12.

4. *Ibid.,* p. 20.

5. Alan Hart, *Arafat: Terrorist or Peacemaker?* (London: Sidgwick & Jackson, 1984), p. 87.

6. Arab names normally include the name of the father and the family and clan names. Abed a-Rachman was Yasir's first name before he changed it. Abed a-Rauf was his father's name, which is attached, according to Arab tradition, to the full name. Arafat al-Qudwah al-Husseini are the family and clan names. Yasir's father dropped the last two names and used only the name Arafat to identify himself. Members of the clan still use the names al-Qudwah al-Husseini as their family name. The al-Husseini name indicates the link to the Husseini clan, which takes its name from the Prophet Mohammed's grandson, Hussein. This clan arrived in Palestine, or southern Syria in those days, from the Arabian Peninsula around the twelfth or thirteenth century A.D.

7. Abu Iyad, *op. cit.,* p. 87.

8. *Ibid.,* p. 89.

9. Interview with Western intelligence official, October 1988.

10. Abu Iyad, *op. cit.,* p. 29.

11. *Ibid.,* pp. 34–35.

12. Some writers refer to each meeting of the PNC as a Palestinian National Congress. It should be noted that in Arabic the Palestinian National Council is al-Maglis (Council) al-Watani (National) el-Falestini (Palestine). Nevertheless, sometime in the late 1960's or early 1970's, the PLO started referring to the PNC in English as the "Palestinian National Congress" or "Palestine National Congress." The change in the English translation was made without altering the PNC's name in Arabic (in Arabic, *muatamar* means "congress"). This has created a good deal of confusion.

13. Major General (ret.) Aharon Yariv, interview, October 26, 1988, Ramat Aviv, Israel. General Yariv also served as a special

adviser for counterterrorism and intelligence matters to the prime minister of Israel. Presently he heads the Jaffe Institute for Strategic Studies at Tel Aviv University.

14. Hart, *op. cit.,* p. 45.

15. Abu Iyad, *op. cit.,* pp. 65 and 131.

16. Information on the PNC, the Central Council, and the Executive Committee is taken, in part, from Dr. Sami Musalem, "Study of the PLO: Functional Structure," *Shu'un Falestinia* (January–February 1987). Published in Arabic on Cyprus, *Shu'un Falestinia* is owned by the PLO.

17. Dr. Sami Musalem, "The PLO Structure," *Shu'un Falestinia* (January–February 1987).

18. U.S. Government, *Terrorist Group Profiles* (Washington, D.C.: U.S. Government Printing Office, 1988), p. 6.

19. Although it generally appears as Nahr al-Bard, the actual name of the Palestinian refugee camp is Nahr *e*l-Bard. Nevertheless, we will use the former spelling so as not to confuse the reader who is accustomed to seeing it that way. In this connection, in Arabic *al* means "the family of," "the clan of," or "the tribe of." *El,* by contrast, is used as an article before a noun, although there are exceptions to this rule.

20. Source: A highly classified intelligence report dated January 1985 based on sources inside the PLO/Fatah.

21. In his book *The American House of Saud,* Steven Emerson devotes a chapter to Gray's representation of Arab governments in Washington. See Steven Emerson, *The American House of Saud* (New York: Franklin Watts, 1985), "The Super Lobbyist," pp. 335–48.

22. The court dismissed the warrant because it had not been formally served on Arafat at an address on Italian soil.

23. Interview with Yariv, *loc. cit.*

24. Yasir Arafat, "Know the Enemy," interview in *Time* (November 7, 1988).

25. Brigadier Atallah Atallah (Abu Zaim) belongs to the second generation of Fatah commanders who managed to reach the top rungs of leadership. He and his brothers joined Fatah in the mid-1960's and rose steadily through the ranks. Atallah Atallah became an intelligence operator at the very outset, joining the Jihaz el-Razd (see Chapter Three). Unlike many of his contemporaries, he did not become a member of Black September. When the Jihaz el-Razd ostensibly was dismantled and the ISA was formed, he was among the first to enlist, and by the mid-1970's he had become chief of ISA and Fatah's top intelligence officer.

Atallah Atallah has always been known for his independent

views, which he is never afraid to express. His sometimes unconventional attitude brought him into conflict with the more doctrinaire elements in Fatah, and he gradually became frustrated when opponents conspired to block his political ambitions. He decided to mount a coup, hoping to enlist the Jordanians in a plot against the "old man" (Arafat) and what he regarded as the intransigent PLO leadership. But the Jordanians wanted no part of his machinations. After his coup failed, he launched an effort to discredit Arafat and other top PLO officials with various charges and by exposing their vices and corruption. While recognizing that he has a vendetta against those he has accused, as a former intelligence chief of Fatah he knows where many of their skeletons are buried.

26. U.S. Government, *Foreign Broadcasting Information Service,* Near East and South Asia daily report, "Sharon Warns Against Talks with PLO," January 30, 1989, p. 34. Original broadcast from the Jerusalem Domestic Service in Hebrew, 0805 GMT, January 28, 1989.

27. Ion Mihai Pacepa, *Red Horizons* (Washington, D.C.: Regnery Gateway, 1987), p. 36.

CHAPTER THREE: COVERT
UNITS AND OPERATIONS

1. Abu Iyad, *My Home, My Land* (New York: Times Books, 1981), pp. 188–89.

2. Ibid., p. 96.

3. U.S. Government, *Foreign Broadcast Information Service,* Near East and South Asia digest, interview with George Habash that appeared in *Al-Safir* (Beirut), January 23, 1989, p. 8.

4. Interview with high-ranking Israeli intelligence source, 1988.

5. The authors have adopted the common English spelling of the Jordanian prime minister's name, Wasfi Tell, even though his surname is pronounced in Arabic "tall" and in our judgement should be written as such.

6. All were Palestinian but Baghdadi, who was an Iraqi.

7. B. Tinnin, with Christensen, *op. cit.,* pp. 36–37.

8. John Richard Thackrah, *Encyclopedia of Terrorism and Political Violence* (London: Routledge & Kegan Paul, 1987), p. 28.

9. In Arabic *jihaz el-razd* means "observation apparatus" or "observation branch."

10. Georgina Rizak, a former Miss Universe from Lebanon, was

Salameh's second wife. His first was a niece of Haj Amin al-Husseini, the grand mufti of Jerusalem.

11. Abu Iyad, *op. cit.,* p. 98.

12. Abu Daoud, testimony published in *Al-Dustur* (Jordan), March 25, 1973.

13. *Ibid.*

14. Interview with former aide to Lebanon's President-elect Bashir Gemayel, October 1988.

15. Interview with former CIA Middle East analyst, December 1988.

16. Source: Highly classified intelligence report dated January 1985 and based on inside sources within Fatah/PLO.

17. It is at the Algerian military academy of Cherchel that a special operations unit called the Commandos of Skikda is trained. Controlled by the Algerian intelligence establishment, the Commandos of Skikda became notorious during the ten-year-old Sahara war for their grisly intelligence activities. They follow Polisario (Popular Front for the Liberation of the Western Saquiet el-Hamra and Río de Oro) units, backed by Algeria, during their raids on Moroccan positions. While they do not actually participate in Polisario military operations, in the aftermath of each engagement they collect tactical/military intelligence about the Moroccan forces, in part by stripping the bodies of the dead. They are also responsible for disposing of the bodies of Polisario guerrillas killed in each operation so as to disguise the number of casualties they have suffered. Often they will simply attach hooks to the bodies of the dead and drag them away behind their Jeeps as much as twenty kilometers from the site of the battle, where they will bury them in the sand.

18. Interview with high-ranking European intelligence official, December 1988.

19. "Lebanese Woman Denies TWA Bombing," Washington *Post,* April 6, 1986.

20. May 15 is also the date designated as "Palestine Struggle Day." As a result of its significance to Palestinians, it is also a date often chosen for terrorist attacks against Israel, the bloodiest being the May 15, 1974, attack on the Israeli border town of Ma'alot, in which twenty-seven Israelis lost their lives.

21. George Rosie, *The Directory of International Terrorism* (New York: Paragon House, 1987), p. 94.

22. Interestingly, both the PFLP and Abu Nidal's Fatah Revolutionary Council attempted to take credit for the incident.

23. PETN should not be confused with the French explosive Peten, which is often used as an enhancer to boost the explosive impact of ordinary explosives.

24. Interview with Israeli antiterrorism analyst, Tel Aviv, October 1988.
25. Abu Iyad, *op. cit.,* p. 139.
26. *Ibid.,* p. 9.
27. *Ibid.,* p. 12.
28. *Ibid.,* p. 21.
29. Eric Rouleau, preface Abu Iyad, *op. cit.,* p. xii.
30. Ibid., p. xii.

CHAPTER FOUR: THE PLO'S COMPLEX FOREIGN RELATIONS

1. U.S. Government, *Foreign Broadcast Information Service,* Near East and South Asia digest, quoting Yasir Arafat, January 30, 1989.
2. Zehdi Terzi, interview contained in *PLO: The Russian Connection,* PBS documentary, September 25, 1979.
3. Colonel Rashid Ahmed, "The Palestinian Delegation to the USSR," January 22, 1981, sent to PLO/CC and to Yasir Arafat.
4. *The New York Times Magazine,* September 24, 1979.
5. London *Daily Telegraph,* July 16, 1979.
6. U.S. Government, *Foreign Broadcast Information Service,* Near East and South Asia digest; statements by Suleiman Najab on April 4, 1988; April 6, 1988.
7. Interview with top Israeli intelligence official, October 28, 1988, Tel Aviv, Israel.
8. Abu Iyad, with Eric Rouleau, *My Home, My Land* (New York: Times Books, 1981), p. viii.
9. U.S. Government, *Foreign Broadcast Information Service,* Near East and South Asia daily report, October 7, 1988, quoting a Baghdad Voice of the PLO Broadcast (in Arabic) on October 6, 1988.
10. At that time the exchange rate was approximately four Lebanese pounds to the U.S. dollar. The following year the Lebanese pound began a steep decline, from which it has yet to recover.
11. See Amir Taheri, *Holy Terror* (Bethesda, Md.: Adler & Adler, 1987), p. 204.
12. A stewardess was wounded in the takeover.
13. Mohammed Reza Shah Pahlavi, statement, *el-Qudes* (Lebanon), December 13, 1974.
14. Samuel Segev, *The Iranian Triangle: The Secret Relations*

Between Israel, Iran, and the USA (Tel Aviv: Ma'ariv, 1981), p. 158. (Translated from Hebrew.)

15. William Shawcross, *The Shah's Last Ride* (New York: Simon & Schuster, 1988), p. 119.

16. Gary Sick, *All Fall Down: America's Tragic Encounter with Iran* (New York: Penguin Books, 1986), p. 264.

17. Yasir Arafat, speech before the General Confederation of Palestinian Writers, quoted in "Arafat Says PLO Aids Foreign Guerrilla Units," *Wall Street Journal,* January 14, 1982, p. 4.

18. Yasir Arafat, Voice of Palestine broadcast (Beirut), April 27, 1979.

19. Yasir Arafat, statement, *Al-Sharq al-Awsat,* October 18, 1985.

20. See, for example, Yasir Arafat, Voice of PLO broadcast, May 15, 1985.

21. See Yasir Arafat, *Al-Sharq al-Awsat,* November 18, 1985, and Yasir Arafat, Baghdad Voice of the PLO, November 27, 1985.

22. For the statement on Libya, see Yasir Arafat, *Al-Sharq al-Awsat,* November 7, 1986.

23. Yasir Arafat, statement, Voice of Palestine (Beirut), August 21, 1981.

24. Yasir Arafat, statement, January 1986.

25. Although Egypt gave the United States little help in bringing the *Achille Lauro* pirates to justice, Arafat decided to punish Egyptian President Hosni Mubarak and the Egyptian government. On November 23, 1985, for example, an Egyptian plane was hijacked to Malta, and Jews and Americans were singled out for execution.

26. Yasir Arafat, *Ukaz,* November 3, 1985.

CHAPTER FIVE: THE PLO'S FINANCIAL EMPIRE

1. Goren had also worked for Israel's military intelligence branch, AMAN, and actually "run" Arab agents for three decades.

2. Reports suggest that Iraq not only is current in meeting its payments to the PNF but reimbursed the PNF, without interest, for missed payments in the early 1980's.

3. The figures published by the PLO were originally denominated in Jordanian dinars. We subsequently converted the figures into U.S. dollars at the rate of 1 Jordanian dinar = 2.5 U.S. dollars.

4. Jaweed al-Ghusain, statement published by the *Arab News* (Kuwait), December 12, 1985.

5. U.S. Government, *Foreign Broadcast Information Service,* Near

East and South Asia report, August 12, 1988, p. 4. See: "Arafat on Jordanian Measures, Other Issues," *al-Sharq al-Aqsat* (London), in Arabic, August 9, 1988, pp. 4–5.

6. Dr. Sami Musalem, "The PLO Structure," *Shu'un Falestinia,* January–February 1987.

7. Interestingly, the Palestinian Central Bureau of Statistics (PCBS), which publishes the *Palestinian Statistical Proceedings,* was also incorporated into the new Economic Department. The PCBS is located in a five-story building near Shah Bandar Square in downtown Damascus.

8. Abu A'ala, statement; at Samed's third conference in Amman, Jordan, July 17, 1985.

9. "PLO Gift Shop," Washington *Times,* January 27, 1986.

10. James Adams, *The Financing of Terror* (New York: Simon & Schuster, 1986), p. 99.

11. U.S. Government, *Foreign Broadcast Information Service,* Near East and South Asia report, August 17, 1988; news report from the Amman Domestic Service in Arabic at 1500 (GMT) on August 13, 1988.

12. U.S. Government, *Foreign Broadcast Information Service,* Near East and South Asia report, October 3, 1988; WAKH dispatch from Baghdad dated September 30, 1988.

13. For further information regarding Sabbagh, see "The Palestinians' Big Backers," *Business Week* (February 22, 1988), pp. 18–20.

14. U.S. Government, *Foreign Broadcast Information Service,* Near East and South Asia report, "Sabbagh Negotiates on Behalf of the PLO with Syria," April 13, 1988.

15. Reportedly Abu Jihad was the only other senior PLO official privy to many of the details concerning the Chairman's Secret Fund.

16. Comment by unnamed Jordanian official, *Wall Street Journal,* July 21, 1986.

17. Twenty-one of the victims were schoolchildren murdered by the terrorists when the Israelis decided to storm the building rather than submit to the DFLP's demands.

18. Although the OPEC attack was a PFLP operation, two of the terrorists, Gabriele Tiedemann and Hans-Joachim Klein, were members of the German Red Army Faction (RAF).

19. The DC-9 carrying the terrorists and forty-two hostages, including eleven oil ministers, flew from Vienna to Algiers, then to Tripoli, and finally back to Algiers.

20. Interview with Lebanese Forces intelligence officer in Washington, D.C., during January 1989.

21. See Neil C. Livingstone and David Halevy, "The Perils of Poverty," *National Review* (April 29, 1988).

22. *Wall Street Journal,* July 21, 1986.

23. Interview with Arab intelligence official in Paris, November 1988.

24. Source: Brigadier General Atallah Atallah.

25. *Ibid.*

26. "The PLO and the Media," Israeli intelligence report, 1985.

27. *Ibid.*

CHAPTER SIX: YESTERDAY'S MAN

1. George Habash, interview, "The Next Generation Will Be Victorious," Washington *Post*, translated from syndicated copy in Hebrew, October 5, 1987.

2. Bassam Abu Sharif, also known as Bassam Towfik Sharif and Bassam Zayad, the spokesman of the PLO.

3. F. Lampert, *Studies in International Terrorism* (London: Routledge and Kegan Paul, 1957), p. 134.

4. For the best description of the hijacking of the El Al plane and related events, see Ehud Yari, *Fatah* (Tel Aviv: A. Levin-Epstein Ltd., 1970).

5. Kennedy is presently a member of the U.S. House of Representatives from Massachusetts.

6. Edward F. Mickolus, *Transnational Terrorism: A Chronology of Events, 1968–1979* (Westport, Conn.: Greenwood Press, 1980), p. 314.

7. Today Barak is a major general and the deputy chief of staff of the IDF. He served as the overall operational commander of the raid on Tunis in which Abu Jihad was killed.

8. Mickolus, *op. cit.,* p. 316.

9. The two camps were in the news again in 1983, when they were the site of Fatah's "last stand" in Lebanon, before Arafat and his organization were forced to evacuate the country once and for all. Completely surrounded by Syrian troops, rebel Fatah units, and pro-Syrian Palestinian splinter groups, Arafat and his loyal troops held out for weeks—involving particularly bitter fighting—in a desperate effort to maintain a foothold in Lebanon.

10. In his book *The Financing of Terror,* James Adams lists some twenty-eight terrorist "conventions" of international terrorists between 1970 and 1984, beginning with a so-called October 1971 conference at Florence, Italy. In reality, the Florence conference was an attempt by the mayor of the Italian city to rekindle the Medi-

terranean Peace Conference held in Florence in the early 1960's. It was not, however, a terrorist summit. See Adams, *op. cit.*, p. 52. In *The Terror Network,* Claire Sterling sees the terrorist summits as an outgrowth or legacy of the January 1966 Tricontinental Conference in Havana, which brought together 513 mostly Marxist delegates from throughout the Third World. See Claire Sterling, *The Terror Network* (New York: Holt, Rinehart and Winston, 1981), p. 14.

11. Dr. George Habash, interview with *Al-Safir* (Beirut), January 23, 1989.

12. *Ibid.*

13. *Ibid.*

CHAPTER SEVEN: AHMED JIBRIL AND THE PFLP-GC

1. Edward F. Mickolus, *Transnational Terrorism: A Chronology of Events, 1968–1979* (Westport, Conn.: Greenwood Press, 1980), p. 336.

2. Abed al-Kader al-Husseini was an Arab guerrilla leader, killed in 1948 during the first Arab-Israeli war. According to Collins and Lapierre, he was "the man the Mufti had sent to Palestine to take command of his Holy War Strugglers. Like his cousin [the grand mufti], Abdul Khader Husseini was a member of Jerusalem's Husseini clan. . . . He was a born leader of men. He possessed great physical courage. Unlike most of the Mufti's lieutenants, he was educated; yet he retained an instinctive understanding of the qualities and shortcomings of his peasant people. He had, despite a limited military background, an intuitive ability to mobilize and use their qualities and resources to their best advantage." See Collins and Lapierre, *op. cit.*, p. 86.

3. Ahmed Jibril, interview, *al-Safir*, July 19, 1981.

4. On January 26, 1984, for example, the Libyan News Agency called for volunteers to fight for the "liberation of Palestine." The volunteers were told to "report to the bureaus of the Popular Front, the General Command." This call for volunteers has been repeated many times over the years.

5. Washington journalist who knows Jibril in conversation with author, Washington, D.C., February 1989.

6. Ahmed Jibril, quoted in *Foreign Broadcast Information Service,* Near East and South Asia daily report, December 13, 1988, p. 4. See "PFLP-GC's Jibril Comments on Israeli Attack."

7. Ahmed Jibril, interview, *al-Auqef al-Arabi* (pro-Libyan magazine published in Paris), February 1983.

CHAPTER EIGHT: ABU NIDAL

1. U.S. Department of Defense [Defense Intelligence Agency], *Terrorist Group Profiles* (Washington, D.C.: U.S. Government Printing Office, 1988), p. 5.

2. In early press reports Sarham was referred to as Ibrahim Mohammed Khaled (see *The New York Times,* March 17, 1987). In an Italian intelligence report he was also called Muhammad Sirhan. Such discrepancies, however, are not unusual, and terrorists often attempt to deceive and confuse investigators with aliases.

3. Intelligence report based on the official Italian investigation of the attack at Fiumicino Airport, dated July 8, 1986.

4. Source: Tunisian and Moroccan intelligence officials involved in the investigation of the passports.

5. Interestingly, Mohammed Abbas used the name Abu Khaled in his ship-to-shore communications with the *Achille Lauro* hijackers, perhaps to divert suspicion from the PLF to Abu Nidal and the FRC.

6. Egyptian intelligence report of the debriefing of a Palestinian source, December 1985.

7. Hanni al-Hassan to Pacepa, *op. cit.,* p. 33. Pacepa also claims that the Romanian intelligence service, DIE, recruited al-Hassan as an agent in 1976 and assigned him the code name Annette. According to Pacepa, al-Hassan was periodically paid various sums of cash for his services, ordinarily between twenty-five hundred and ten thousand dollars.

8. The source of the information regarding Janine al-Banna is a Lebanese Forces intelligence report dated July, 1986.

CHAPTER NINE: ABU ABBAS, THE PLF, AND THE HIJACKING OF THE ACHILLE LAURO

1. Classified Lebanese intelligence report, December 1986.
2. *Foreign Broadcast Information Service,* October 6, 1985.

3. Mohammed Abbas in an interview with the Egyptian News Agency, which was reported in the Washington *Post* on October 14, 1985. Similarly, an October 10, 1985, *New York Times* story quoted Abbas as saying that he had traveled to Port Said "at Mr. Arafat's behest reportedly to mediate an end to the hijacking."

4. Shore-to-ship telephone conversations, taped, transmitted by IDF/AMAN to Rome and Washington. On October 16, 1985, the tapes were released in Israel.

5. Washington *Post,* October 15, 1985.

6. Washington *Post,* October 17, 1985.

7. For a detailed account of the interception of the EgyptAir flight see David Halevy and Neil C. Livingstone, "The Ollie We Knew," *Washingtonian* (July 1987).

8. The interception was opposed by Secretary of Defense Caspar Weinberger who told President Reagan, "This will destroy our relations with Egypt."

9. William Webster, interview with CBS News, October 13, 1985.

10. "Italy Defends Release of Achille Lauro Suspect," Washington *Post,* June 25, 1986.

11. "Italians Say Abbas Masterminded Ship Hijacking," *The New York Times,* June 11, 1986.

12. U.S. Department of State, announcement, November 25, 1985.

13. "Justice Dept. Drops Warrant in Achille Lauro Hijacking," Washington *Post,* January 17, 1988.

14. *The New York Times,* October 8, 1985.

15. *The New York Times,* October 9, 1985.

16. *The New York Times,* October 10, 1985.

17. Washington *Post,* October 11, 1985.

18. Yasir Arafat, interview, Budapest Television Service, November 28, 1985.

19. Mohammed Abbas, interview, *al-Ittihad al-Usbui,* December 5, 1985.

20. "Abbas Threatens Reagan, All Americans," Washington *Times,* May 6, 1986.

21. *Ibid.*

22. "PLO Official Suggests Wife Killed Klinghoffer," Washington *Post,* December 5, 1985.

23. "Hijacker Dismisses the Achille Lauro Killing," *The New York Times,* November 14, 1988.

24. *Ibid.*

25. Mohammed Abbas, interview, *Journal Dimanche* (Paris), May 5, 1987.

CHAPTER TEN: THE PLO AND HIZBALLAH

1. Secret Hizballah document obtained by the authors describing the organization's chain of command and organizational structure.

2. Mugniyeh was identified by U.S. and Lebanese intelligence sources as responsible for the embassy bombing. In 1985 and 1986 Lieutenant Colonel Oliver North also described to colleagues Mugniyeh's complicity in the embassy attack.

3. Interview with former Lebanese intelligence official in Paris, November 3, 1988.

4. Interviews with Lieutenant Colonel Oliver North, 1985–86; interview with Israeli intelligence official in Tel Aviv on October 14, 1988; and interview with high-ranking intelligence source in Washington, D.C., on November 21, 1988.

5. Fadlallah's position in the Hizballah structure is confirmed by the secret Hizballah document obtained by the authors.

6. "Sheik Named in Bombing Says He Is Nonviolent," Washington *Post*, October 30, 1983.

7. In Arabic the assassins were known as the *hashshashin*, the consumers of hashish.

8. For the best account of Salameh's death see: Michael Bar-Zohar and Eitan Haber, *The Quest for the Red Prince* (New York: William Morrow & Company, 1983), pp. 215–22.

9. Interview with high-ranking intelligence source in Washington on November 18, 1988.

10. Interview with high-ranking intelligence source in Washington, November 21, 1988.

11. *Ibid.*

12. Interview with high-ranking intelligence official, 1987.

13. Interview with high-ranking intelligence source in Washington, on November 21, 1988.

14. Interview with high-ranking Israeli intelligence official.

CHAPTER ELEVEN: OPERATION COLD RIVER

1. *Times* of London, reports on the Sudanese government investigation into the Khartoum incident, March 11, 1973.

2. Interview with former high-ranking intelligence official, October 1988.

3. The day after the Israeli raid on Nahr al-Bard, the Israelis shot down a Libyan jetliner that had strayed over the occupied Sinai after it became lost in a sandstorm. The Israelis feared that the plane was part of a terrorist plot to crash an explosives-laden aircraft into an important military site or heavily populated area.

4. Interview with a former high-ranking intelligence official, October, 1988.

5. Cable from the U.S. Embassy in Beirut to the U.S. Department of State (Beirut 2543), March 5, 1973, p. 2.

6. U.S. government, cable from the U.S. Embassy in Beirut to the U.S. Department of State (Beirut A2543 A51923Z), p. 4.

7. U.S. State Department cable, "PLO Role in Surrender of Khartoum Terrorists," Beirut A2543 A51923Z, March 5, 1973, pp. 02–03.

8. Shlomo Cohen Abarbanel, interview, July 1973, Tel Aviv.

9. U.S. State Department cable, "PLO Role in Surrender of Khartoum Terrorists," Beirut A2543 A51923Z, March 5, 1973, pp. 02–03.

10. Beirut *Daily Star,* November 20, 1973.

11. U.S. Government, *Foreign Broadcast Information Service,* Near East and South Asia digest, August 12, 1988. See Arafat interview with *Al-Sharq al-Awsat,* August 9, 1988.

12. Edwin Black, "Arafat Indictment Sought in '73 Sudan Murders," *Jewish Exponent* (Philadelphia), November 29, 1985, p. 77.

13. Cable from the U.S. Embassy in Khartoum to the Department of State in Washington. Reference number: 939764.

14. Cable from U.S. Embassy in Khartoum to secretary of state, (KHARTO 08471 0712492 46 C Action INRO-07), March 7, 1973.

15. Interview with high-ranking former intelligence official, October 1988.

16. See Thomas B. Ross, "Cover-up in '73 Sudan Slaying of Diplomats," Chicago *Sun-Times,* June 13, 1974.

17. U.S. Government, Foreign Broadcast Information Service (FBIS), Near East and South Asia daily report, "First Official Meeting Begins," December 19, 1988, p. 3.

CHAPTER TWELVE: THE FUTURE OF THE PLO

1. Abu Iyad, *Al-Anbaa* (Kuwait), December 18, 1988. (in Arabic)

2. Yitzhak Rabin, interview; October 27, 1988, Tel Aviv, Israel.

3. U.S. Government, *Foreign Broadcast Information Service,* Near East and South Asia digest, statement by Anwar Sadat (0922 GMT, November 17, 1977), November 17, 1977.

4. Rabin, *op. cit.*

Select Bibliography

Abu Iyad, with Eric Rouleau. *My Home, My Land.* New York: Times Books, 1981.

Adams, James. *The Funding of Terror.* New York: Simon & Schuster, 1986.

Alnwick, Kenneth J., and Thomas A. Fabyanic, eds. *Warfare in Lebanon.* Washington, D.C.: National Defense University, 1988.

Bar-Zohar, Michael, and Eitan Haber. *The Quest for the Red Prince.* New York: William Morrow and Co., 1983.

Becker, Jillian. *The PLO: The Rise and Fall of the Palestine Liberation Organization.* New York: St. Martin's Press, 1984.

Benvenisti, Meron. *The Sling and the Club.* Jerusalem: Keter Publishing House, 1988.

Cline, Ray S., and Yonah Alexander. *Terrorism: The Soviet Connection.* New York: Crane Russak, 1984.

Collins, Larry, and Dominique Lapierre. *O Jerusalem.* New York: Simon & Schuster, 1988.

Cooley, John K. *Libyan Sandstorm.* New York: Holt, Rinehart and Winston, 1982.

Dobson, Christopher. *Black September: Its Short, Violent History.* New York: Macmillan, 1974.

Emerson, Steven. *The American House of Saud.* New York: Franklin Watts, 1985.

Fontaine, Roger. *Terrorism: The Cuban Connection.* New York: Crane Russak, 1988.

Gabriel, Richard A., ed. *Fighting Armies: Antagonists in the Middle East, a Combat Assessment.* Westport, Conn.: Greenwood Press, 1983.

Golan, Galia. *The Soviet Union and the Palestine Liberation Organization: An Uneasy Alliance.* New York: Praeger, 1980.

Hadawi, Sami. *Bitter Harvest: Palestine Between 1914–1979.* Delmar, N.Y.: Caravan Books, 1979.

Hareven, Alouph. *Towards Peace, or Another War?* Jerusalem: Van Leer Jerusalem Institute, 1988.

Harkabi, Yehoshafat. *Fatah in the Arab Strategy.* Tel Aviv: Marachot Publishers/Israeli Defense Forces, 1969.

——. *The Palestinians from Quiescence to Awakening.* Jerusalem: Magnes Press/Hebrew University, 1979.

Hart, Alan. *Arafat: Terrorist or Peacemaker?* London: Sidgwick & Jackson, 1984.

Ivianski, Zeev. *Individual Terror: Theory and Deed.* Tel Aviv: Hakibbutz Hameuchad Publishing House, 1977.

Kazziha, Walid. *Revolutionary Transformation in the Arab World: Habash and His Comrades from Nationalism to Marxism.* New York: St. Martin's Press, 1975.

Khalidi, Rashid. *Under Siege: PLO Decision-Making During the 1982 War.* Tel Aviv: Marachot Publishers/Israeli Defense Forces, 1988.

Kiernan, Thomas. *Arafat: The Man and the Myth.* New York: Norton, 1976.

Kurz, Anat, and Ariel Merari. *ASALA: International Terrorism or Political Tool?* Jerusalem: Jerusalem Post and Westview Press, 1985.

Ledeen, Michael. *Perilous Statecraft.* New York: Charles Scribner's Sons, 1988.

Lesch, Ann Mosley. *Political Perception of the Palestinians on the West Bank and the Gaza Strip.* Washington, D.C.: Middle East Institute, 1980.

Livingstone, Neil C. *The War Against Terrorism.* Lexington, Mass.: Lexington Books, 1982.

Livingstone, Neil C., and Terrell E. Arnold. *Fighting Back: Winning the War Against Terrorism.* Lexington, Mass.: Lexington Books, 1986.

——. *Beyond the Iran-Contra Crisis: The Shape of U.S. Anti-Terrorism Policy in the Post-Reagan Era.* Lexington, Mass.: Lexington Books, 1988.

Martin, David C., and John Walcott. *Best Laid Plans.* New York: Harper & Row, 1988.

Melman, Yossi. *The Master Terrorist: The True Story Behind Abu Nidal.* New York: Adama Books, 1986.

Merari, Ariel, and Shlomi Elad. *The International Dimension and Palestinian Terrorism.* Boulder, Colo.: Westview Press, 1986.

Meyer, Herbert E. *Real-World Intelligence.* New York: Weidenfeld & Nicolson, 1987.

Mickolus, Edward F. *Transnational Terrorism: A Chronology of Events, 1968–1979.* Westport, Conn.: Greenwood Press, 1980.

————; Todd Sandler; and Jean M. Murdock. *International Terrorism in the 1980s, a Chronology of Events, 1980–1983,* vol. I. Ames, Iowa: Iowa State University Press, 1989.

Pacepa, Lieutenant General Ion Mihai. *Red Horizons.* Washington, D.C.: Regnery Gateway, 1987.

Pakradouni, Karim. *The Lost Peace: The Presidency of Elias Sarkis (1976–1982).* Tel Aviv: Marachot Publishers/Israeli Defense Forces, 1986.

Pintak, Larry. *Beirut Outtakes.* Lexington, Mass.: Lexington Books, 1988.

Ra'anan, Uri; Robert L. Pfaltzgraff, Jr.; Richard H. Shultz, Ernst Halperin; and Igor Lukes, eds. *The Hydra of Carnage.* Lexington, Mass.: Lexington Books, 1986.

Randal, Jonathan C. *Going All the Way.* New York: Viking Press, 1983.

Richelson, Jeffrey T. *Foreign Intelligence Organizations.* Cambridge, Mass.: Ballinger Publishing Co., 1988.

Rubenberg, Cheryl. *The Palestine Liberation Organization: Its International Infrastructure.* Belmont, Mass.: Institute of Arab Studies, 1983.

Sahliyeh, Emil. *The PLO After the Lebanon War.* Boulder, Colo.: Westview Press, 1985.

Said, Eduard W. *The Question of Palestine.* New York: Times Books, 1979.

Seale, Patrick. *Assad of Syria: The Struggle for the Middle East.* London: I. B. Tauris & Co., Ltd., 1988.

Segal, Jerome M. *Creating the Palestinian State.* Chicago: Lawrence Hill Books, 1989.

Shawcross, William. *The Shah's Last Ride.* New York: Simon & Schuster, 1988.

Sivan, Emmanuel. *Radical Islam: Medieval Theology and Modern Policies.* Tel Aviv: Am Oved Publisher Ltd., 1985.

Sterling, Claire. *The Terror Network*. New York: Holt, Rinehart and Winston, 1981.

Susser, Asher. *The PLO After the War in Lebanon: The Quest for Survival*. Tel Aviv: Hakibbutz Hameuchad Publishing House, 1985.

Taheri, Amir. *Holy Terror*. Bethesda, Md.: Adler & Adler, 1987.

Tlas, General Mustafa. *The Israeli Invasion of Lebanon*. Tel Aviv: Marachot Publishers/Israeli Defense Forces, 1988.

Ward, Richard J.; Don Peretz; and Evan M. Wilson. *The Palestine State*. Port Washington, N.Y.: Lennikat Press, 1977.

Yari, Ehud. *Fatah*. Tel Aviv: A. Levin-Epstein Ltd., 1970.

Yodfat, Aryeh Y., and Yuval Arnon-Ohanna. *PLO Strategy and Tactics*. London: Croom Helm Ltd., 1981.

Index

325